Psychoneural Reduction
The New Wave

John Bickle

A Bradford Book
The MIT Press
Cambridge, Massachusetts
London, England

This book was set in Sabon on the Monotype "Prism Plus" PostScript Imagesetter by Asco Trade Typesetting Ltd., Hong Kong, and was printed and bound in the United States of America.

First printing, 1998.

Library of Congress Cataloging-in-Publication Data

Bickle, John.
 Psychoneural reduction : the new wave / John Bickle.
     p.   cm.
 "A Bradford book."
 Includes bibliographical references and index.
 ISBN 0-262-02432-2 (alk. paper)
 1. Psychology—Philosophy. I. Title.
BF38.B48   1998
128'.2—dc21   97-28252
                                              CIP

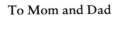
To Mom and Dad

Contents

Preface

The philosophy of psychology seems like an overly specialized area in a discipline continually dominated by specialties. Yet one of its central problems—its most interesting one, by my lights—requires a wide array of philosophical and empirical knowledge. This is the problem of how various levels of explanation concerning human behavior relate to one another. To say something interesting about this issue, one must have a passing knowledge of empirical research and developments in the relevant sciences. These include areas of cognitive psychology, both theoretical and experimental, and the mathematics that psychologists increasingly use to express their results; computational modeling and artificial intelligence, which by now include a wide range of sophisticated mathematics; the neurosciences, from the level of neural modules down to the biochemistry of synapses and cellular processes; and the relevant and related areas of biology and chemistry that ground the neurosciences. The amount of knowledge at every one of these levels has exploded over the past three decades. Gone are the days when a philosopher interested in how these levels relate could get by with the cursory knowledge of these sciences that one acquires through a standard liberal-arts education.

Second, the philosopher of psychology needs a firm grounding in the philosophy of science. The questions he or she is addressing, in the capacity of a *philosopher* of psychology (as opposed to a philosophically interested psychologist, cognitive scientist, intelligence modeler, or neurobiologist) are really quite general questions from the philosophy of science, tailored specifically to the behavioral and brain sciences. The question of how psychological theories relate to neuroscience is no different from, e.g., the question of how theories in chemistry relate to their counterparts in physics. The object-level theories are different, and maybe the relationship between levels is different, but the question at issue is the same. Thus the would-be philosopher of psychology needs working knowledge of the general philosophy of science informing the specific questions he or she is asking.

Finally, the philosopher of psychology needs firsthand knowledge of the philosophy of mind. The real interest in philosophy of psychology is the light that the behavioral and brain sciences shed on that old philosophical chestnut, the mind-body problem. The question of how levels of theories in the behavioral and brain sciences relate to one another is but a short and updated version of how minds relate to physical bodies. To bring out this important aspect of his or her endeavors, the philosopher of psychology needs to know how philosophers have addressed and continue to address this worry, and also the related questions their investigations have spawned: about the semantics of content, the nature and status of representation, and the structure of our self-knowledge.

This book seeks to succeed on all these levels. Perhaps this goal is unrealistic. Specialists in any one of these areas will no doubt know about some missing argument or development that is relevant to what I have to say. But to eschew this goal is to eschew what Wilfrid Sellars (1962) dubbed "the synoptic vision," the"eye on the whole" that distinguishes philosophers from philosophically minded specialists. If there is no such perspective, or if such a perspective contributes nothing to our intellectual endeavors, then there is no *philosophy* of psychology.

Since my interest in this overarching project goes back to my doctoral dissertation, I owe many thanks. David Woodruff Smith, Brian Skyrms, Karel Lambert, and Peter Woodruff at the University of California, Irvine, initially encouraged my philosophical interest in these issues and my continual pursuit of the required education in the brain and behavioral sciences. Norman Weinberger and Mary-Louise Kean at the Bonney Center for the Neurobiology of Learning and Memory at the University of California, Irvine, helped guide me through the neurosciences. Terence Horgan became almost a second teacher when my first job out of graduate school took me near Memphis. Paul Churchland helped out several times. Throughout, this manuscript reflects my debt to his vision of the important issues and how to do philosophy. Valerie Hardcastle, Ronald

Endicott, and Terry Horgan, along with two others who remain anonymous, refereed the manuscript for the MIT Press. Much rewriting and restructuring followed from the referees' helpful comments. Ken Aizawa, Anne Beizuidenhout, John Heil, Max Hocutt, Robert McCauley, John Post, William Ramsey, John Tienson, Ted Warfield, and Mort Winston read and commented on papers of mine, now published, on which I draw at various points. Nicolas Georgalis and Ümit Yalçin, colleagues at East Carolina University, read and commented on the entire manuscript. Susan Greene Osgood constructed the original figures and tables. Thanks also to Betty Stanton and the editorial staff at the MIT Press, especially my copy editor, Alan Thwaits. His suggestions led to many stylistic improvements.

Finally, and most importantly, thank you Marica Bernstein, loving partner.

1

Why Reduction? And Why a New-Wave Version?

1 Reductionism Revived as a Program

Consensus holds that reductionism is dead.[1] Well-known arguments by Donald Davidson, Hilary Putnam, Jerry Fodor, Richard Boyd, Ned Block, and others show that reductionism is either superfluous or false. And consensus is quite inclusive. Being a reductionist nowadays, as Jaegwon Kim notes, "is a bit like being a logical positivist or a member of the Old Left: an aura of doctrinaire naiveté hangs over such a person" (1989b, 32). However, not even the most fervent "autonomist" about psychology claims that none of it will reduce. Citing associative processes and the effects of emotion on perception and belief, even the Jerry Fodor of 1975 insisted that "explaining them is left to lower-level (probably biological) investigation" (1975, 203). Yet Fodor has long denied that reduction is viable for theories about genuinely cognitive phenomena.

Why this selective skepticism? The typical answer focuses on the indispensable explanatory need for representations and computations over their contents. This is a widely acknowledged "mark" separating cognitive psychology from the rest of the discipline. James Garfield, for example, writes that cognitive scientists are committed to an approach that "involves at least taking seriously ... the notion that intelligent behavior is, or at least is made possible by, the manipulation of symbolic *representations*" and that "the operations on those representations can be described, at least at some theoretically useful level of analysis, as *computations*" (1990, xxi–xxii; my emphases). Zenon Pylyshyn is equally explicit about this mark of the cognitive: "What, then, is the common nature of the members of the class of cognizers? I will suggest that one of the main things cognizers have in common is, they act on the basis of *representations*" (1984, xii; author's emphasis).

This mark serves as the first premise of a generic antireductionist argument:

1. We can only explain genuinely cognitive psychological phenomena by generalizations adverting to the contents of mental representations and to computations over these contents.
2. Psychological theories adverting to contents and computations over them do not reduce to purely neurobiological theories.
3. Therefore, cognitive psychological theories do not reduce to neurobiological theories.

Versions of this argument built on different defenses of premise (2) pervade contemporary philosophy of mind. Ernest LePore and Barry Loewer correctly reflect current consensus when they write, "Recent discussions of content properties have focused on a number of features ... which have been thought to show either that they are *not reducible* to physical properties which ground causal relations ... or *not reducible* to physical properties at all.... It is *practically received wisdom* among philosophers of mind that psychological properties (including content properties) are *not identical* to neurophysiological or other physical properties" (1989, 179; my emphases). This passage clearly expresses premise (2) of the generic antireductionist argument.

However, rejection of reductionism has not produced an explicit revival of dualism. The scientific spirit of our times is partly responsible for this. But another force is at work. Many physicalists are convinced that they can articulate some alternative, *nonreductive* relation to ground their philosophy of mind. The currently popular idea is one-way *dependence* of the mental on the physical. Mental properties, events, processes, states, sentences, truths, etc., are said to *supervene upon*, be *determined by*, or *realized in* physical properties, states, etc. A variety of distinct *nonreductive physicalisms* employing distinct dependency relations inhabit the recent literature. Nothing like a "dominant" version has emerged. Yet one can assert without serious challenge that nonreductive physicalism in some form or other is *the* currently accepted solution to the mind-body problem, at least within Anglo-American philosophy of mind.

This book starts with that view of the current landscape. I am addressing physicalists. Here I won't defend physicalism from, for example, qualia-based arguments (like those in Jackson 1982) or view-from-nowhere objections (Nagel 1989).[2] My overarching goal is to convince physicalists that a *kind of reduction* is the relationship to champion. What I seek is a relation stronger than one-way dependency that nevertheless sidesteps the arguments that sank "classical" reductionism. Such a result should attract anyone with physicalist inclinations. If successful, I expect to attract many current "nonreductive physicalists" (not all, however, for reasons I'll explore in the next section).

What are the classical antireductionist arguments? Four are prominent. First and most influential is *multiple realizability*. A variety of distinct physical kinds sharing nothing significant at any physical level of description can still realize the same mental kind. For example, distinct brain states plausibly realize my belief and Barry Switzer's belief that the Dallas Cowboys will win another Super Bowl by the year 2000. Distinct brain states plausibly realize my belief about the Cowboys now and my belief on Super Bowl Sunday 1999 before the Cowboys kick off. The larger context and environment embedding the brains differ, and so presumably do the exact neural realizations of the mental state. Antireductionists argue that such multiple realizability is inconsistent with reduction. The second argument is based on *mental anomalousness*. According to an important tradition in recent philosophy of mind, no strict laws govern mental phenomena, in contrast with "nomolous" physical phenomena. Again, antireductionists claim that this difference is inconsistent with reduction of the former to the latter. Third are the *methodological caveats*, worries about stultifying effects on theory development in special sciences when reductionism is imposed as a methodological constraint. If reductionist methodology stultifies theory development, so much the worse for reductionism on broadly empirical grounds. Fourth is the *put up or shut up* challenge. Where are the reductive successes promised for genuinely cognitive theories in the current behavioral and brain sciences? Nowhere, says the antireductionist, to the empirical detriment of reductionism.

To see why these arguments and features, especially the first two, are so telling against classical reductionism, we need to backtrack three decades to when they first appeared. In the philosophy of science at that time, there was a received view of intertheoretic reduction. Ernest Nagel's (1961, chap. 11) account was most influential, but there were several variations on its basic theme. Nagel understood reduction as a relation between theories construed syntactically as sets of sentences expressible in first-order logic. Reduction was *deduction*, of the reduced theory T_R from the reducing (or "basic") theory T_B. For interesting theory reductions—"heterogeneous" ones, as Nagel called them, where the T_R contains descriptive terms not contained in the vocabulary of T_B—T_B alone is insufficient for anything but a trivial derivation of T_R. In such cases, *connecting principles* ("bridge laws," "correspondence rules") must be conjoined with T_B to effect the deduction. Typically assumed to be biconditionals, these principles relate every descriptive term of T_R not present in T_B with some term or terms of the latter. Specifying the logical status of these principles turned out to be a difficult problem for the received view. Except for some willing to treat them as "mere conventions," most took these principles to express at least accidental coextension of the terms related. Some took an even stronger reading: nomic coextension or even type identity.

Here classical reductionism runs afoul of the first two antireductionist arguments. Many potential psychoneural intertheoretic reductions are heterogeneous. Psychological theories often contain terms not present in their neurobiological counterparts. Any classical reductions will thus require appropriate connecting principles. *But multiple realizability and mental anomaly nix the required principles.* I present the detailed arguments for this claim in chapter 4, but the basic ideas are straightforward. Multiple realizability implies that any connecting principles will be one-many, relating a single psychological predicate to a disjunction of lower-level predicates denoting the various kinds realizing it. This is inconsistent with the nature of connecting principles required in many versions of the received view. Mental anomaly implies that the connecting principles cannot be *laws*, since they must contain psychological predicates. This runs counter to some influential accounts of their required status. If appropriate connecting principles (i.e., one-one, lawful ones) cannot be formulated, then classical psychoneural reductions will not come forth.

My defense of new-wave reductionism will deny neither these features of the psychological nor their toll on classical reductionism. However, it is crucial to understand why they are decisive against the latter. *They doom classical reductionism because of the detailed nature of the reduction relation that the project assumes.* But in the philosophy of science, intertheoretic reduction characterized classically is only a species of the reduction relation—a prevalent species in Anglo-American philosophy, but just a species nonetheless. Other theories of intertheoretic reduction, *competitors* in the philosophy of science with the received account, are less susceptible to these antireductionist arguments. *Hence a "new wave" psychoneural reductionism grounded on one of these alternative theories remains viable in light of these objections to classical reductionism.* (The emphasized sentences of this paragraph will be continual themes throughout this book.) In fact, a "new wave" reductionism has even emerged over the past two decades. The problem is that it has emerged piecemeal. A comprehensive statement and defense of it does not exist.[3] This book fills that gap.

To put the goal of this book bluntly, I'm willing to make numerous concessions to classical antireductionism, yet I still hold out for a relation between psychology and neurobiology that shares *some* of the key aims, features, and consequences of classical reduction. I am even willing to give up the label "reductionism" if it causes too much cognitive dissonance. I will keep that label in this work, because the intertheoretic relation I am going to adopt and further develop is called "reduction" by its proponents in the philosophy of science. Fighting over labels can be invigorating but is ultimately fruitless. The reader must realize from the outset that the "new wave" part of "new-wave reductionism" is where the stress lies. In the next two chapters I will articulate a relation in the spirit of one called "reduction" in the philosophy of science that nevertheless differs in fundamental ways from the received view. (Unfortunately, the received view remains the only account of intertheoretic reduction that many Anglo-American philosophers of mind are familiar with.) I will argue that viewed from the philosophy of science generally, this relation is strong enough to rule out counterexamples of theories standing in this relation while obviously not constituting genuine reduction pairs. I will articulate the ontological consequences of this relation for higher-level ("reduced") kinds, defend its sufficiency for physicalism (about the mental), and argue that some popular "dependency" relations lack this sufficiency. In chapter 4 I will show how this relation sidesteps the arguments sinking classical reduction. In chapter 5 I will apply this relation to some existing psychological and neurobiological theories of genuinely cognitive phenomena. Toward the end of chapter 2, I will survey what traditional solutions amount to when the mind-body problem is reformulated around this account of reduction. In chapter 6 I'll argue that current empirical evidence supports one of these solutions: *revisionary physicalism*. New-wave reductionism will explicitly reject some features, aims, and consequences of classical reduction. But it will retain and deepen some crucial methodological and ontological views of a position deserving the "reduction" label.[4]

So while we will be wading through a good deal of recent work in both the philosophy of science and the empirical brain and behavioral sciences, this book is ultimately a contribution to the philosophy of mind. Its fundamental goal is to articulate a relation between psychological and neurobiological theories that adequately grounds physicalism. This relation must accommodate those features of the mental that doomed classical reductionism. It must be based on how levels of scientific explanation in general relate, and actual examples of it must obtain in cognitive science. Finally, the relation must provide a physicalist account of the ontological nature of mental kinds.

2   A Puzzle about Nonreductive Physicalism

There is one concession to contemporary antireductionism that I refuse to make. The relation I seek must be stronger than one-way dependence of psychological theories and kinds on neurobiological theories and kinds. I say this because of a puzzling and sometimes overlooked observation about "nonreductive physicalisms" built on such relations. All nonreductive *physicalists* must commit to the priority of physics in some sense. Usually this gets cashed out as the claim that all existing objects have physical properties. However, many nonreductive physicalists also insist that their favored relations have ontological consequences *weaker than* identity between mental and physical properties or events (or revision or elimination of the mental). This suggests an entity or substance monism but a property or event dualism. The puzzle is whether this combination constitutes physicalism. Prima facie, it does not.

To insure that I am not misconstruing nonreductive physicalism, consider a triplet of recent characterizations. John Post writes, "Part of what nonreductive physicalism envisages, then, is a monism of entities (the mathematical-physical) *combined with a dualism of their properties* (the nonphysical and the physical).... Thereby we are ... prevented from saying that everything is *nothing but* a physical entity—meaning that all of its properties are or are reducible to physical properties—even though nothing but physical entities exist" (1987, 197). Jaegwon Kim provides a similar exposition: "The leading idea ... has been the thought that we can assuage our physicalist qualms by embracing 'ontological physicalism,' the claim that all that exists in spacetime is physical, but, at the same time, accept 'property dualism,' a dualism about psychological and physical attributes, insisting that psychological concepts or properties form an irreducible, autonomous domain" (1989b, 32). Finally, Ronald McClamrock, expressly concerned with phenomenological properties, writes, "Even if it turns out that there is no objective characterization of subjective facts or properties as such, and that any such properties are importantly perspective-bound, this shouldn't be viewed at all as being anti-materialist. Non-reductive identity materialism explicitly claims that not all properties are physical properties—that's what distinguishes it from the more reductive accounts" (1992, 186). These quotes noted, one may be excused for wondering whether recent philosophy of mind has lost a once-honored distinction, that between physicalism and *property dualism.*

Traditionally, their rejection of nonphysical soul stuff in which mental properties inhere distinguishes property from substance dualists. Mental properties are properties of the brain (and presumably of any physical system complex and organized enough to produce or support them). But property dualism remains dualism, since it denies that even a matured physical science could exhaustively explain the essence of the mental. Paul Churchland nicely articulates these distinctions: "The basic idea [of property dualism] is that while there is no *substance* to be dealt with here beyond the physical brain, the brain has a special set of *properties* possessed by no other kind of physical object. It is these special properties that are nonphysical: hence the term *property dualism....* These are the properties that are characteristic of conscious intelligence. They are held to be nonphysical in the sense that they cannot ever be reduced to or explained solely in terms of the concepts of the familiar physical sciences. They will require a wholly new and autonomous science—the 'science of mental phenomena'—if they are ever to be adequately understood" (1987, 10). Thus contemporary nonreductive physicalism is identical to property dualism, traditionally conceived. Much current "nonreductive physicalism" is not physicalism at all. It is instead a less extreme form of dualism, a dualism not of substances but of their properties.

This consequence has not passed unnoticed by all nonreductive physicalists. Post, for example, notes humorously that his "resulting philosophy, despite adhering to the minimal physicalist principles, is not happily called physicalism.... A far happier name, surely, would be 'post-physicalism'" (1987, 18). Joseph Margolis, whose *Persons and Minds* (1979) was an early attempt to explicitly formulate a nonreductive physicalism, contrasts "attribute" with "ontic" materialism. The latter holds that everything that exists has physical attributes. The former, which Margolis associates with J. J. C. Smart, is the stronger thesis that "all mental and psychological attributes are physical or material attributes," in that the relevant predicates are "extensionally equivalent ... and, for reasons of theoretical economy, the attributes designated are said to be one and the same" (1979, 5). According to Margolis, his theory is compatible with ontic materialism but not with attribute materialism. This leads to the key admission: "Often, since dualism is opposed to materialism, it is claimed that the rejection of attribute materialism is tantamount to the adoption of dualism. *If so, so be it*" (1979, 5; my emphasis).

Thus many nonreductive physicalists won't balk at the "property dualist" label. However, two considerations demonstrate just how robust their property dualism is. First, consider the history of supervenience, a popular relation among nonreductive physicalists. Most advocates of this notion in philosophy of mind blithely (and correctly) trace it back to G. E. Moore's ethical writings.[5] Though he did not use the term, Moore claimed that goodness supervened on natural properties. Two objects not differing in their natural properties could not differ in their goodness. *However, Moore was unabashedly a dualist about descriptive and normative properties.* Goodness supervenes on natural properties but is nonetheless—and, I might add, *thereby*—a *nonnatural* property. Moore explicitly rejected all forms of ethical naturalism. That was one point of his famous open-question argument and his labeling such views as committing the "naturalistic fallacy." How, then, can some heir of Moore's notion adequately ground a nonreductive psychological naturalism, say nothing of a nonreductive *physicalism*?

To my knowledge, Terence Horgan (1984) is the only nonreductive physicalist sensitive to this worry.[6] In that work, Horgan is concerned with materialist "cosmic hermeneutics," which investigates claims beyond supervenience required to determine all the truths in a possible world that is physically accessible on the basis of that world's microphysical truths.[7] One approach he considers is a generalization of G. E. Moore's attempt to ground evaluative truths on natural/descriptive truths. Moorean supervenience rests "upon certain fundamental, sui generis, necessary truths: truths to the effect that acts or agents or objects with such-and-such descriptive properties always have so-and-so valuational properties" (Horgan 1984, 24). Horgan notices two troubles with this approach to materialist cosmic hermeneutics. First, these fundamental "bridging principles" state facts about the world just as basic as microphysical facts. So the latter alone don't determine all truths. Instead, the conjunction of the microphysical truths and the bridging principles linking the supervening and basic truths determine all other truths. Second and more important, the supervenience thesis is thereby compatible with Moore's meta-ethics, a view that "explicitly rejected any doctrine of descriptive/normative property identity, and instead held that terms like 'good' express properties distinct from any property expressed by descriptive language" (Horgan 1984, 24). This approach thus makes the supervenience thesis unsatisfactory as an explication of physicalism. What more is needed? Horgan insists, "To obtain a satisfactory explication, we need to supplement [the supervenience thesis] with a materialistically-acceptable account of the principles of cosmic hermeneutics. I take it that one acid-test of such an account will be that it rules out *objective non-naturalist* metaethical theories such as Moore's" (1984, 24–25). Otherwise, strong property-dualist, and hence antiphysicalist, implications are unavoidable.

Second, consider a recent argument by Jaegwon Kim. For the past few years Kim has been a vocal opponent of nonreductive physicalism. Most of his arguments rest on his doctrine of "causal-explanatory exclusion," which holds that a full, sufficient causal explanation of an event excludes other independent causal explanations of it (1989a, 1989b). This doctrine, coupled with the causal closure of the physical domain (a doctrine that any physicalist seems required to accept), yields the problem of how a mentalistic explanation of a behavioral event can coexist with a physical explanation. The obvious "noneliminativist" solution is to identify psychological and physical causes. But commitment to an ontological relation weaker than property identity bars this solution to the nonreductive physicalist.

Kim's explanatory-exclusion arguments have sparked some discussion (Horgan 1993a, 1993b). At this stage I do not assume that he has shown nonreductive physicalism to be an "unstable" position. But one of his recent installments does bring out nicely the strong property-dualistic implications of the position. Clearly, any position that denies the identity of mental and physical properties and is committed to "downward causation"—the doctrine that mental properties have causal effects on the physical level not had by even the physical properties on which they depend—is a robust version of property dualism. Despite their protestations to the contrary, Kim (1992) argues that many nonreductive physicalists commit to downward causation. He compares some key doctrines of recent "supervenient" nonreductive physicalism with British emergentism from earlier in this century. The British emergentists explicitly committed to mental realism, the rejection of epiphenomenalism (which is tantamount to the reality of mental causes), the emergence of mental properties from a physical-biological base, and the irreducibility of mental properties to their emergent base. Substitute supervenience for emergence and much contemporary nonreductive physicalism commits to exactly this set of doctrines.

Yet from this set a commitment to downward causation follows. Kim argues by separating cases (1992, 136). Both the emergentist tradition and contemporary nonreductive physicalism are committed to mental properties possessing novel causal powers not had by their base properties. Otherwise, given the nonidentity of mental and physical properties, epiphenomenalism would be their lot. These causal powers must manifest themselves by causing either physical or mental events. If the former, then that alone is commitment to downward causation. So Kim considers the latter and seeks to show that it is possible only if the mental property M, which by hypothesis causes another mental property M^*, also causes some physical property. Being a mental property, M^* is itself an emergent property (or supervenient property, or realized property, or whatever nonreductive relation one favors). Thus it occurs on a given occasion only because its base physical property P^* occurs on that occasion. In light of M^*'s dependence on P^*, Kim asks what we are to make of its (M^*'s) causal dependence on M. His answer is that "these two claims concerning why M^* is present on this occasion must be reconciled, and ... the only viable way of accomplishing it is to suppose that M caused M^* by causing its emergent base P^*. In general, the principle involved here is this: *the only way to cause an emergent property to be instantiated is by causing its emergence base property to be instantiated.* And this means that the 'same- level' causation of an emergent property presupposes the downward causation of its emergent base. That briefly is why emergentism is committed to downward causation. I believe that this argument remains plausible when emergence is replaced by physical realization at appropriate places" (1992, 136; author's emphasis). Commitment to downward causation is tantamount to a robust form of property dualism. If Kim's argument is sound, then nonreductive physicalism built on one-way-dependency relations commits to the former— and by implication, the latter.

At this point, nonreductive physicalists often talk about "token" physicalism and identity. Supposedly, this commitment distinguishes them from real property dualists. Speaking for nonreductive physicalism, J. D. Trout insists that Fodor's well-known example of the variety of ways of realizing monetary exchanges shows "that we can be good physicalists without being reductionists, because we can claim that each token higher-level state is identical to a token physical state without claiming that there are smooth identities" (1991, 390).[8] However, this appeal to token physicalism won't extricate nonreductive physicalists from property or event dualism. The combination of their characteristic doctrine, the nonidentity of mental and physical properties, with token state or event identity is conceptually unstable, at least on what arguably remains the best account of the latter: Kim's "property exemplification" account (1966, 1969, 1976).

A deductive account of explanation lies at the heart of Kim's theory of events. Explicans must entail explicandum. Hence explanation is a relation between propositions, with the explicandum typically attributing a property to an object (e.g., that the bridge collapsed). However, we also often speak of explaining events, rather than the propositions referring to them. How is it possible to hold both claims: that explicanda of explanations are (sometimes) individual events, and that explanation in general is a deductive relation between propositions? According to Kim, both claims are possible if there is a relation between individual events and the propositions that occur in their explanations. The propositions must refer to or describe individual events. When an explicans explains the truth of some proposition p, p refers to or describes some event e. Furthermore, e must be uniquely related to p in this way. And since p, recall, typically attributes a property to an object, being of the form "x exemplifies F," the event uniquely referred to by p is x's exemplifying property F. Finally, since an object can exemplify a property more than once, the uniqueness of the explicandum requires a temporal modifier. Thus events are exemplifications of properties by objects at times. This leads to Kim's criterion of event identity. Identical concrete (i.e., token) events must be the same object exemplifying *the same property* at the same time (Lombard 1986, 54; after Kim 1976, 161; my emphasis). The tie-in with explanation is straightforward. If a proposition p attributes to x the property F at time t and another proposition p' attributes to x' the property F' at t', then the facts explaining why p is true will explain why p' is true only if $x = x'$, $F = F'$, and $t = t'$.

Obviously, Kim's criterion for event identity will not help the anti-reductionist who wishes to take refuge from the charge of property or event dualism by appeal to token event identity. On Kim's theory, denying the identity of mental and physical properties implies that a token mental event m (subject x's exemplifying a mental property M at time t)

cannot be identical to a token physical (e.g., neural) event n (x's exemplifying a neural property N at t). This holds no matter how complex the property m is. Even if m is a complex event exemplifying a conjunction of mental and physical properties, it cannot be identical (on Kim's event theory) to a purely physical event exemplifying only physical properties as long as mental and physical properties are not identical.[9]

Lombard (1986, 61–62) criticizes Kim's theory for being less a theory of events and more a theory of *states*. I won't take up the issue of whether this criticism is cogent, but notice that it does clearly show that nonidentity of mental and physical properties and token identity of mental and physical *states* together are unstable. (Notice also that Trout appeals directly to token *state* identity in the passage cited above.) If mental fproperties are not identical to physical properties, as nonreductive physicalists characteristically hold, and if Kim's identity criterion is unobjectionable for states, then token mental states cannot be identical to token physical states. This holds even if the mental and physical properties inhere in the same objects (e.g., brains).

Perhaps one of the more coarse-grained theories of events proposed as alternatives to Kim's view can help the nonreductive physicalist here.[10] However, such theories are notoriously susceptible to counterexamples. Short of providing an acceptable general theory of events that permits event identities along side of property nonidentities, the only apparent way to maintain token physicalism is to accept some form of property identity. But this move is anathema to many nonreductive physicalists. Hence nonreductive physicalists uncomfortable with these strong property-dualistic implications might find new-wave reductionism more to their liking.

It is crucial to be absolutely clear on what I am claiming in this section. I don't (now) intend my claim that much of recent nonreductive physicalism is actually committed to property dualism as a criticism of it. Even after we later wade through some recent work in the cognitive and brain sciences, the empirical case against "nonreductive physicalism" won't be closed. For all we now know, some relation weaker than new-wave reduction might turn out finally to be the strongest relation that obtains between psychological and physical theories and kinds. At this stage, everybody's position is a broadly empirical prediction about the outcome of developing science. My point is that if the typical nonreductive relations championed now pan out, then physicalism stands repudiated. Dualism of a sort—property (or state or event) dualism—will be our ontological lot.

Prima facie, then, the "nonreductive physicalist" can't have it both ways: nonreductive *and* physicalist. I present new-wave reduction as the weakest available relation that a full-blooded physicalist (as opposed to a property dualist) can hold out for. To the extent that various "nonreductive" relations prove equivalent to new-wave reduction, these positions deserve the "reduction" label (modulo the new-wave rejection of classical reductionism discussed in the previous section). On the other hand, those grounded on relations weaker than new-wave reduction deserve the "property dualism" label. Referring to attempts to characterize supervenience as the appropriate relation, Kim nicely states this dilemma: "It has not been easy to find such a relation. The main difficulty has been this: if a relation is weak enough to be nonreductive, it tends to be too weak to serve as a dependence relation; conversely, when a relation is strong enough to give us dependence, it tends to be too strong—strong enough to imply reducibility" (1989b, 40).[11] At this point, I don't intend this labeling of much nonreductive physicalism as property dualism as a criticism. Empirical arguments for new-wave reducibility will come later. The concern of this section is to get the position properly located in ontological space.

3   The Mind-Body Problem as a "Levels" Problem

This talk about the requirements of physicalism and this labeling much of nonreductive physicalism as really property dualism raise a problem for new-wave reductionism from an unexpected quarter. John Searle (1992) has recently charged that the relation between mind and brain remains a philosophical "problem" only because all parties continue to use an obsolete seventeenth-century vocabulary and set of assumptions. The oppositions implicit in this vocabulary—"physical" versus "mental," "body" versus "mind," "materialism" versus "mentalism," "matter" versus "spirit"—prohibit us from stating what we know to be true from both personal experience and science. This state of affairs is intellectually inexcusable, since science itself showed the inadequacy of this vocabulary and set of assumptions long ago. In its talk about physicalism versus property dualism, new-wave reductionism apparently still wallows in this inadequacy.

Searle scatters passages indicative of this attitude throughout the first two chapters of *The Rediscovery of the Mind* (1992). I cite two to reveal their general flavor. "I am now convinced, after several years of discussing these issues, that with very few exceptions all of the parties to the disputes in the current issues in the philosophy of mind are captive to a certain set of verbal categories. They are the prisoners of a certain terminology, a terminology that goes back at least to Descartes if not before" (1992, 31). "The weird feature about this entire discussion is that materialism inherits the worst assumption of dualism.... It accepts the terms in which Descartes set the debate. It accepts, in short, the idea that the vocabulary of the mental and the physical, of material and immaterial, of mind and body, is perfectly adequate as it stands.... What I believe is that the vocabulary, and the accompanying categories, are the source of our deepest philosophical difficulties" (1992, 54). Searle's prescription for "solving" the mind-body "problem" is simply to give up the outdated vocabulary and set of categories. This will enable everyone to see that "the famous mind-body problem ... has a simple solution," one "available to any educated person since serious work began on the brain nearly a century ago, and, in a sense, we all know to be true." That solution is *biological naturalism*, encapsulated in the slogan "Mental phenomena are caused by neurophysiological processes in the brain and are themselves features of the brain" (1992, 1).

Although it receives its most extended treatment in his 1992 book, Searle has been pointing out the outdated nature of this vocabulary and set of categories since his *Minds, Brains, and Science* (1984). In the introduction to that earlier work, Searle insisted, "A third theme that runs, subliminally, through these chapters is that the traditional terminology we have for discussing these problems is in various ways inadequate.... The use of the noun 'mind' is dangerously inhabited by the ghosts of old philosophical theories" (1984, 10–11). When commenting on the macro/micro-properties analogy he uses to illustrate the relation between mind and brain inherent in his biological naturalism, Searle writes, "In objecting to this someone might say that liquidity, solidity, and so on are identical with features of the microstructure [as opposed to being caused by and realized in microstructural features].... This point seems to me correct but not really an objection to the analysis I am proposing.... One can ... say either that solidity just is the lattice structure of the system of molecules and that solidity so defined causes, for example, resistance to touch and pressure. Or one can say that solidity consists of such high level features as rigidity and resistance to touch and pressure and that it is caused by the behavior of the elements at the micro-level" (1984, 21–22). One very plausible interpretation of this passage is that Searle is claiming that it doesn't matter which of these two things one says, because the purported distinction is spurious. If we apply this reading to the mind-body relation, where "caused by" and "realized in" have exactly the sense that they have in the macro/micro distinction between physical properties, Searle's point is that the "distinction" between the identity theory and a kind of property dualism is equally spurious. One can "say either." It really doesn't matter, once the vocabulary is purged of its seventeenth-century connotations.

Although it is not his explicit target, Searle is wrong in his diagnosis of the source of a genuine problem about how "mind" relates to "brain." Even if we eschew the seventeenth-century vocabulary and set of assumptions, a real problem remains fully in force. It isn't the traditional mind-body problem. Searle may well be correct in his diagnosis and dismissal of that. Rather, it is a problem stemming from the existence of *distinct levels of theory and explanation* for a range of phenomena (behavior), and in particular about *how these distinct levels relate* when our concerns are ontological (when we are theorizing about what there is). My argument for Searle's misdiagnosis is straightforward. I can raise the real problem without invoking the vocabulary and categories that Searle insists is the culprit. Here goes. How do theories invoking causal states with propositional content comport with theories invoking brain processes and subsequent effects on the motor system? Do they comport as, e.g., theories from chemistry comport with theories from physics? Or do they stand in some other cross-theoretic relation?

In raising this question about inter*theoretic* levels, I raise an issue closely related to the traditional mind-body question. In fact, as we will see in the next chapter, different answers to this levels question carry in their stead consequences equivalent to traditional answers given to the traditional problem. If explanations from intentional psychology remain the best we can offer, we remain committed to the independent, autonomous existence of the entities or properties postulated in those explanations. Different varieties of this answer generate the traditional varieties of dualism. On the other hand, if theories pitched at the neurobiological level develop the potential to explain everything explained by intentional psychology, we have grounds for simplifying our ontology of the *independent* or *fundamental* existence of the entities and properties postulated by the latter. Depending upon the successful lower-level theories and the nature of the relation obtaining, different varieties of this answer generate the traditional varieties of materialism.[12]

On this reformulated mind-body problem, ontological conclusions *follow from* the nature of the appropriate relation between inter*theoretic* levels. Ontological claims are *secondary to and dependent on* how theories from different levels relate. Reductionism amounts to the thesis that intertheoretic reduction (properly understood, in "new wave" fashion) is the cross-level relation appropriate for exploring ontological questions. Physicalism is the *prediction* that theories from intentional psychology ultimately will reduce to theories pitched at the level of physical mechanisms (theories from neurobiology, in this case). Contra Searle's diagnosis, the existence of distinct levels of theory and explanation for a class of observable phenomena generates a genuine problem, importantly related to the traditional mind-body problem. Everybody's solution to this levels-of-theory question, John Searle's "biological naturalism" included, is a broadly empirical *prediction* about future scientific developments.

This emphasis on levels of theory and explanation, and on reduction being the appropriate relation to explore between these levels when ontological questions are at stake, in turn raises another potential worry. New-wave reductionism might now remind some of Paul Oppenheim and Hilary Putnam's (1958) "unity of science" hypothesis. Is new-wave reduction nothing more than a specific application of Oppenheim and Putnam's unity of science, restricted in scope to psychology and neuroscience? If so, is it not susceptible to the well-known problems haunting the latter? It is neither. For despite shared emphasis on levels of theory and on reduction as the crucial intertheoretic relation, one key contrast is more striking than the similarities.

Oppenheim and Putnam base unity of science exclusively on *microreduction*. Besides meeting the general conditions on reduction introduced by Kemeny and Oppenheim (1956), microreduction also requires that the objects in the universe of discourse of the reduced theory be wholes that decompose without remainder into proper parts all of which belong to the universe of the reducing theory. Microreductions thus move in the direction of both unity of terms and unity of laws, since a consequence is that "we can use [microreducing] B_1 in place of [microreduced] B_2" (Oppenheim and Putnam 1958, 5).[13]

Microreductions in Oppenheim and Putnam's sense, when obtainable, are clearly steps toward physicalism and the unity of science. But Oppenheim and Putnam defend a stronger claim: "The *only* method of attaining unitary science that appears to be seriously available at present is microreduction" (1958, 6; my emphasis). Microreductions aren't just sufficient for the project; they are *necessary*. They offer two arguments in defense of this stronger claim. First, it seems doubtful that one branch of science could genuinely reduce another if the elements of the universe of discourse of the latter are neither elements of the universe of the former nor possess a complete decomposition into those elements. Otherwise, the two branches seem not to be "speaking about the same things." Second, when the branches do have different universes, we need the whole-part-decomposition condition to rule out problematic implications of the general theory of reduction. For example, we surely want our reductionism to rule out the possibility of, e.g., physics reducing to psychology. Limiting ourselves to microreduction rules out such problematic possibilities. Even if the general conditions on reduction obtain in these unwanted directions, there is still no sense in which inorganic matter is decomposable into psychological parts.

Do psychological theories *microreduce* to neurobiological theories? Or is another sense of reduction at work? Interestingly, Oppenheim and Putnam's treatment of psychology and neuroscience within the unity of science, given their exclusive concern with microreduction, is curiously inconsistent. On the one hand, the following three levels lie at the top of Oppenheim and Putnam's hierarchy (ordered via their universes of discourse and the whole-parts decomposition relation) (see 1958, 9):

6. Social groups
5. Multicellular living things
4. Cells

Given this grouping, psychological and neurobiological theories lie *on the same level* (as competitors?), namely, level 5, since both pertain to multicellular living things. Being at the same level, with these levels distinguished and ordered by decomposition, psychological theories could not *micro*reduce to neurobiological theories (though they might *reduce*, i.e., meet the conditions on reduction laid down by Kemeny and Oppenheim). But then if microreduction is the *only* way to achieve unified science, psychology-to-neuroscience reductions are not steps toward it. This consequence, however, is in direct opposition to strong intuition. I take it that everybody agrees that successful psychology-to-neuroscience reductions would be monumental steps toward unified science. Even more important, this consequence stands in opposition to much of what Oppenheim and Putnam say later in the essay when defending the "credibility" of unity of science as a "working hypothesis." Then-existing work relating psychological and neurobiological theories figured prominently. One of their prime examples of a microreduction in progress is "a theory of the brain advanced by Hebb" that accounts for many *psychological* phenomena, including "association, memory, motivation, emotional disturbance, and some of the phenomena connected with learning, intelligence and perception" (Oppenheim and Putnam 1958, 19). But the universe of discourse for both Hebb's theory of the brain *and* for psychological theories addressing these phenomena are multicellular living things: entities at the same level in Oppenheim and Putnam's scientific hierarchy based on decomposition relations. So by definition these theories are not *micro*reducible to one another.

To see this, consider briefly Hebb's theory. Hebb's central explanatory notion is the *cell assembly*, "a diffuse structure comprising cells in the cortex and diencephalon (and also, perhaps, in the basal ganglia of the cerebellum), capable of acting briefly as a closed system, delivering facilitation to other such systems and usually having a specific motor

facilitation" (1949, xix). Even the cell assembly, obviously a feature of
multicellular living things, is only a building block in Hebb's neurophysiological account of psychological processes. He also writes, "A
series of such events [growth of cell assemblies] constitutes a "phase
sequence"—the thought process" (1949, xix). He explicitly denied pitch-
ing his theory at the level of individual cellular processes: "It [his theory]
does not, further, make any single nerve cell or pathway essential to any
habit or perception" (1949, xix). He even calls his theory "a form of
connectionism" (1949, xix)! Perhaps Hebb's famed "neurophysiological
postulate" about the growth of the cell assembly confuses Oppenheim
and Putnam into assuming that his theory rests at level 4 of their hierarchy. Hebb writes, "When an axon of cell *A* is near enough to excite a
cell *B* and repeatedly or persistently takes part in firing it, some growth
process or metabolic change takes place in one or both cells such that *A*'s
efficiency, as one of the cells firing *B*, is increased" (1949, 62). This passage formulates the basis of "Hebbian learning," by now a well-explored
hypothesis in connectionist artificial intelligence and neural-network
modeling. But while the individual events producing the cell assembly
take place in individual neurons, the cell assembly itself is a feature
of multicellular nervous systems. It is the cell assembly that figures into
Hebb's neuropsychological explanations of "association, memory, motivation, emotional disturbance, learning, intelligence, and perception."
Both psychological theories and Hebb's neuropsychology are located at
level 5 of Oppenheim and Putnam's hierarchy. Hence by definition the
former cannot microreduce to the latter. So by the strong condition on
the unity of science, such reductions are not evidence for it. Something
has to give in Oppenheim and Putnam's account.

   One possible solution is to retain an exclusive emphasis on microreduction for unity of science but change the number of levels. Perhaps a
level (the cell-network level?) needs to be inserted between (5) and (4).
Psychological theories would then remain at (5), while neural theories
like Hebb's would be located at this intermediate level.[14] However, there
is another option. One can give up the exclusive emphasis on microreduction and argue that another type of reduction relation and distinction between scientific levels are both present in numerous cases of

reduction from the history of science and to be expected in psychology-to-neuroscience cases. In keeping with the basic theme outlined in section 1, I'll adopt this second option. The result will be in contrast to Oppenheim and Putnam's exclusive concern with microreduction. Of course, my alternative intertheoretic-reduction relation must be common across levels in science generally. It cannot be simply an ad hoc addition to bring psychology underneath the reductionist umbrella.

In addition, the relation that new-wave reductionism supplements microreduction with must meet certain demands. Microreduction must emerge as a special case of the general reduction relation, since micro-reductions do sometimes obtain and are obviously important for physicalism and the unity of science when they do. The general intertheoretic-reduction relation must meet a "too weak to be adequate" challenge, a generalization of the "two theories don't speak about the same things" argument that drove Oppenheim and Putnam to an exclusive emphasis on microreduction. The problem is that when we extend reduction beyond microreduction, the general account appears to capture too many theory pairs. It seems to count as reductions either historical or imagined cases that meet the general conditions on the relation but which aren't real reductions. This problem must be addressed (and will be addressed, in chapter 3, section 4, below).

In eschewing an exclusive appeal to microreductions, new-wave reductionism proves itself more than a specific application of Oppenheim and Putnam's unity-of-science hypothesis. Nevertheless, physicalism reformulated according to new-wave reductionism shares an important feature with one of their basic themes. It has the same status, and permits the same sort of defense, as Oppenheim and Putnam's "unity of science as a working hypothesis." That it can be "fully realized" is an "overarching meta-scientific hypothesis" (1958, 4), a broadly empirical *prediction*, as I called it above. Accepting this prediction is more than a "mere act of faith," since it can and will be defended as credible on the grounds Oppenheim and Putnam cite for their hypothesis.

Motivating the promise of new-wave reductionism was the purpose of this chapter. Now the hard work begins. What is the intertheoretic relation grounding the project? Articulating this will take the next two chapters. Chapter 2 presents Clifford Hooker's key insight about scientific reduction and applies it to an important historical case. Chapter 3 captures Hooker's insight within an illuminating approach to the structure of scientific theories and relations. This broad approach is particularly helpful, since it permits an elegant, semiformal presentation of the reduction relation and develops resources that avoid the problems that sunk classical reductionism.

2

Exploiting Hooker's Insights

1 Clifford Hooker's General Theory of Reduction

Before developing the new-wave account of intertheoretic reduction, I
first make explicit a presupposition that I won't here defend. I view the
philosophy of science primarily as a descriptive rather than a prescriptive
enterprise. Its task is to start with cases the scientific community calls,
e.g., "reductions" (or "explanations" or "theories," etc.) and to seek
conditions that unite this and only this class. I do not take its primary
task to be imposing a set of prior epistemic conditions that reductions (or
explanations or theories, etc.) must meet. This isn't to say that philosophy of science cannot discover inconsistencies or mistakes in scientific
discourse. Once we find a set of conditions that unite all and only
"paradigm" instances of reduction (explanation, theory), we might discover either cases not counted as instances that should be counted or
cases counted as instances that shouldn't. It also does not rule out using
formal resources in theorizing about the conditions. It's just that scientific
practice and judgment come first and are presumed correct until proven
wrong. As with the earlier assumption of a minimal scientific realism,
I trust that most readers will accept this descriptive approach to the
philosophy of science, at least for the sake of argument.

The new-wave account of intertheoretic reduction begins with some
key insights from Clifford Hooker's work (1979, 1981). The clearest way
to present Hooker's insights is to locate them in historical context. His
general theory appeared as a response to well-known criticisms of the
"received view" stemming from Ernest Nagel and logical empiricism. As
noted in chapter 1, section 1, above, that view takes reduction to be

deduction of the reduced theory T_R *from the reducing theory* T_B. This feature of the received view creates a need for cross-theoretic connecting principles ("bridge laws," "correspondence rules") in heterogeneous cases where T_R contains terms not contained in the vocabulary of T_B.

A much-discussed difficulty looms right at this point. Modus tollens alone requires that if T_R is false, then T_B must be false as well, in contradiction to its assumed truth (at least at the time when the reduction is discovered).[1] And it does appear that some "textbook" cases of intertheoretic reduction from the history of science involve, strictly speaking, false T_Rs. Falling bodies near the surface of the earth do not exhibit uniform vertical acceleration over any finite interval, yet this uniformity is a central assumption of Galilean mechanics. Galilean mechanics is empirically false. It does not correctly describe the behavior of falling bodies in any part of the actual physical universe. So the "textbook" reduction of Galilean mechanics to Newtonian mechanics (with the latter assumed true at the time the reduction was discovered) does not fit Nagel's account. In a similar vein, as Paul Feyerabend liked to point out (see especially the middle sections of his 1962 work), a logical consequence of Nagel's account is that T_B must be logically consistent with T_R. This condition is likewise violated in this and other "textbook" cases of theory reduction in science.

One can avoid this worry in at least two ways. First, one can supplement the reducing complex (the premises of the deduction) with various boundary conditions and limiting assumptions, some counter to fact. For example, one can conjoin to Newton's laws and the connecting principles either a counterfactual assumption describing conditions near the surface of the earth that allow for uniform vertical acceleration over some finite interval of distance, or a counterfactual assumption limiting the applicability of Newton's laws to bodies falling distances only negligibly greater than zero. From the supplemented reducing complex T_B & CP & C_R, (where CP are the cross-theoretic connecting principles and C_R are the possibly counterfactual limiting assumptions and boundary conditions), the laws of an empirically false T_R can be validly (and nontrivially) derived from a T_B assumed true. The falsity of T_R is thus explained by and safely confined to the counterfactual conditions of C_R. This satisfies the requirements of modus tollens and logical consistency for the reducing complex without implying the falsity of T_B.

Alternatively, one can address these worries in a fashion championed by Kenneth Schaffner (1967). Instead of deriving the original T_R, one derives a *corrected version* T_R^* *of* T_R from a reducing complex T_B & CP. Following Quine, Schaffner speaks not of "connecting principles" but of "reduction functions" whose values "exhaust the universe" of T_R^* for "arguments in the universe" of T_B (1967, 144). Each reduction function must "be specifiable, have empirical support, and in general be interpretable as expressing synthetic identity" (1967, 144). These conditions are exactly the requirements that the received view places on the connecting principles CP. The corrected version T_R^* must provide more accurate experimentally verified predictions than T_R did in almost all cases and should show why T_R worked as well as it did. T_R^* must also bear a "close similarity" to T_R by producing numerical predictions "very close" to T_R and by standing in a "large positive analogy" to it. One example Schaffner provides is the "corrected" transmission genetics of today, which employs the concepts cistron, muton, and recon, in contrast with the Mendelian genetics of the 1950s (1967, 142–144). On his approach, the falsity of the original T_R is eliminated in the corrected T_R^*, with the corrections to the original T_R motivated directly by the reducing T_B. This removes the worries about deriving a false conclusion from premises assumed true and about the logical consistency of premises and conclusion. However, given the conditions Schaffner stipulates on the reduction functions from the "universe" of T_B onto that of T_R^*, it is clear that the latter remains expressible within the vocabulary and conceptual framework of the reduced T_R. Otherwise, the reduction functions would not be necessary. On this point, Schaffner's approach agrees with the received view.

Neither of these approaches handles every problem raised by reductions of empirically false T_Rs. Sometimes a theory reducible to (some portion of) its successor turns out to be so radically false (in certain respects) that central elements of its ontology must be rejected as empirically uninstantiated. This creates a problem for interpreting the connecting principles or reduction functions. Referents of terms of T_B cannot be synthetically identical to, or even nomically coextensive with, "referents" of terms of T_R (or of T_R^*) if the latter completely lack actual extension.

One might think that this problem of radical falsity only arises in a narrow range of theory successions (e.g., phlogiston chemistry, caloric-fluid heat theory). If this were true, then the obvious response would be to distinguish genuine reductions from mere theory successions. One could then classify the troublesome cases as instances of the latter, and hence as unproblematic for a theory of reduction. Unfortunately, this move fails to appreciate the number of "textbook" *reductions* involving radical falsity of this sort. Relativistic mass, a two-place *relation* between an object and countless reference frames, cannot be identical to classical mass, a one-place *property* of objects. Relativistic mass is never even coextensive with classical mass at any actual velocity. Strictly speaking, there is no such thing as classical mass. No actual physical object possesses it. So what is the status of a principle or function meeting the conditions Schaffner specifies that "connects" the relevant expressions or referents? Similar remarks hold for the reduction of equilibrium thermodynamics to statistical mechanics (Nagel's treatment of it notwithstanding [1961, chap. 11]). Temperature is only identical with mean molecular kinetic energy when the particles of the gas are in perfectly random motion. The problem is, they never are. Most statistical-mechanical results that mimic thermodynamical laws are calculated only in the "thermodynamical limit," which involves an infinite number of particles and where a gas's volume is indefinitely large in comparison to the mean distance between colliding particles. These conditions are never actually realized. If we purge all cases involving significant ontological correction to the T_R from the domain of intertheoretic reduction, very few cases of genuine reduction remain.

There remain ways of coping with this problem. One could follow many logical empiricists toward an instrumentalist interpretation of scientific theories, treating all theoretical terms as "mere computational devices," helpful only for deriving additional observational predictions. Or one could follow Feyerabend, giving up the idea that reduction involves deduction (and hence requires logical consistency between reduced and reducing theories), instead viewing "reduction" as *replacement* of

T_R's ontology with that of the possibly incommensurable T_B. Or one could adopt Schaffner's strategy of "fall[ing] back on something like the Kemeny-Oppenheim paradigm" in these problematic cases and conclude that there is "no theory relation in [these] case[s]—only adequate explanation of the observational predictions of the previous theory" (1967, 145). Each move faces serious and familiar difficulties.

What has gone wrong? Notice that despite the differences between these accounts, a single diagnosis applies. The problematic cases arise from their treating reduction not just as deduction but as deduction of a *structure specified within the vocabulary and framework of the reduced theory*—either T_R itself or some corrected version T_R^*. What happens if we give up this feature? One thing we can get is Feyerabend's ontological-replacement view. But another, less radical possibility is Clifford Hooker's general model:

> *Within* T_B construct an analog, T_R^*, of T_R under certain conditions C_R such that T_B and C_R entails T_R^* and argue that the analog relation, AR, between T_R and T_R^* warrants claiming (some kind of) reduction relation, R, between T_R and T_B. Thus $(T_B \ \& \ C_R \supset T_R^*) \ \& \ (T_R^* \ AR \ T_R)$ warrants $(T_B \ R \ T_R)$. What this discussion indicates so far is that, while the construction of T_R^* within T_B may be a complicated affair—C_R might be fearfully complex (cf. biological reductions), counterfactual (e.g., assume continuity), necessarily counterfactual *qua* realization (e.g., "force free") and so on—the ultimate relation between T_B and T_R^* remains straightforward deduction. The importance of this is that T_B continues to directly explain T_R^* and this is the basis for T_B's indirect explanation of T_R's erstwhile scientific role. (1981, 49; my emphasis)[2]

On Hooker's account, neither T_R itself nor any structure constructed from its vocabulary and explanatory resources gets deduced in a reduction, not even in the smoothest cases. Rather, as Paul Churchland puts it, T_R is always the target of a kind of *complex mimicry* (1985, 11). This difference over what gets deduced is Hooker's first important insight about intertheoretic reduction.[3]

I borrow a helpful schematic illustration of Hooker's account from Paul Churchland (1985, 3), changing some of Churchland's notational conventions:

T_B and restricting conditions C_R (limiting assumptions, boundary conditions)

    logically entails

T_R^* (a set of theorems of [restricted] T_B),

e.g., $(x)(Ax \supset Bx), (x)((Bx \ \& \ Cx) \supset Dx)$,

   which is relevantly isomorphic with

T_R,

e.g., $(x)(Jx \supset Kx), (x)((Kx \ \& \ Lx) \supset Mx)$

Churchland's simplified example should not be taken as a serious attempt to analyze the notion of analog relation *AR*. Unfortunately, neither he nor Hooker have since carried the analysis much beyond this simplified illustration. I will pick up this problem at the end of this chapter. It provides an important segue into my theory of reduction, developed in the next chapter.

There are several similarities between Hooker's account and Nagel's orthodox empiricist account. For both, reduction is a proof of displacement (in principle), showing that a (typically) more comprehensive theory contains explanatory and predictive resources that parallel those of the reduced theory. In this fashion, reductions achieve explanatory unification. Contra Feyerabend, deduction remains at the heart of Hooker's reduction relation. Only what gets deduced has changed. For Nagel (and others), the reduced theory T_R itself (or a corrected version of it) is the conclusion. On Hooker's account, the conclusion of the deductive component of a reduction is a structure already within the vocabulary of the reducing theory T_B.

This single change addresses the "radical falsity" worry for paradigm cases of intertheoretic reduction within a realist philosophy of science. Neither connecting principles nor reductive functions play any role in the derivation of Hooker's T_R^*. There is no need for them. T_R^* is already specified within (a restricted portion of) the vocabulary of T_B. Elements analogous in some respects to connecting principles occur within Hooker's account, when we explore both the nature of the analog relation *AR* obtaining between T_R^* and T_R and the ontological consequences of a given reduction. But these elements are merely ordered pairs of terms, drawn from the nonlogical vocabularies of the two theories. Their sole function is to indicate the term substitutions in T_R^* that will yield the laws of T_R (or approximations of those laws, depending upon the extent to which the reduction corrects T_R). No worry arises about the "logical status" of ordered pairs of terms, even when one of a pair has no empirical extension. By themselves, these ordered pairs imply neither synonymy, synthetic identity, nor coextension.

How does Hooker's account capture ontological unification, his second-stated aim of reduction? A higher-order property of the reduction relation, its relative smoothness, justifies cross-theoretic identity claims. If the C_R does not contain numerous and wildly counterfactual restricting conditions and if most of the laws of T_R find close syntactic analogs within T_R^* (that is, if AR amounts to a "strong positive analogy"), this warrants our asserting (material) identities between the referents of the terms conjoined in the cross-theoretic ordered pairs. Put simply, cross-theoretic entity and property identities obtain when reductions don't entail large-scale corrections to the reduced theory. The direction of implication between the intertheoretic-reduction relation and the onto-logical consequences is the crucial point. As Paul Churchland puts it, "it is smooth intertheoretic reductions that motivate and sustain statements of cross-theoretic identity, and not the other way around" (1985, 11). Smooth intertheoretic reductions show that the reduced and reducing theories have latched onto the same entities or properties and have char-acterized them differently: respectively less and more fundamentally in terms of their ultimate constituents. As I will continually emphasize, this direction of implication—theory reduction first, ontological consequences second and dependent upon it—is a central component of new-wave reductionism.

Sometimes, however, we achieve ontological "unification" by *elimi-nating* the "referents" or "extension" of the terms of T_R. This occurs in the cases producing the worry discussed above for orthodox logical-empiricist accounts. How does Hooker's account capture this type of ontological simplification? Again, the same kind of higher-order property is the key: the reduction's relative *lack* of smoothness. In these cases, the C_R required to derive T_R^* from T_B contains numerous and wildly counterfactual restricting conditions, and even with the help of these conditions the analog relation AR between T_R^* and T_R remains weak. (T_R^* at best only grossly mimics the structure of the laws of T_R.)

This distinction between smooth and bumpy reduction shows another important feature of Hooker's account. Owing to the nature of the analog relation *AR*, there is a spectrum or continuum of cases lying between the smooth and bumpy endpoints. This is not a binary distinction, smooth or bumpy. Cases shade off from either endpoint, depending upon the extent and nature of the counterfactual elements of C_R and the strength of the analogy achieved.

I can illustrate this feature by locating some historically significant intertheoretic reductions according to an intuitive ordering of relative smoothness (figure 2.1, top arrow).[4] In the case of physical optics and electromagnetic theory, only minor corrections to the laws of physical

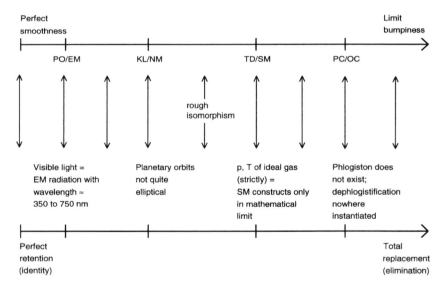

Figure 2.1
Top arrow: the intertheoretic reduction spectrum. Some historical cases are ranked (ordinally) according to the amount of correction to the reduced theory. Bottom arrow: the ontology spectrum. Cross-theoretic ontological consequences affiliated with these historical cases are ranked (ordinally) from retentive to eliminative. PO: physical optics (wave theory of light); EM: Maxwell's electromagnetic theory; KL: Kepler's laws of planetary motion; NM: Newtonian mechanics; TD: classical equilibrium thermodynamics; SM: statistical mechanics (kinetic/corpuscular theory of heat); PC: phlogiston chemistry; OC: oxygen chemistry. (From Bickle 1996.)

optics result (e.g., electromagnetic theory predicts an exponentially attenuated penetrating wave at reflection, physical optics does not). In the case of Kepler's laws and Newtonian mechanics, the latter corrects all the laws of the former, but only to a small degree of predictive difference. Newtonian mechanics leaves the conceptual apparatus of Kepler's laws in place. In the reduction of thermodynamics to statistical mechanics and kinetic theory, the implied amount of correction to the former is more extreme, concerning both its conceptual apparatus and nomic structure. Thermodynamic processes are intrinsically irreversible; statistical-mechanical processes are not. The theoretical constructs of thermodynamics obtain within statistical mechanics only under certain mathematical (and not empirically realizable) limiting conditions. In the reduction of phlogiston chemistry to oxidation chemistry, correction to the former is so extreme that only a few, quite pedestrian "observation" statements of phlogiston chemistry are retained. Not even the direction of dynamic processes are the same. Phlogiston is *released* during exothermic reactions; oxygen is *gained*. (See Hooker 1979, sec. 5, and 1981, sec. 3, for a more detailed discussion of these and other historical cases and their ordinal ranking on the intertheoretic-reduction spectrum.)

We can now see how ontological consequences depend upon the nature of the reduction relation in a nonarbitrary, non–*ad hoc* fashion. Compare the intertheoretic reduction spectrum, the top half of figure 2.1, with the ontological consequence spectrum, the bottom half of figure 2.1. This lower spectrum provides an intuitive ordering of the same cases concerning the retention, revision, or elimination of key posited entities and properties. The cross-theoretic ontological consequences are robustly retentive for cases falling near the "retention" endpoint. Cross-theoretic entity and property identities obtain. Consequences grow respectively more revisionary and finally eliminative for cases falling toward the rightmost endpoint. Notice that there is a rough isomorphism between the location of cases on the two spectrums. Relatively smooth intertheoretic reductions are affiliated with robustly retentive ontological consequences, while relatively bumpy reductions are affiliated with eliminativist conclusions.

Consider now one final wrinkle that Hooker (1981) introduces into his general theory of reduction. He wishes to distinguish genuine theory reduction from mere historical theory succession. To do so, he separates cases located too far from the "smooth" endpoint of the intertheoretic-reduction spectrum (top arrow of figure 2.1). "Reduction" is reserved for the smoother cases only. He gives two reasons for drawing this distinction. First, collapsing theory reduction into historical succession "relinquishes pursuit of the aims of reduction" (1981, 43), namely, explanatory and ontological unification. Second, it renders the theory of intertheoretic reduction "unintersting ... because the notion of a [theory's] domain is itself a theoretical construct from the science of the day" (1981, 43). I don't find either of these reasons compelling. The relevance of the second reason is not apparent, and the first just seems false. Both explanatory and ontological "unification" result in even the bumpiest cases by eliminating the explanatory use of the reduced/replaced theory and its ontology. (West Germany and the former East Germany were "unified," but the East German government and its institutions were replaced!) Thus *these reasons* don't compel me to distinguish theory reduction from mere historical succession. However, my commitment to scientific discourse and practice does. I've known few physicists willing to call the change from, e.g., phlogiston to oxygen chemistry a "reduction." Nevertheless, it remains interesting (and relevant for drawing ontological consequences) that a similar type of intertheoretic relation obtains in genuine reductions and many cases of historical succession. So while I will also distinguish genuine reductions from mere historical successions when I present my own theory in the next chapter, I will do so for reasons different from Hooker's. Also, my general approach to theory and intertheoretic relations allows me to provide a semiformal, quantitative account of this distinction, something Hooker (1981) admits he is unable to provide. I'll pick up with this limitation on Hooker's theory in the final section of this chapter.

We thus have the beginnings of a research program. To discover the projected ontological consequences of a potential intertheoretic reduction, first find where the case appears on the intertheoretic-reduction spectrum (top arrow of Figure 2.1). What sorts of counterfactual C_R conditions appear necessary to derive a T_R^* strongly analogous to the nomic structure of T_R? How strong an analogy can we construct, and how counterfactual are the limiting assumptions and boundary conditions required? On the basis of the isomorphism between the two spectrums, draw the appropriate ontological conclusion affiliated with this point on the intertheoretic reduction spectrum by drawing a line downward from the top arrow to the bottom arrow of the figure. This is the program of new-wave reductionism, applied specifically to potential reductions of psychological theories to neuroscientific theories. It is a specific application of this general procedure.

In the rest of this chapter I seek to accomplish three tasks. First, I will show how fruitful Hooker's approach to intertheoretic reduction is by constructing a Hooker reduction of the simple thermodynamics of gases to the kinetic theory supplemented with statistical mechanics. This case is both interesting in its own right and important for some later arguments. Second, I will show what the traditional mind-body problem looks like when reformulated in terms the project sketched in the previous paragraph. Third, I will raise an important problem for Hooker's general theory of reduction. This is a problem Hooker himself notes in his 1981 work but fails to solve. The problem is important enough to seek to realize Hooker's insights about reduction within an entirely different approach to the structure of theories and intertheoretic relations. This will set the stage for my own theory of intertheoretic reduction in chapter 3.

2   Applying Hooker's Theory: The Reduction of the Simple Thermodynamics of Gases to Kinetic Theory and Statistical Mechanics

The reduction of the simple thermodynamics of gases to the kinetic theory (microphysics) and statistical mechanics is familiar in the philosophy-of-science literature. Here I'll reconstruct some features of it in Hooker-reduction terms and draw some general conclusions for a theory of reduction. Beyond showing that this case is a genuine instance of intertheoretic reduction and illustrating the fruitfulness of Hooker's insights about reduction for general philosophy of science, this will also provide a case study for my own account of intertheoretic reduction developed in the next chapter and a concrete instance of an analogue structure T_R^*. (Hooker never provides the latter.) It will also play a key role (in chapter 4) in showing how new-wave reductionism is immune to the multiple-realizability challenge that helped sink classical psychophysical reduction.

A centerpiece of this reduction relates the *combined ideal gas law* of classical thermodynamics to an important theorem of statistical mechanics and the kinetic theory of gases.[5] At sufficiently low pressures and high temperatures, classical *ideal gases* obey three laws relating volume, pressure, and temperature. (An ideal gas does not undergo change in chemical complexity when pressure or temperature varies.) When temperature is kept constant, volume varies inversely with pressure. Mathematically, pressure multiplied by volume remains constant. This is Boyle's law:[6]

$$p_1 \cdot V_1 = p_2 \cdot V_2$$

At constant pressure, volume varies directly with absolute temperature (measured in degrees Kelvin). This is Charles's law:

$$\frac{V_1}{T_1} = \frac{V_2}{T_2}$$

At constant volume, pressure varies directly with absolute temperature. This is Gay-Lussac's law:

$$\frac{p_1}{T_1} = \frac{p_2}{T_2}$$

One can use any of these three laws to derive a law applying to all possible combinations of changes. This is the combined gas law, applicable to a fixed mass of gas, typically written in one of two ways:

$$\frac{p_1 \cdot V_1}{T_1} = \frac{p_2 \cdot V_2}{T_2} = \text{constant} \quad \text{or} \quad V_2 = V_1 \cdot \frac{T_2}{T_1} \cdot \frac{p_1}{p_2}$$

As volume increases (for a fixed mass of ideal gas), density (mass per unit volume) decreases proportionately. Thus density varies inversely with volume. For an ideal gas, it follows from the combined law that

$$d_2 = d_1 \cdot \frac{V_1}{V_2} = d_1 \cdot \frac{T_1}{T_2} \cdot \frac{p_2}{p_1}$$

(where *d* stands for density). These laws strictly hold only for ideal gases. That all gases can be liquefied (and hence made to undergo a change in chemical complexity) if sufficiently compressed and cooled shows that all gases become nonideal at high pressures and low temperatures. Note that the kinetic theory *explains* this "brute fact" from the perspective of thermodynamics. This displays one intuitive condition on reduction: increased explanatory power of the reducing theory in comparison with the reduced theory.

Avogadro's hypothesis says that equal volumes of all gases under the same conditions of temperature and pressure contain the same number of molecules. This is important for determining molecular weights of gases. Conjoined with the fact that 1 mole of any gas has the same number of molecules, N_A, as 1 mole of any other gas, it follows that 1 mole of gas has the same volume at S.T.P. as 1 mole of any other gas. This standard molar volume is 22.4 L (liters). S.T.P. is standard temperature and pressure, namely 273.15°K (0°C) and normal atmospheric pressure (760 torr, approximately the average pressure of the atmosphere at sea level). A mole, abbreviated mol., is a standard unit for an amount of a substance, a dimensionally independent quantity. A mole of atoms of any element is the amount of substance containing the same number of atoms as in exactly 12 grams of pure carbon (^{12}C). This number is Avogadro's constant, N_A; it is related to atomic mass, μ, as follows:

$$\text{mass of one mol of }^{12}C\text{ atoms} = N_A \cdot (\text{mass of one }^{12}C\text{ atom})$$

$$12\text{ g} \cdot \text{mol}^{-1} = N_A \cdot 12\mu$$

$$N_A = \frac{1\text{ g} \cdot \text{mol}^{-1}}{1\mu} = \frac{1\text{ g} \cdot \text{mol}^{-1}}{1.66 \cdot 10^{-27}\text{ kg} \cdot 10^3\text{ g} \cdot \text{kg}^{-1}} = 6.02 \cdot 10^{23}\text{ mol}^{-1}$$

We can now apply the combined gas law to 1 mole of an ideal gas. Following standard notational conventions, I let the subscript 0 denote standard conditions (S.T.P.):

$$\frac{pV}{T} = \frac{p_0 V_0}{T_0} = \frac{(1\text{ atm}) \cdot (22.4\text{ L/mol})}{273\text{ K}} = 0.08\text{ L} \cdot \text{atm} \cdot \text{K}^{-1} \cdot \text{mol}^{-1}$$

The quantity $R = 0.08\text{ L} \cdot \text{atm} \cdot \text{K}^{-1} \cdot \text{mol}^{-1}$ is the *universal gas constant*. For n moles of ideal gas at the same temperature and pressure, volume is n times greater. Thus $pV/T = nR$, or more standard, $pV = nRT$. This is the ideal gas law, with the above quantity for R when p is in atmospheres, V is in liters, T is in kelvins, and n is in moles. (When p is in pascals and V in cubic meters, $R = 8.314\text{ J} \cdot \text{K}^{-1} \cdot \text{mol}^{-1}$, where J stands for joules.) For an ideal gas, V is proportional to n when p and T are fixed. This fact enables us to calculate gas-volume relations from statements of chemical equations.

As mentioned above, a key step (though not the only step) in the reduction of classical thermodynamics to the kinetic theory involves showing how microscopic properties of gas molecules relate to macroscopic properties of ideal gases captured by the combined gas law. This argument involves some assumptions about the nature of molecules and the application of laws from Newtonian mechanics. Details of the kinetic theory of gases can be found in virtually every elementary physics text. I won't explicitly state them but instead will simply use them in the mechanical argument concluding that temperature is directly proportional to mean molecular kinetic energy (indicating such assumptions with an "A"). Suppose that we contain an ideal gas in a rectangular volume with length (x axis) $= l$, height (y axis) $= h$, and width (z axis) $= w$. The volume of this container $V = l \cdot h \cdot w$ (cubic meters, say). Suppose that the number of molecules is N, each with mass m and moving at velocity v (meters per second). We can analyze the motion of the molecules as a vector sum of three components at right angles to each other, selecting one direction parallel to the length of the container (v_x), one to the height (v_y), and one to the width (v_z). Since molecules are in a state of constant random motion with no net motion in one direction (A), we can assume that each component making up the motion vector sum contains an equal share of the motion (1/3).

Consider now a molecule traveling parallel to the x axis that collides with the side of the container. Its momentum is mv. So since all molecular collisions are perfectly elastic (there is no change to the kinetic energy of the molecule following a collision) (A), its change of momentum is $-mv - mv = -2mv$ (in the opposite direction from which the molecule came). The impulse imparted on the wall of the container from this collision is thus $+2mv$ (in the original same direction). Given that the molecule's diameter is negligible compared to length l (A), the time interval between this collision and the next one of this molecule at the same wall is $2l/v$. Hence the number of times this molecule will collide with this wall during a unit time interval is $v/2l$ (since the distance it travels back and forth along the x axis is $2l$). By Newton's Second Law, the force exerted by this molecule on the side is the rate at which the molecule transfers momentum to it, that is, the impulse of a single collision multiplied by the number of collisions per unit time (A):

$$2mv \cdot \frac{v}{2l} = \frac{mv^2}{l}$$

The total force delivered in a unit time on that wall of the container is the product of the force delivered by all the molecules striking it. By the supposition above that 1/3 of the molecules are moving parallel to the x axis, the total force on the wall per unit time is as follows:

$$\frac{N}{3} \cdot \frac{mv^2}{l} = \frac{Nmv^2}{3l}$$

The width and height of the container, respectively w and h, bound the wall we are considering. Its area is thus wh square units. We can now calculate the force per square unit by dividing the total force on the side by the number of square units:

$$\frac{Nmv^2}{3l} \cdot \frac{1}{wh} = \frac{Nmv^2}{3lwh} = \frac{N}{3lwh} mv^2 = \frac{2N}{3lwh} \cdot \frac{1}{2} mv^2$$

Rearranging, we get equation 1:

Equation 1 $$\frac{Nmv^2}{3lwh} \cdot lwh = \frac{2N}{3} \cdot \frac{1}{2} mv^2$$

So far, all calculations have involved resources solely from kinetic theory (i.e., microphysics), statistics, and Newtonian mechanics. I applied no resources from the simple thermodynamics of gases. I can now introduce some cross-theoretic ordered pairs of terms:

$$\langle \text{"}p\text{"}, \text{"}Nmv^2/3lwh\text{"} \rangle$$

$$\langle \text{"}V\text{"}, \text{"}lwh\text{"} \rangle$$

The first pair represents pressure and force exerted against a unit area, and in the second pair, both quantities are measures of volume.

Furthermore, in Newtonian mechanics the quantity $(1/2)mv^2$ represents kinetic energy e_k, the work that must be done to move a body of mass m at velocity v, and hence the kinetic energy contained in a body of mass m moving at velocity v. Thus we also have the following cross-theoretic pair:

$$\langle \text{"}\tfrac{1}{2} mv^2\text{"}, \text{"}e_k\text{"} \rangle$$

Substituting these terms into equation 1, we get

$$pV = \frac{2N}{3} e_k$$

But $2N/3$ is a constant, since the number of molecules N in the gas remains constant, so pressure times volume is directly proportional to the kinetic energy of the gas's molecules. The classical ideal gas law says that pressure multiplied by volume is directly proportional to temperature, which implies that temperature is directly proportional to the kinetic energy of the molecules constituting an ideal gas.

In terms of Hooker's theory of reduction, we have derived within statistical mechanics and the kinetic theory (T_B) *an analog structure* (T_R^*) (equation 1) of the combined gas law of the simple thermodynamics of gases (T_R). The assumptions of the portion of kinetic theory we have used here embody two counterfactual C_R conditions: that there are no attractive forces among the constituent molecules of a gas and that molecules are so small that their volume is negligible compared to the space between them. The first assumption is false, strictly speaking, because there are always weak attractive forces obtaining between actual molecules. The second is false, strictly speaking, because the volume of a molecule is not really zero. Relaxing these counterfactual conditions allows the kinetic theory to handle experimental results with real gases that deviate from the ideal gas laws.

We can further develop this analog structure T_R^* (equation 1) to mimic more features of the simple thermodynamics of gases. A further C_R condition built into the assumptions of the kinetic theory as developed so far is that all the molecules of a gas have identical velocities. This is not true. As molecules collide, momentum gets transferred randomly, although the total momentum remains constant. The distribution of velocities is predictable, however, by the Maxwell-Boltzmann distribution. Since there is a distribution of velocities among the molecules, there is a distribution of kinetic energies. We can map these on a graph relating molecular velocity per unit distance per unit time (x axis) to the fraction of molecules at the various distributions (y axis). The resulting curve for actual temperatures is roughly bell-shaped (though it flattens out as temperatures approach absolute zero, $0°K$ or $-273°C$). Three velocities are important: the *most* *probable velocity* v_{mp}, the velocity at which the distribution curve has maximum value on the y axis; the slightly higher *average (or mean) velocity* v_{avg}; and the even slightly higher *root-mean-squared velocity* v_{rms}, the velocity for which a molecule's kinetic energy would be equal to the average kinetic energy over the entire aggregate. Now v_{rms} relates mathematically to v_{avg} by the following equation:

$$\tfrac{1}{2} m(v_{rms})^2 = (\tfrac{1}{2} mv^2)_{avg}$$

For the Maxwell-Boltzmann distribution we get the following relationship:

$$v_{rms} = \frac{(3kT)^{1/2}}{m}$$

Here the Boltzmann constant $k = 1.38 \times 10^{-23}$ J/K (joules per Kelvin, a measure of energy related to absolute temperature) and T is shorthand for kinetic energy per molecule (given that we have already established that temperature is directly proportional to kinetic energy). Thus from equation 1 and these latest equations, and by simplifying, we get this:

$$\frac{Nmv^2}{3lwh} \cdot lwh = \frac{2}{3} N \left[\frac{1}{2} m(v_{rms})^2 \right] = \frac{2}{3} N \left[\frac{1}{2} m \frac{3kT}{m} \right] = \frac{2}{3} N \frac{3kT}{2} = NkT$$

Since N (number of molecules comprising the gas) $= nN_A$ (the number of moles n multiplied by the number of molecules per mole, Avogadro's constant N_A), and if we make the cross-theoretic term substitutions into the analog structure (equation 1), the result is the combined gas law with $N_A k$ for R:

$$pV = nN_A kT$$

We thus obtain as the value of R (when p and V are expressed in S.I. values, respectively pascals and cubic meters):

$$R = N_A k = (6.02 \times 10^{23} \text{ mol}^{-1}) \cdot (1.38 \times 10^{-23} \text{J/K})$$

$$= 8.31 \text{J} \cdot \text{K}^{-1} \cdot \text{mol}^{-1}$$

This, of course, is the same value for R obtained from the combined ideal gas law of thermodynamics.

We can thus reconstruct the relation between the simple thermodynamics of gases and statistical mechanics plus kinetic theory (microphysics) in terms of Hooker's account of intertheoretic reduction. We derive an analog structure of the combined ideal gas law of the former (equation 1) as a theorem of the latter.[7] With this important illustration in place, let's now turn to the second task mentioned at the end of the last section to see how Hooker's insights about intertheoretic reduction can help us fruitfully reformulate the philosophical mind-body problem.

3   The Intertheoretic-Reduction Reformulation of the Mind-Body Problem

In its traditional guise, the philosophical mind-body problem is ontological.[8] It concerns the fundamental constituents of the universe, the basic stuff or stuffs out of which nature compounds cognizers. Philosophers often state the problem in question form. What is the nature of mind? How do mental events relate to physical events, especially the physical events occurring in functioning nervous systems? Is the mind identical with, the same thing as, the functioning brain? Or is mind something more than, something beyond, the workings of purely physical objects?

Some contemporary philosophers have argued that this issue needs reformulating, that we need to find a better way to state and address the real problem. One recent reformulation begins by asserting that our commonsense conception of the mental is a *theory*. We can then reformulate the mind-body problem into a question about a future *intertheoretic reduction*. The problem concerns how two theories of human behavior (or two theoretical frameworks), a commonsense or "folk" psychology and some future theory from the brain and behavioral sciences, will (or will not) cohere. The defensible ontological conclusion becomes secondary to and dependent upon this logically prior issue of intertheoretic reduction.

A key motivation here is the insight that its exclusive ontological focus is perhaps what keeps the mind-body problem unsolved, even after a century of groundbreaking work in the brain and behavioral sciences. Vague and unclear notions often infect and distract investigations proceeding strictly at the ontological level. Patricia Churchland once pointed out,

When we raise the question of whether mental states are reducible to brain states, this question must be posed first in terms of whether some theory concerning the nature of mental states is reducible to a theory describing how the neuronal ensembles work, and second in terms of whether it reduces in such a way that the mental states of T_R can be identified with the neuronal states of T_B. *A good deal of muddle concerning reduction can be avoided with this initial clarification regarding reductive relations.* (1986, 279; my emphasis)

I will refer to this proposal as the *intertheoretic-reduction reformulation* of the mind-body problem, or for short, the *IR reformulation*.[9]

On the IR reformulation, we must first inquire into the candidate reduced and reducing theories to reformulate the traditional issue. Since modern interest is whether mental states and events are states and events of higher terrestrial nervous systems, it is uncontroversial that the candidate T_B is some future theory from the cognitive and brain sciences.[10] Both psychology and the neurosciences are currently a long way from providing a comprehensive explanatory framework for cognition, and there is no guarantee that they ever will. But progress has been impressive, especially recently. No one knows just how far we will progress toward the distant goal of comprehensive explanation, but there is no reason to believe that the relevant sciences are presently near their theoretical limits.

What theory is the candidate T_R? Which theoretical framework posits our mentalistic ontology? The prima facie answer is obvious: some ideal (and not yet existent) *scientific psychology*, some "integrated body of generalizations describing the high-level states and processes and their causal interactions that underlie behavior" (Patricia Churchland 1986, 295). As many have pointed out, the possibility of future neuroscientific reduction is not in serious question for many established psychological generalizations and principles. This includes generalizations from learning theory, perception, and memory; some of developmental psychology; and elements of clinical and abnormal psychology. What remains at issue? What remains the source of worries about the claim that a developed scientific psychology, as a whole, will reduce to future cognitive neuroscience?

Patricia Churchland provides an interesting answer. She claims that once we clear away confusions and misunderstandings about reduction, antireductionist worries rest upon the intuition that some aspects of our *ordinary, commonsense understanding of mental states and processes,* our *folk psychology,* are both correct and irreducible to neuroscientific theory: "Virtually all arguments against reduction, if they are not just confusions about what intertheoretic reduction is, depend on the designation of some aspect of our *common sense framework* as correct and irreducible" (1986, 299; my emphasis). The designated aspects might be conscious awareness or the qualitative character of experienced mental events or their essential subjectivity or the special access cognizers have to their mental states, as dualists have historically emphasized. Or the correct and irreducible aspect of folk psychology might be the representational character, the "intentionality," of mental states and events, as more recent antireductionists have stressed. Despite the aspect of mind antireductionists invoke, Churchland's insight suggests a reductionist agenda. Responses must focus directly on folk psychology, this "common sense framework, its relation to scientific psychology, and its epistemological status" (Patricia Churchland 1986, 299). It must be the target of intertheoretic reduction if the IR reformulation is to capture the point at issue in the traditional philosophical mind-body problem.

I can also cast this conclusion historically. Historically, the mind-body problem has concerned the fundamental nature of mental phenomena *as ordinarily conceived and experienced.* "Ordinary language" arguments of the twentieth century, based on analysis of everyday discourse about the mental, is only the culmination of this tradition. At issue has been the status of those mental states, processes, and events that are entertained by all and that all persons are subject to and aware of as such. Thus if the IR reformulation is to offer a *historically* adequate reformulation of the traditional mind-body question, it must capture this fact about what has traditionally been at issue. It does this by treating folk psychology as the theory on which the integrity of the historically relevant mentalistic ontology rides.

What generalizations make up folk psychology? A homey example is illustrative. You ask why Alonzo isn't joining us at the pub tonight. I reply that he has an important deadline to meet at work tomorrow. You understand. But what has done the explaining? One plausible answer is that you have a tacit grasp of the explanatory generalization or law underwriting my abbreviated response. What is that generalization or law? It applies to more than just Alonzo's behavior, behavior when deadlines are looming, and behavior concerning pubs. Instead, it is something to the effect that whenever person p wishes to bring about a state of affairs s and believes that engaging in activity a is incompatible (or at least in strong tension) with bringing about s, then typically (ceteris paribus) p will not engage in a. Substitute "Alonzo" for "p," "meeting tomorrow's deadline" for "s," and "joining us at the pub tonight" for "a," and you have (a very pedantic version of) my explanation of Alonzo's behavior. Folk psychology is that vast collection of abstract generalizations appealing to the propositional or otherwise linguistic attitudes (wishes, beliefs, actions), and logical interactions between their contents, that underlie and inform our everyday psychological understanding of one another.[11]

However, construing folk psychology as the candidate T_R in the IR reformulation presupposes what many now take to be a controversial claim: that folk psychology is a *theory*. Whether it is or not has sparked a voluminous literature of late, including both conceptual arguments and empirical studies.[12] My attitude toward this literature is that it is beside the point of *this use* of folk psychology as theory. (There are other uses of the thesis, and no doubt this literature is relevant to these.) To treat folk psychology as the targeted reduced theory in the IR reformulation, all that matters is that we *can* construe our commonsense conception of the mental as a theory. It doesn't matter whether it is actually "stored in the head" as a theory (see the theory-theory-versus-simulation literature cited in note 12) or whether it constitutes more than just a theory (i.e., plays roles other than generating predictions and explanations of behavior). All that matters for the IR reformulation is that folk psychology *can be treated* as the theory that our commonsense ontology of the mental belongs with. In view of how generalizations seem to underwrite our everyday use of mentalistic terminology, it is difficult to deny that folk psychology is a theory in this minimal sense.

So the IR reformulation holds that the mind-body problem is primarily an issue in theory reduction. Folk psychology is the targeted reduced theory, and some future cognitive or brain science is the targeted reducing theory. What does the IR reformulation accomplish? What do we get by reformulating the mind-body problem in this fashion? First, if it adequately captures the traditional issue, the IR reformulation promises significant advantages toward a rational resolution over what more traditional (i.e., exclusively ontological) approaches have yielded. The central reason is that it puts to work a well-studied, well-illustrated central notion: intertheoretic reduction. Replacing the murky notion of ontological reduction with this better understood notion is the primary advantage of the IR reformulation over more traditional approaches. To again borrow a line from Patricia Churchland, "By making theories the fundamental relata [of the reduction relation], much of the metaphysical bewilderment and dottiness concerning how entities or properties could be reduced simply vanish[es]" (1986, 280–281). We can appeal to examples from the history of science concerning the amount of correction entailed to the reduced theory and the subsequent ontological conclusions drawn, in keeping with the general program illustrated in figure 2.1. When we add the IR reformulation to new-wave reductionism, we will have a sophisticated and well-grounded account of intertheoretic reduction at our behest.

Subsequent advantages of the IR reformulation follow from this primary one. Taking intertheoretic reduction as the primary issue, we obtain clear and justifiable criteria for the relevance of particular sorts of evidence and argument. The relevant criteria are just those sorts relevant toward solving any other theory-reduction question. How closely do the explanatory and predictive resources of the reducing theory mimic the nomological structure of the reduced theory? What is the explanatory scope of the reducing theory via the reduced theory? How much correction does the reducing theory imply to the reduced theory? These are the criteria stemming from Hooker's insights about reduction, and they greatly streamline the kinds of arguments relevant to the mind-body problem. Even a brief tour through the dialectical thicket created by the traditional mind-body problem reveals the advantages of having a defensible litmus test for admissible arguments and evidence. For example, one kind of argument, popular in the mid twentieth century (and not entirely absent now), is clearly irrelevant to the issue of IR reformulation. This is the "ordinary language" strategy of arguing that mental states and events cannot be identical to brain states and events because neurobiological terminology and explanations are incompatible with everyday discourse about minds and mental events. Jerome Shaffer's often-cited (and still anthologized) passage is a good example:

> The fact that it *makes no sense at all* to speak of mental events as occurring at some point within the body has the result that the identity theory cannot be true. This is because the corresponding physical events do occur at some point within the body, and if those physical events are identical with mental events, then those mental events must occur at the same point within the body. But those mental events do not occur at any point within the body because *any statement to the effect that they occur here, or there, would be senseless.* Hence the mental events cannot meet the conditions of coexistence in space, and therefore cannot be identical with physical events. (1968, 48–49; my emphasis)

This argument simply begs the question posed by IR reformulation, since the very propriety of these ordinary linguistic practices encapsulated in folk psychology is exactly the point at issue.

A catchy way of phrasing this point is to say that on the IR reformulation, philosophy of mind becomes a specialized part of applied philosophy of science, although a part with a special intrigue, since its subject matter is ourselves. This reformulation also renders many rigorous and rich resources from twentieth-century philosophy of science directly applicable to this traditional philosophical issue. We can finally address questions about the ontology of mind from the perspective of a rigorous philosophy of science.

4 The "Place for Everything" Argument

Beyond these metaphilosophical advantages, however, lies the strongest argument for the IR reformulation. The latter finds a place around the intertheoretic-reduction spectrum for all of the traditional solutions to the mind-body problem in a way that illustrates the relations between seemingly disparate theses.[13] Call this the "place for everything" argument. Each traditional solution gets reformulated as a *prediction* concerning the reductive fate of folk psychology. Consider first the varieties of *dualism*. Traditionally, dualists claim that mental states and processes, as ordinarily conceived and experienced, are in a realm of either substances or properties forever beyond explanation by physical science. Translated into the IR reformulation, this amounts to a prediction of the explanatory success and irreducibility of folk psychology for at least some domain of behavior. It is the prediction that folk psychology will continue to provide the best explanation for that domain beyond anything the physical sciences will develop. We thus remain ontologically committed to the referents of its explanatory resources, mental states and processes as ordinarily conceived and experienced, just as we remain ontologically committed to the explanatory resources of all successful irreducible theories. An example of this general point is the commitment we maintain to electrical charge as a fundamental property of physical objects, given the failure of electromagnetics to intertheoretically reduce to mechanics.

The electrical-charge example nicely illustrates another thing: how *property dualism* gets reformulated. Electromagnetics, though irreducible to mechanics, remains a branch of physics. So its irreducibility doesn't show that something other than physical *objects* exist. Instead, it shows that mechanics doesn't exhaust the physical *properties* of the universe. Besides mass, length, velocity, and gravitation, there is in addition the property of electrical charge. The irreducibility of folk psychology might yield a similar lesson. The objects subject to the irreducible laws of folk psychology might also be subject to the laws of physics. In this case the ontological lesson to be drawn from the irreducibility of folk psychology would be not that there are nonphysical *substances* in the universe but rather that there are nonphysical *properties* of some physical objects. Only here, in a disanalogy with electrodynamics, these mental properties will be distinct from the whole of physical science, including mechanics, electromagnetism, quantum theory, and the rest. Such a result is IR-reformulated *property dualism*.

We can even carry dualism beyond this prediction. It might seem unfair to saddle all dualists with commitment to folk psychology, in view of the latter's homely origins and the progressive capacity of science. The key to dualism, on the IR reformulation, is irreducibility of theory at the level of psychology to lower-level theories in reductive contact with basic physics. So we can imagine a dualist insisting that folk psychology will itself someday smoothly reduce, only to a more comprehensive psychological theory that does not itself reduce further. Interestingly, some landmarks in the functionalist literature from two decades back sound remarkably like IR-reformulated "reductive dualism." Fodor, for example, once wrote,

> If we think about what these [commonsense mentalistic] generalizations are like, what's striking is that all of the candidates—literally *all* of them—are generalizations that apply to propositional attitudes in virtue of the content of the propositional attitudes.... The point of such examples is not, of course, that any of [these] are likely to figure in a serious cognitive psychology. It's rather that our attempts at a serious cognitive psychology are founded on the hope that *this kind* of generalization can be systematized and made rigorous. (1981, 25–26)

Folk psychology won't constitute the ultimate cognitive science, but cognitive scientists will adopt its basic explanatory strategy, and in this sense it will maintain reductive contact with our best and irreducible science of the mental. This point nicely supplements the charge made in chapter 1, section 2, that much functionalism and subsequent nonreductive materialisms are actually property dualisms in thin disguise. On this view, we remain ontologically committed to the explanatory resources of this comprehensive successor, to which the entities or properties of folk psychology enjoy cross-theoretic ontological identification via the smooth intertheoretic reduction but which don't reduce further to the physical sciences.

We can even imagine a quite unorthodox dualist who insists that we will only achieve a very bumpy reduction of folk psychology to some successful yet irreducible psychological successor. Hence we eliminate the ontology of folk psychology in favor of this more penetrating explanatory framework of nonphysical reality and wind up with an almost paradoxical-sounding "eliminative dualism." (The mystical tradition, in both its popular and scholarly forms, might provide examples.)

Next let us consider *functionalist* solutions in a bit more detail. A priori functionalism insists that mental states and processes, as ordinarily conceived and experienced, are really abstract "functional" or "computational" states and processes. These mediate causally between sensory inputs, other internal functional or computational states, and behavioral outputs.[14] By recognizing the need to posit these internal states and processes to avoid the well-known problems sinking purely behavioral analyses of mental kinds, functionalism succeeds philosophical behaviorism.[15] Functionalists also insist that these functional or computational properties are never ontologically reducible to (identical with) specific physical properties of any organism instantiating the relevant functional network, owing to multiple realizability. Physically very diverse substrata can instantiate identical functional networks. Translated into the IR reformulation, a priori functionalism amounts to the prediction that folk psychology will remain the best account of at least some domains of human behavior, with its kinds interpreted functionally or computationally. So interpreted, folk psychology will not reduce to any future theory of the physical details of any one of its many possible instantiations. On this basis, we will remain ontologically committed to folk-psychological kinds interpreted as abstract functional kinds.

We can imagine functionalist variations on the IR reformulation. One kind of functionalist (which Block [1978] dubs a "psychofunctionalist") insists that folk psychology, interpreted computationally, will smoothly reduce to part of some more comprehensive computational psychology. This more comprehensive framework will not reduce to physical science. Some of Jerry Fodor's writings seem naturally interpreted in this fashion. Fodor once wrote, "We were driven to functionalism (hence to the autonomy of psychology) by the suspicion that there are empirical generalizations about mental states that can't be formulated in the vocabulary of neurological or physical theories: neurology and physics don't, we supposed, provide projectible kind-predicates that subtend the domains of these generalizations" (1981, 25). Furthermore, these generalizations borrow their basic structure from folk psychology, as they "apply to propositional attitudes in virtue of the content of the propositional attitudes." On the IR reformulation, Fodor's claim here is tantamount to predicting that folk psychology will enjoy a relatively smooth intertheoretic reduction to this more systematic and rigorous "serious scientific psychology." We would thus remain ontologically committed to the explanatory kinds of this successor science, to its physically irreducible functional or computational posits, and hence to folk psychology's ontology as cross-theoretically identified with these kinds via the smooth intertheoretic reduction.

On the other hand, a scientifically inspired "psychofunctionalist" might predict an eliminative result. On the IR reformulation, this amounts to the prediction that only a bumpy reduction will obtain for folk psychology to some future computational psychology. We might interpret Stephen Stich's (1983) perspective on the fate of folk psychology in this way.[16] Stich argues that folk psychology greatly restricts its domain of application because it types mental states according to their propositional contents. The problem is that content ascription, a necessary component of this typing, necessarily involves context-dependent "similarity assessments" between ascriber and ascribee. These assessments grow problematic as we move away from subjects cognitively like ourselves and finally become downright impossible in cases involving very young children, primitive peoples, and the clinically abnormal. Thus a cognitive psychology continuous with folk psychology, which is committed to generalizations couched in terms of propositional contents, will fail to provide an adequate developmental, comparative, and abnormal psychology. Furthermore, (according to Stich 1983, chapter 8), an alternative strategy for cognitive science, the Syntactic Theory of Mind (STM), is not so restricted. This strategy types mental states in terms of purely syntactic mental sentences. STM is thus committed to a "narrow causal account" of content, with content typed strictly by a state's causal antecedents and effects. This allows cognitive science to capture any generalizations that our own behavior shares with exotic folk. However, it finds no place for the ontology of folk psychology. By typing mental contents strictly along narrow causal lines, it counts as type-identical many mental-state tokens that folk psychology distinguishes, and vice versa.

Translated into the IR reformulation, Stich's position predicts a very bumpy intertheoretic reduction of folk psychology to a future cognitive psychology built on STM. This will entail large-scale correction to the explanatory structure of the former. In keeping with the ontological consequences of bumpy intertheoretic reductions, this amounts to an "eliminative functionalism."

I've already noted similarities from the IR-reformulation perspective between some landmark statements of functionalism and property dualism. These similarities should not be surprising in view of the comparison in chapter 1 between contemporary nonreductive physicalism and traditional property dualism. Much recent nonreductive physicalism is the direct heir of functionalism. It simply adopts classical functionalist arguments against reduction but couples these with a disdain for the way functionalists individuate mental content (Horgan 1994). Familiar Twin Earth thought experiments ground the disdain. The intuition pumped is that an earthling and his or her Twin Earth doppelgänger could be in identical functional states while entertaining mental states with distinct content. My state is about water, my doppelgänger's is about twater (whose chemical composition is XYZ).[17] Nevertheless, in one respect the functionalism of twenty years ago is not as objectionable on this point as contemporary nonreductive physicalism. By identifying mental properties with abstract functional or computational properties, functionalism provides what is for many an unobjectionable special status for these nonphysical properties. It is perhaps not intractably mysterious to allow into one's ontology a distinction between physical and functional/computational properties. Solving philosophical problems besides the mind-body problem might also warrant this. However, most contemporary nonreductive physicalists, who deny even the identity between mental properties and functional/computational properties, cannot help themselves to this perhaps unobjectionable ontological category. Their mental properties and events are again as ontologically mysterious as those of any admitted property or event dualist. (See again chapter 1, section 2, above.)

This brings us finally to the traditional materialist solutions. First there is *reductive materialism*, or the *mind-brain identity theory*. Its central theme is that mental states and processes, as ordinarily conceived and experienced, are numerically identical to states and processes in the working central nervous systems of higher organisms. Translated into the IR reformulation, this becomes the prediction that folk psychology will smoothly reduce to some future neuroscientific successor, yielding the cross-theoretic identifications afforded by reductions at this end of the intertheoretic-reduction spectrum. This reformulated claim provides a natural interpretation of many passages by influential identity theorists. Despite admitting his attraction for Feyerabend's more radical materialism, J. J. C. Smart once still insisted, "Just as J. K. Galbraith in his book *The Affluent Society* prefers where possible to argue against what he calls 'the conventional wisdom' on its own grounds, so I think that it is worthwhile trying to meet some of my own philosophical friends as far as possible on their own grounds, *which is the analysis of ordinary language*" (1963, 170). The ordinary language at issue is commonsense discourse about the mental. Smart is here insisting that part of the materialist's task is to show (to the extent possible) that ordinary mentalistic discourse is not beyond materialistic (e.g., neurobiological) analysis or translation. On the IR reformulation, this amounts to the prediction that a good portion of folk psychology, the theory informing ordinary mentalistic discourse, will smoothly reduce to future neurobiology.

Then there is a materialist alternative of more recent vintage: *eliminative materialism*. Eliminativists like to compare the ontological status of mind in light of a (future) developed neuroscience to those of caloric fluid pressure and dephlogistification in light of, respectively, kinetic heat theory and oxidative chemistry. The eliminativist's general theme is that sometimes a novel explanatory theory, significantly more powerful than its predecessor, affords no straightforward translation of the previous theory's explanatory kinds. We then simply abandon the less successful framework, along with its affiliated ontology. To one eliminative materialist, Rorty (1965), the materialist assertion that mental states and processes are really brain states and processes resembles the assertion that demonic possession is really a form of hallucinatory psychosis. The latter claim is elliptical for "What people used to call 'demonic possession' is really a form of hallucinatory psychosis." In turn this entails that there is no such thing as demonic possession as previously conceptualized. Eliminativists urge a similar lesson about mentalistic ascriptions and kinds.

It is crucial to bear in mind that eliminative materialists typically have as their target mental states and processes as ordinarily conceived and experienced. The appeal of Feyerabend's eliminativism to otherwise staunch reductive materialists, like Smart (1963, 1967) and Feigl (1968), was the path it provided around objections, offered by ordinary-language philosophers, to their "translational" forms of the identity theory. These objections typically purported to show that a detailed analysis of what we *ordinarily mean* by "sensation," "pain," "believes that *p*," and so on, shows how radically different these ordinary mental concepts are from those of the physical sciences. Hence no physicalist translation of them could hope to capture their meanings or adequately characterize the properties they express. To these sorts of arguments, the eliminativist offers full assent. The scientific concept of pain is neither synonymous nor even coextensive with the ordinary-language concept. Because "Every interesting discussion, that is every discussion which leads to an advance of knowledge, terminates in a situation where some decisive change of meaning has occurred.... A new theory of pains will not change the pains.... It will change the meaning of 'I am in pain'" (Feyerabend 1962, 58). In addition, the scientific concept is part of a potentially much more powerful explanatory framework than the ordinary concept. So, given the incommensurability of the two frameworks, adopting the scientific framework requires us to jettison our ordinary mentalistic kinds.

Translated into the IR reformulation, eliminative materialism is the prediction that folk psychology will enjoy at best an extremely bumpy reduction to some future cognitive neuroscience. It will fall in with the reduction of caloric fluid to kinetic theory and the reduction of phlogiston to oxygen chemistry on the intertheoretic-reduction spectrum (top arrow of figure 2.1). In keeping with the ontological consequences of intertheoretic reductions at this location, we will eliminate mental states and processes as ordinarily conceived and experienced from our future scientific ontology.

Rephrased in terms of the IR reformulation, every traditional solution to the mind-body problem finds a place around the intertheoretic-reduction spectrum showing the possible fates of folk psychology. Furthermore, we get an interesting answer to a question that has not received much attention. Why, traditionally, have so few solutions to the mind-body problem warranted serious consideration? One might think that since so many intellectual giants have investigated the problem for so long, many different solutions would be on the table. This is simply not so. All we really have are the two basic varieties of dualism (substance and property), functionalism, and reductive and eliminative physicalism. Why so few?

The IR reformulation offers an answer. These traditional alternatives pretty much exhaust the possibilities for an intertheoretic reduction of folk psychology to some scientific successor, given the available scientific alternatives. Some of folk psychology might not reduce. This gives us the varieties of dualism. Contemporary science provides two basic research methodologies with pretensions of comprehensive explanations: cognitive/computational psychology and neurobiology. Hence we have functionalism (and nonreductive physicalism) and reductive materialism. Finally, there is the possibility of bumpy reduction to its scientific successor. This gives the varieties of eliminativism. That about exhausts the possible reductive outcomes for folk psychology, or so it has seemed to the tradition.

I conclude that the IR reformulation built on a theory of intertheoretic reduction adequate for the methodology and ontology of science generally is an advantageous and adequate reformulation of the traditional philosophical mind-body problem. I also contend that Hooker's insights about intertheoretic reduction carry us a long way toward an adequate theory of scientific reduction. But they don't carry us quite far enough. This was the third point I stressed at the end of section 1 of this chapter. For the purposes of new-wave reduction and the IR reformulation, Hooker's theory is incomplete. This incompleteness affects one of the key features of new-wave reduction: the spectrum of intertheoretic reductions (top arrow of figure 2.1). This is a limitation that Hooker himself acknowledges. After developing a detailed account of cross-theoretic identities as working hypotheses in potential reductions, Hooker writes, "Against this theoretical background, what can be said about a theory of the retention/replacement distinction? ... Unhappily, I can think of no neat formal conditions which would intuitively separate the two—we are dealing with a continuum which grades off across examples from retention to replacement" (1981, 223). Crucial is formal representation of the preservation of the nomic role of properties and objects: "The key lies in the importance of properties in mathematical sciences as organising focii for sets of nomic relations and the conditions of contingent identity as requiring preservation of nomic role" (Hooker 1981, 223). Hooker even hints at how to construct a measure of property preservation, and a subsequent account of object retention based upon preservation of their theoretically central properties: "Comparative preservation indices may be definable by ranking the properties (mathematical structures) and weighing these rankings with some measure of their preservation. (For example, intuitively the local preservation of euclidean structure in General Relativity is more nearly a preservation than is the retention of algebraic structure between thermodynamics and statistical mechanics.) ... Retention of objects can be assigned a degree by assessing the degree of retention of their theoretically central properties (as measured by their ranking order in the abstract mathematical hierarchy)" (1981, 223–224). But his upshot is honest: "All of this is very programmatic and as yet lacking in deep yet simple insight" (1981, 224). To my knowledge, since his 1981 work Hooker has not returned to address this lack. I insist that addressing it is crucial to defending new-wave reductionism. The next chapter is offered in this spirit.

Here some sympathizers to new-wave reduction will demur. Some question any need to find a formally specifiable measure for the inter-theoretic-reduction spectrum. Patricia Churchland, for example, writes, "Determining when the fit [reduction relation] is close enough to claim identities between properties of the old [theory] and those of the new *is not a matter for formal criteria....* I do not think it matters very much that we establish criteria for determining when the reduced and reducing theory resemble each other sufficiently to herald identity of properties" (1986, 283–284; my emphasis). But we should not ignore the disastrous limitations of this attitude if we wish to draw ontological conclusions based on the nature of the intertheoretic-reduction relation. Because of her anti-formal-criteria view about the intertheoretic-reduction spectrum, Churchland is forced to conclude that her ontological eliminativism emerges primarily at the behest of "a variety of social and pragmatic considerations," including "the whim of the central investigators, ... the opportunities for publicizing the theory, cadging grants, and attracting disciples" (1986, 283). That is an interesting upshot. Sounding at first so brash, radical, and empirically motivated, Churchland's ontological eliminativism now appears to be little more than an episode in the sociology of science (see Bickle 1993a, 359–361). I, for one, won't have my ontology rest on that foundation without a fight.

Finally, addressing this limitation in Hooker's account of reduction in turn addresses another popular criticism of some work in the new-wave-reductionist program. It is often said by philosophers of science about, e.g., the Churchlands' work, that the underlying theory of intertheoretic reduction is shallow and unsophisticated (relative, I suppose, to prevailing standards in contemporary philosophy of science). This criticism is already somewhat insensitive, in light of the Churchlands' constant referral to Hooker's (1981) work on reduction. Nevertheless, it is worthwhile to carry Hooker's work further, for the attempt at formal explication (to the extent possible) keeps the overarching account honest. Handwaving over precise details can permit sloppy claims occasionally to pass through. I turn now to such an attempt.

3

A Theory of Intertheoretic Reduction

I now seek to show that the general theory of intertheoretic reduction undergirding new-wave reductionism is consistent, formally specifiable to a significant degree, sufficient to represent important reductions from the history of science, and sufficient to address a worry about the class of approaches to which it belongs (the "too weak to be adequate" challenge). In addition to its providing the key foundational plank for new-wave reductionism, I also intend this chapter as a contribution to the philosophy of science. I'm going to borrow and further develop some resources from the "structuralist program," one of the few approaches that still maintains an interest in the "logic" of intertheoretic reduction.[1] Structuralist results are not well known among Anglo-American philosophers of science, so I hope to introduce some details of this program to a larger audience. It is rich in resources and results, and it deserves more attention than it has received. At the same time, much structuralist writing ignores some important connections with issues that have interested Anglo-American philosophers. So this chapter should also interest structuralists, since it displays further development, application, and relevance of their work. Finally, this chapter will introduce resources that I will use in the last three chapters of the book to show the philosophical advantages of new-wave reductionism over classical versions.

In the previous chapter I noted how new-wave reductionism exploits some of Clifford Hooker's insights about the nature and consequences of scientific reduction. These included the spectrum of reductions ranging from smooth to bumpy according to the amount of correction entailed to the reduced theory; the resulting reformulation of the philosophical mind-body problem, with ontological conclusions secondary to and depending on the nature of the reduction relation obtaining and with a place for each traditional solution tied to some location on or related to the intertheoretic-reduction spectrum; the derivation of an analog structure T_R^* already specified within the theoretical vocabulary and framework of the reducing theory T_B (the nomic structure of reduced theory T_R is always mimicked, never derived); and, as an example, the resulting reconstruction of the reduction of simple gas thermodynamics to kinetic theory plus statistical mechanics. However, we saw toward the end of the last chapter a limitation in Hooker's general account. I now seek to embed Hooker's insights within an approach to the structure of scientific theories and intertheoretic relations that at least provides a start on a precise, formal account of the implied amount of correction to the reduced theory. Hooker himself recognized that his approach failed to provide this.

At the outset, however, I issue a warning about this chapter: it is not easy reading. Those not wishing to get bogged down in the formal details of the underlying theory of intertheoretic reduction at this point might now skip forward to the next chapter.

1   The Structuralist Model of Theories

To accomplish the goal stated two paragraphs above, I introduce two departures from tradition within Anglo-American philosophy of mind. Any account of intertheoretic reduction presupposes an underlying account of theory structure. I will adopt a *nonsentential* account, construing theories as something other than collections of statements or propositions. I borrow from a fairly recent tradition in the philosophy of science that has come to be called the *semantic* view or approach. Besides being controversial, this move might also appear tangential toward a defense of psychoneural reductionism. So it deserves some preliminary discussion.[2]

The semantic view of theories is a misnomer. It comprises a family of related approaches toward explicating the structure of scientific theories. Each member of this family shares at least two assumptions. These assumptions distinguish the approach from the "received" view of theories rooted in logical empiricism, which depicts a theory as a symbolic calculus formalizable in first-order logic and (partially) interpretable by connecting principles (bridge laws, correspondence rules). These assumptions are the following (see Mormann 1991):

• Scientific theories are properly conceived *not* primarily as linguistic entities (i.e., as sets of sentences), but instead in terms of their *models*.

• The appropriate tool for the formal explication of the structure of scientific theories is not first-order logic and metamathematics, but instead *mathematics*.

Advocates of the semantic view differ in their choice of mathematical formalisms, some preferring a geometrical "state space" approach (van Fraassen 1972; Suppe 1974), others preferring set theory (Suppes 1956, 1967; Sneed 1971; Stegmüller 1976), still others preferring set theory supplemented with category theory (Balzer, Moulines, and Sneed 1987), and one even appealing to computational resources from recent cognitive science (Giere 1988). Kuhn's, Feyerabend's, and Hanson's well-known criticisms of the "received" view of theories and their functions (e.g., explanation), and of intertheoretic relations (e.g., reduction), figure prominently in many arguments for the semantic view (see especially Suppe 1974, 221–230; van Fraassen 1987; and Stegmüller 1976, part 2). But independent defenses of the semantic view also exist. In fact, the initial arguments of Suppes (1956) predate the appeal to these well-known criticisms.

Suppes's initial defense of the semantic view (not his term) was more pragmatic than principled. He was concerned with axiomatizing theories that "assume more than first-order logic as already available for use in [their] statement and development." For such theories, "it is *neither natural nor simple* to formalize [them] in first-order logic" (1956, 248; my emphasis). He admitted that theoretically one could simultaneously axiomatize in first-order logic both the theory in question and the relevant portions of whatever more was assumed (e.g., set theory). But "this is *awkward and unduly laborious*" (1956, 248; my emphasis). For theories that assume real numbers and functions on them "formalization ... in first-order logic is *utterly impractical*" (1956, 250; my emphasis). In his own words, the "essential methodological purpose" of his alternate account of theory structure was to "demonstrate that the same standards of clarity and precision may be achieved in axiomatizing complicated theories within set theory as are achieved by axiomatizing relatively simple theories directly in first-order logic" (1956, 250).

Van Fraassen (1970, 1972) also initially emphasized pragmatic over principled advantages. But lately (1980, chap. 3; 1987) he has grown bolder. He originally undertook to extend the approach of physicist Evert Beth into a general philosophy of science. Even then, van Fraassen argued that Beth's state-space account offered a "much more deep-going analysis of the structure of scientific theories" than did the "very shallow" reconstructions offered by the received view (1970, 325–326, 337–338). He also claimed that the received view failed to "present anything like a faithful picture of actual foundational work in physics" (1970, 337). Nevertheless, he still thought that there remained "natural interrelations" between syntactical and semantical approaches to the formal study of languages (i.e., those described by generalized completeness proofs), and these interrelations "make implausible any claim of philosophical superiority for either" (1970, 326).

Referring to this very quote, van Fraassen has recently said that he has long ago changed his mind about both the theoretical and practical significance of these claims. On the theoretical side are the provable limitations of syntax. When one presents a theory by defining its class of models, "that class of structures cannot generally be identified with an elementary class of models in any first-order language" (1987, 120). A simple illustration is any theory whose models include the real-number continuum. There is no elementary class of models of any denumerable first-order language each of which includes the real numbers. There also exist relationships between models that are "peculiarly semantic," "clearly very important for the comparison and evaluation of theories," and "not accessible to the syntactic approach". An example is that every model of one theory can be relatively embedded in a model of another that is syntactically inconsistent with the first (1980, 41–44). On the practical side, van Fraassen continues to emphasize "the enormous distance" between actual research on the foundations of science and "syntactically capturable axiomatics" (1980, 65–67; 1987, 114–118). He concludes that "while this disparity will not affect philosophical points which hinge only on what is possible 'in principle,' it may certainly affect the real possibility of understanding and clarification" (1987, 120).

Any brief survey of recent defenses of the semantic view should also include Ronald Giere's (1988) "cognitivist" approach toward explaining science. By dubbing his approach "cognitivist," Giere intends it as part of a science of scientific activity. He draws explanatory resources directly from recent cognitive science, especially work on the nature of human representation and judgment. His advocating a semantic view of theories rests upon his argument (1988, Chapter 3) for the conclusion that "recent work in the cognitive sciences provides the inspiration, and some resources, for going further in directions already indicated by ... Suppes, ... van Fraassen, ... and Suppe" (1988, 62). According to Giere, scientific theories contain two elements: a family of models and a class of "theoretical hypotheses" linking these models to real-world systems. A *similarity* relation determines whether a particular model counts as a member of the family comprising the theory. Giere's explication of this similarity relation employs recent work from cognitive science (see especially Giere 1988, 81–82, 88–89). Giere also argues that his version of the semantic view provides a much more accurate account of the way textbooks present theories than does the received view. This point is an important pragmatic advantage, since textbooks remain the primary vehicle of a scientific education.

But what does all of this have to do with a theory of reduction? Return to Suppes's initial work. One of his standard defenses of this account of theory structure appeals to the account of *intertheoretic reduction* it provides. Suppes writes, "[One] example of the use of models concerns the discussion of reductionism in the philosophy of science. Many of the problems formulated in connection with the question of reducing one science to another may be formulated as a series of problems using the notion of a representation theorem for the models of a theory. For instance, the thesis that psychology may be reduced to physiology would be for many people appropriately established if one could show that for any model of a psychological theory it was possible to construct an isomorphic model within physiological theory" (1956, 59). While Suppes's account of intertheoretic reduction based on set-theoretic isomorphism proved far too weak, his appeal to the formal resources of the semantic view to develop a theory of intertheoretic reduction continues in at least one program in formal philosophy of science: the structuralist program.

This brings me to my second controversial point in my choice of an underlying account of theory structure. I'm going to adopt the semantic view's specific account of theories at work in structuralist philosophy of science. We've already seen that characterizing a theory in terms of its models, with the notion of model being the familiar one from model theory in formal semantics, is a common feature of semantic approaches. Models here are not representations of things depicted by a theory. Instead, they *are* the things depicted. As Balzer, Moulines, and Sneed put this point in their monumental 1987 work, where the structuralist program receives its fullest formal and philosophical treatment, "Instead of saying that certain equations are a model of subatomic or economic phenomena, we propose to say that the subatomic or economic phenomena are models of the theory represented by those equations" (1987, 2).

Set theory is the structuralists' mathematics of choice for formally characterizing the structure shared by all models of a theory **T**. The empirical assertions of **T** are claims that a given empirical ("real world") system is a model of **T**, i.e., has the set-theoretic structure characteristic of models of **T**. Classical collision mechanics provides a simple illustration. A structuralist construal begins with the definition of the set-theoretic predicate "is a model of classical collision mechanics (**CCM**)":[3]

x is a **CCM** iff there exist P, T, v, m such that

(1) $x = \langle P, T, \Re, v, m \rangle$

(2) P is a finite, nonempty set

(3) T is an ordered-pair set $\langle t_1, t_2 \rangle$

(4) $v : P \times T \to \Re \times \Re \times \Re$

(5) $m : P \to \Re^+$

(6) $\sum_{p \in P} m(p) \cdot v(p, t_1) = \sum_{p \in P} m(p) \cdot v(p, t_2)$

A model m of **CCM** ($m \in M(\mathbf{CCM})$) is any mathematical or empirical ("real world") system satisfying the predicate "is a **CCM**." Structuralists distinguish models of a theory, even "real world" models, from its *intended empirical* ("real world") *applications I*. For example, in all $i \in I(\text{CCM})$, P is a set of particles, T a set of time instances (with t_1 being before, and t_2 after, the collision), v is the velocity relation (assigning a triplet of real numbers ($\Re$) to particles at times), m is the mass relation (assigning positive real numbers to particles) , and (6) expresses the theory's fundamental law, the conservation of momentum following a collision (the sum for all particles of a particle's mass times velocity is the same before and after the collision). The *empirical claim* of **CCM** is that the entire set of intended empirical applications I is a subset of the set of models of **CCM** (that $I(\text{CCM}) \subseteq M(\text{CCM})$).

Models, however, are not the fundamental units of a structuralist analysis of theories. Models are themselves a special subset of the *potential models* of a theory, $M_p(\text{T})$. Using Stegmüller's (1976) helpful phrase, potential models are the structures about which it "makes sense" to ask whether they are actual models. In this **CCM** example, notice the difference between conditions (1) to (5) and condition (6). Conditions (1) to (5) characterize the formal conceptual structure of the models of **CCM**, with each component characterized individually. Condition (6), on the other hand, combines these components and characterizes the theory's fundamental law. The potential models $M_p(\text{CCM})$ are those structures (both purely mathematical and "real world") meeting conditions (1) to (5), while the actual models $M(\text{CCM})$ are those potential models that, in addition, meet condition (6). Roughly speaking, the distinction between model and potential model is parallel to the more familiar distinction between lawlike and nonlawlike axiomatic statements. Structuralists have formally characterized this distinction using Bourbaki's concept of a *structure species* (Balzer, Moulines, and Sneed 1987, chap. 1, sec. 1.3). I ignore these complexities, since they are important for characterizing a formal account of "theoreticity," and so are tangential to my concern with intertheoretic reduction.

The structuralist notion of potential model goes back to the inception of the program in Sneed 1971. It is a very attractive feature. Structuralists have shown, for example, that it plays an important role in formal treatments of some features of science emphasized by "radical" critics of logical empiricism. Interestingly, both Thomas Kuhn (1976) and Paul Feyerabend (1977) wrote favorable reviews of early books by Sneed and

Stegmüller. Kuhn in particular noticed the importance of potential models for formal treatment of some of his concerns (see Kuhn 1976, sec. 2).

For our purposes, then, $M(T) \subseteq M_p(T)$ (and seemingly without exception $M(T) \subset M_p(T)$), $I(T) \subseteq M_p(T)$, and typically at any given time $I(T) \cap M(T) \neq \varnothing$ but $I(T) \nsubseteq M(T)$. That is, at any given time a theory T will have some intended empirical applications already confirmed to be actual models, but the empirical claim of T goes beyond its confirmed intended empirical applications. Thus according to the structuralist program, and simplified for my purposes, a theory T is an ordered triple $\langle M_p(T), M(T), I(T)\rangle$ meeting the conditions just stated. I illustrate these conditions in figure 3.1.[4]

Now for some commentary. Notice that the formula $I(T) \nsubseteq M(T)$ admits of a stronger reading than the one offered in the paragraph above. One might read it as saying that some intended empirical applications of a theory T are *incompatible with* the theory's actual models. C. U. Moulines (private correspondence) informs me that structuralists typically intend this stronger reading, as indicative of the actual state of scientific theories. Nothing in this chapter hinges on which reading one adopts.[5]

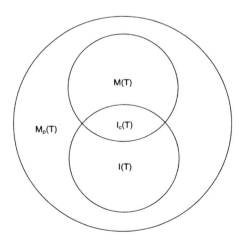

Figure 3.1
The structuralist account of theory structure (with the simplifications described in the text).

Beyond this ambiguity, however, one must avoid a potential *mis*reading of this condition. One might think that this condition violates the earlier definition of the empirical claim of a theory that $I(T) \subseteq M(T)$. But there is no contradiction. A theory's empirical claim is exactly that: an empirical *claim*. The condition stated in this formula concerns the status of the theory's empirical claim *at any given time*. In other words, a theory's empirical *claim* at any given time extends beyond its actual grasp.[6]

2   The Reduction Relation ρ

Building on this account of theory structure, structuralists have developed a number of accounts of intertheoretic reduction.[7] None, however, capture Hooker's insight about what gets deduced in a reduction (an analog structure T_R^*, rather than T_R itself, specified within the framework of the reducing theory T_B and designed to mimic the structure of T_R). From a pure philosophy-of-science perspective, this is not by itself a criticism of structuralist accounts. (Besides, no structuralist has tried to capture Hooker's insights.) Even the structuralist theory that most closely captures Nagel's condition on reduction, that of Balzer, Moulines, and Sneed (1987, chap. 6), avoids the well-known problem of accounting for the status of the "coordinating definitions" ("bridge laws," "correspondence rules") in reductions implying correction to the reduced theory (discussed above in chapter 2, section 1). Since structuralists construe theories in terms of their models instead of their linguistic expressions, analogs of Nagel's "derivability" and "connectability" conditions nowhere require problematic analogs of coordinating definitions. However, my overarching purpose in this chapter goes beyond the philosophy of science. We've seen how Hooker's insights get around the problem of understanding the nature of the reduction relation obtaining in cases implying significant correction to the reduced theory. We've seen how his insights can be used to fruitfully reconstruct an important historical case. In the next chapter and throughout the rest of this work, we'll see other work performed by Hooker's insight about what gets deduced in a reduction. I thus propose to reconstruct Hooker's notion of the structure and role of T_R^* within the basic structuralist framework of theories and reduction, rather than adopt any existing structuralist account.

Structuralists construe reduction as a "global" relation ρ from the potential models of T_B into those of T_R that meet particular restricting conditions. Formally, ρ is a set of ordered pairs with $\text{Dom}(\rho) = M_p(T_B)$ and $\text{Rng}(\rho) = M_p(T_R)$. The trick to constructing an adequate theory of reduction is to characterize the right set of conditions on ρ that captures the right set of ordered pairs with the right higher-order properties characteristic of intertheoretic reduction.

I begin with Hooker's notion of the analog structure T_R^*. T_R^* is a structure specified within a restricted portion of T_B that is analogous to T_R. We capture the first feature by characterizing T_R^* as a subset of $M_p(T_B)$ that, besides meeting the conditions on $M_p(T_B)$, also meets whatever conditions—possibly counterfactual—that enable it to stand in the appropriate relation to T_R. Figure 3.2 illustrates the structure of T_R^*. As an illustration, consider the reduction of the ideal gas law of the simple thermodynamics of gases to the kinetic theory and statistical mechanics (chapter 2, section 2, above). Equation 1 (p. 37) is the analog structure

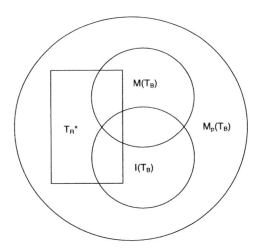

Figure 3.2
The analog structure T_R^*. The extent to which T_R^* intersects with $M(T_B)$ and $I(T_B)$ depends on the extent and nature of the counterfactual assumptions separating it from the rest of $M_p(T_B)$.

for the ideal gas law within the kinetic theory. Its derivation requires various assumptions, some counterfactual, besides the central characteristics of gases postulated by the kinetic theory. Key assumptions and characteristics include the following: Gas molecules are in constant random motion with no net motion in any direction. Collisions are perfectly elastic. A molecule's diameter is negligible compared to the length of the container enclosing the gas. There are no attractive forces among the molecules. Molecular volume is negligible compared to the spaces between molecules.

On a structuralist reconstruction, these additional assumptions are additional clauses ("axioms") conjoined to the definition of the set-theoretic predicate "is a (potential model of the) kinetic theory." That is, the basic assumptions of the theory characterize the potential models, the models, and the intended empirical applications in the fashion specified in the previous section. We then introduce the additional assumptions needed to derive equation 1 as further conditions that carve off another subset of potential models. This additional subset, consisting of potential models that also meet the additional assumptions, is the analog structure T_R^*, the square subset illustrated in figure 3.2. Notice that if any of the additional assumptions are counterfactual, as occurs in reductions implying even small corrections to the reduced theory, then at least some elements of T_R^* will not be actual models of T_B. At least part of T_R^* will lie outside $M(T_B)$. I'll take up the interesting technical and philosophical issues this raises later in this chapter and again in chapter 6.

With T_R^* now characterized set-theoretically, what sense can we make of Hooker's "analog relation" AR obtaining between T_R^* and the reduced theory T_R? Following structuralist notational conventions, I'll dub this relation ρ and begin with a quite strong set of two conditions on it (following Balzer, Moulines, and Sneed [BMS] 1987, chap. 6). These conditions are possibly too strong to account for all of the actual historical cases that scientists have dubbed "reductions." After presenting it and drawing out some of its consequences, I'll suggest a weaker set of conditions (following Mayr 1976).

The reduction relation ρ is a relation with $\text{Dom}(\rho) = T_R^*$ and $\text{Rng}(\rho) \subseteq M_p(T_R)$ (see figure 3.3). In the spirit of the BMS account (with

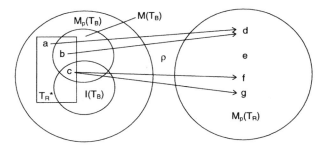

Figure 3.3
The domain and range of ρ. $\mathrm{Dom}(\rho) = T_R^*$; $\mathrm{Rng}(\rho) \subseteq M_p(T_R)$. The reduction relation ρ is into $M_p(T_R)$. It can be many-one (e.g., $\langle a, d \rangle, \langle b, d \rangle \in \rho$) or one-many (e.g., $\langle c, f \rangle, \langle c, g \rangle \in \rho$).

the simplifications on theory element introduced in the previous section), the first of the two conditions on ρ is as follows:[8]

(1)   For all $x' \in T_R^*$, $x \in M_p(T_R)$: if $x' \in M(T_B)$ and $\langle x', x \rangle \in \rho$, then $x \in M(T_R)$.

(In English, for all elements x' of the analog structure in the reducing theory and all elements x of the potential models of the reduced theory, if x' is also a model of the reducing theory and x' and x are related by the reduction relation, then x must be a model of the reducing theory.) Condition (1) requires that ρ relate only actual models of T_R to actual models of T_B that also belong to T_R^*, i.e., that ρ never relate an actual model of T_B also contained in T_R^* to a merely potential model of T_R. This condition is interesting when conjoined with auxiliary condition (a), which follows from the fact that seemingly without exception in actual theories, $M(T) \subset M_p(T)$.

(a) $\mathrm{Rng}\,(\rho) \nsubseteq M(T_R)$.

(In English, ρ relates some elements of T_R^* to merely potential models of T_R.) Auxiliary condition (a) provides an "independence" requirement, ruling out a trivial way of meeting condition (1) by simply defining ρ as $\langle x', x \rangle \in \rho$ iff $x' \in T_R^*$ and $x \in M(T_R)$. Together, these two conditions seem to give ρ the strength of Nagel's "condition of derivability," that "all the laws of the secondary [reduced] science ... must be logically derivable from the theoretical premises ... in the primary [reducing] dis-

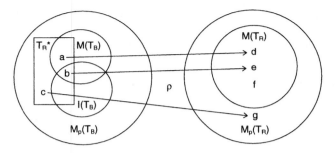

Figure 3.4
BMS-inspired condition (1). When $\mathrm{Dom}(\rho)$ is restricted to the intersection of T_R^* and $M(T_B)$, $\mathrm{Rng}(\rho)$ must include only actual models of the reduced theory $M(T_R)$. (Notice that this diagram also meets auxiliary condition (a).)

cipline" (Nagel 1961, 354). Balzer, Moulines, and Sneed even phrase their version of this condition as a "general condition of derivability," the "requirement that the laws of T_R should be derived from those of T_B through the mediation of ρ" (1987, 275; interestingly, *not* mentioning Nagel in this context). They even seek to provide a formal proof that their version of this condition is a derivability requirement (1987, 308–310). I don't need to get involved in that debate here, since it is irrelevant to my current concerns. As I've noted, Hooker denies that his relation AR between T_R^* and T_R needs to be as strong as derivability, even in the smoothest cases of reduction. Notice, however, that condition (1) trivially obtains in reductions implying significant correction to T_R (as in the reduction of simple thermodynamics of gases to kinetic theory and statistical mechanics). Since all additional assumptions necessary to construct T_R^* are counterfactual, none of its elements belong to $M(T_B)$, and so the antecedent of (1) will be false. The importance of this fact will be at issue in section 4 of this chapter. (For an illustration of condition (1), see figure 3.4.)[9]

Condition (2) obtains between *confirmed* intended empirical applications of the analog structure and the reduced theory:

(2)   For all $x \in I_C(T_R)$, there exists some $x' \in T_R^* \cap I_C(T_B)$ such that $\langle x', x \rangle \in \rho$ (where $I_C(T) = I(T) \cap M(T)$)

(In English, for all elements x of the confirmed intended empirical applications of the reduced theory, there is some element x' belonging to the intersection of the analog structure with the confirmed intended empirical applications of the reducing theory such that x' and x stand in the reduction relation. The confirmed intended empirical applications of a theory are those elements in the intersection of the theory's intended empirical applications and its actual models.) Condition (2) requires that p relate a *confirmed* intended empirical application of T_B—a "real world" potential model in $I(T_B)$ already shown to be an actual model— also belonging to T_R^* to each confirmed intended empirical application of T_R. As Balzer, Moulines, and Sneed say of their version of this condition, it constitutes "a minimal pragmatic condition which seems to be satisfied in all conceivable examples [of actual reductions in science]" (1987, 277). (For an illustration of this condition, see figure 3.5. For a simple illustration displaying all these BMS-inspired conditions on p, see figure 3.6.)

Using (their versions of) these conditions on p, Balzer, Moulines, and Sneed precisely reconstruct several historical reductions, including collision mechanics to classical particle mechanics (1987, 255–267) and rigid body mechanics to classical particle mechanics (1987, 267–275).[10] These demonstrations are important steps toward justifying the historical adequacy of this account of reduction without handwaving. Still, there is reason to wonder whether these conditions on p are adequate for other

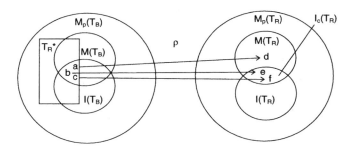

Figure 3.5
BMS-inspired condition (2). All confirmed intended empirical applications of the reduced theory $I_C(T_R)$ must be included in $\text{Rng}(p)$ when $\text{Dom}(p)$ is restricted to the intersection of T_R^* and $I_C(T_B)$ (confirmed intended empirical applications of the reducing theory). That T_B actually develops a subclass of confirmed intended empirical applications meeting this condition is a strong requirement on the reduction relation.

historical reductions. These conditions are very much in the spirit of Ernest Nagel's (1961, chap. 11) formal conditions on reduction (especially when stated without the use of T_R^*). As is well-known, it was appeals to actual historical cases by "radical" critics of orthodox logical empiricism (Kuhn, Feyerabend, Hanson) that seriously undermined Nagel's account. (One might recall Feyerabend's claim that when one extends Nagel's account to "such comprehensive structures of thought" as Aristotelian mechanics, the medieval impetus theory, Newton's celestial mechanics, Maxwell's electrodynamics, relativity theory, and the quantum theory, "then complete failure is the result" (1962, 44).) Furthermore, in the structuralist literature, one finds alternate conditions on reduction very much in the spirit of proposals by these radical critics (although explicit mention of these radical critics often goes unstated). For example, Dieter Mayr (1976) develops a set-theoretic account of "anomaly" and includes the *explication of anomalies* as an explicit condition on ρ. Is Mayr's alternate set of conditions more adequate for many historical cases of intertheoretic reduction?

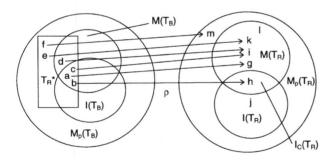

Figure 3.6
A simple model meeting all BMS-inspired conditions on ρ. $\text{Dom}(\rho) = T_R^*$, $\text{Rng}(\rho) \subseteq M_p(T_R)$. The reduction relation ρ is many-one (since $\langle c, i \rangle, \langle d, i \rangle \in \rho$). $\text{Rng}(\rho \not\subseteq M(T_R)$ (since $\langle f, m \rangle \in \rho$). $\text{Rng}(\rho)$ is restricted to actual models of the reduced theory $M(T_R)$ when $\text{Dom}(\rho)$ is restricted to the intersection of T_R^* and actual models of the reducing theory $M(T_B)$ (since $T_R^* \cap M(T_B) = \{a, b, c, d\}$ and $\langle a, g \rangle, \langle b, h \rangle, \langle c, i \rangle, \langle d, i \rangle, \in \rho$ and $g, h, i \in M(T_R)$): actual models of T_R^* are related only to actual models of T_R, never to merely potential models. All confirmed intended empirical applications of the reduced theory $I_C(T_R)$ are contained in $\text{Rng}(\rho)$ when $\text{Dom}(\rho)$ is restricted to confirmed intended empirical applications $I_C(T_B)$ contained in T_R^* (since $\{h\} = I_C(T_R)$, $b \in T_R^* \cap I_C(T_B)$, and $\langle b, h \rangle, \in \rho$).

We can define an *anomaly of a theory element* T as an element of the set-theoretic difference of $I(T)$ with respect to $M(T)$. Formally, this is stated as follows:[11]

x is an anomaly of a theory element T iff $x \in I(T) - M(T)$.

An anomaly is an intended empirical application that has not been confirmed, and perhaps *cannot* be confirmed, as an actual model of T. (Being an element of $I(T)$, an anomaly meets the structural conditions of the set-theoretic predicate "is a T," but it has not been shown to meet the lawlike conditions.) To illustrate his notion, Mayr (1976) appeals to a familiar historical example, the movement of Mercury's perihelion. Using informal structuralist terminology, he writes, "In Newton's gravitational theory the actual orbit of Mercury is no solution of the differential equations, although Mercury, as part of our solar system, falls in the range of application of Newton's theory" (1976, 291). Mercury's orbit is hence an element of the set-theoretic difference between the intended empirical applications of Newton's theory and the actual models.

With anomalies of T now defined, I specify an alternate, Mayr-inspired condition on the reduction relation ρ. The analog structure T_R^* must resolve (explain) anomalies of T_R.[12] Formally, this is stated as follows:

(3)   For some $x' \in T_R^*$, $x \in M_p(T_R)$: $x' \in T_R^* \cap I(T_B) \cap M(T_B)$ and $x \in I(T_R) - M(T_R)$ and $\langle x', x \rangle \in \rho$.

(In English, for some element x' of the analog structure of the reducing theory and some element x of the potential models of the reduced theory, x' is an element of the intersection of the analog structure, the intended empirical applications, and the models of the reducing theory; x is an element of the intended empirical applications of the reduced theory not included in the models; and x' and x stand in the reduction relation.) That is, ρ must contain at least one ordered pair whose first element is a *confirmed* intended empirical application of T_B also contained in T_R^* and whose second element is an anomaly of T_R. This condition captures Kuhn's Lakatos's claim that the reducing (or replacing) theory has a specific kind of increased explanatory power over the reduced (replaced) theory, though Kuhn 1977 and Lakatos 1970 curiously go unmentioned by Mayr as a source for his account.[13]

Condition (3) is interesting for another reason. Notice that it is the contradictory of condition (1) of the BMS-inspired account. An ordered pair meeting condition (3) is a *model* of T_B related by ρ to a merely *potential model* of T_R. (Anomalies are by definition potential models that are not actual models.) Such an ordered pair provides a counterexample to (1). Hence a structuralist rendering of Nagelian reduction conditions and an alternative in the spirit of his "radical" critics reveals a precise point of conflict: Nagel's derivability condition (instead of his "connectability" condition) versus an explanation-of-anomalies condition.

Must we choose which conditions on ρ to adopt (at the expense of the others)? Not necessarily. Perhaps intertheoretic reduction in science is ambiguous. Our pretheoretic intuitions might lead us to expect uniform treatment, but actual scientific practice might use different notions. The cases that science lumps together as "reductions" might be a motley crew. Reduction would not be the first scientific concept to fragment under scrutiny. Perhaps some cases meet one set of conditions, while others meet another.

Even with all this machinery, however, I still can't hint at how to reconstruct the one historical case of reduction central to the new-wave-reductionist program: that of simple thermodynamics of gases to the kinetic theory and statistical mechanics. I've already noted that this reduction requires counterfactual assumptions to carve off T_R^* from T_B, leaving empty the intersection of T_R^* and the actual models of T_B (including the confirmed intended empirical applications of T_B). This case thus trivially satisfies BMS-inspired conditions (1) and (2), because their antecedents are false, and fails to satisfy Mayr-inspired (3), because its first conjunct is false. I've already explained the falsity of the antecedent of (1). The antecedent of (2) is false because T_R contains no confirmed intended empirical applications. At best, some of its real-world intended empirical applications will approximate actual models of T_R. The first conjunct of (3) is false because the intersection of T_R^* and $M(T_B)$ is empty. These limitations obtain in every historical reduction requiring counterfactual assumptions to carve off all of T_R^* from T_B, i.e., in cases implying significant correction to the reduced theory. Somehow I must supplement the conditions on ρ to account for these important historical cases. Along these same lines, I must also fulfill my promise at the end of chapter 2, section 1, to distinguish genuine theory reduction from mere historical theory progression. Finally, I've yet to provide any precise account of a given reduction's location on the spectrum separating smooth (retentive) from bumpy (replacement) cases.

Before I address these missing pieces, however, I'm first going to turn my attention to a challenge to the very class of reduction theories to which this one belongs. Relation ρ, as developed so far, falls squarely within a class of reduction theories subjected to a devastating criticism by Kenneth Schaffner (1967) almost three decades ago. I dub this the "too-weak-to-be-adequate challenge." To meet it, I will introduce a resource—additional structure to the potential models of a theory element—that will also be helpful for addressing the other outstanding challenges. If I can't meet the too-weak-to-be-adequate challenge, then it is pointless to continue investigating this account of reduction.

3   The "Too Weak to Be Adequate" Challenge

As I mentioned above, one of Patrick Suppes's favorite arguments for his set-theoretic account of scientific theories was the account of intertheoretic reduction it provides. His argument failed to convince everyone. In his classic 1967 essay, Kenneth Schaffner (among other things) offered a critique of the "Suppes Reduction Paradigm" and a challenge to its proponents. His critique concluded that the approach is "so weak as it stands that it will not do as an adequate reduction paradigm" (1967, 145). His challenge is implicit in his final evaluation: "I do not think the Suppes approach is one that is workable, *without some additional criteria of reduction conjoined to it*" (1967, 145; my emphasis).

Suppes account of reduction uses the set-theoretic notion of an *isomorphism*. Reflecting on a familiar historical example, Suppes writes, "To show in a sharp sense that thermodynamics may be reduced to statistical mechanics, we would need to axiomatize both disciplines by defining appropriate set-theoretical predicates, and then show that given any model T of thermodynamics we may find a model of statistical mechanics on the basis of which we may construct a model *isomorphic to* T" (1956, 271; my emphasis). While he admits that a "satisfactory general definition of isomorphism for two set-theoretic entities of any kind is difficult if not impossible to formulate" and that when "the n-tuples are as complicated as in the case of models for the theory of particle mechanics, it is sometimes difficult to decide exactly what is meant by two isomorphic models" (1956, 262), it is clear from his discussion of isomorphisms on simple binary-relation structures that he has the standard sense of same formal structure in mind. Where A and B are any sets, R a binary relation in A, and S a binary relation in B, $\langle A, R \rangle$ is isomorphic to $\langle B, S \rangle$ just in case there is a function f such that $\mathrm{Dom}(f) = A$; $\mathrm{Rng}(f) = B$; f is 1 to 1; and if x, $y \in A$, then $\langle x, y \rangle \in R$ iff $\langle f(x), f(y) \rangle \in S$.[14]

With Suppes's sense of isomorphism clarified, Schaffner (1967) launches his critique. First, he establishes the relationship between Suppes's account and one of the other four paradigms under investigation, the account of Nagel, Woodger, and Quine (NWQ), by proving the following theorem: if it is possible to construct an NWQ reduction for two theories, then a Suppes reduction can also be constructed. The proof rests on the fact that the NWQ reduction functions insure the conditions necessary to establish the isomorphism of models. This theorem establishes that the Suppes account "is a weaker form of the NWQ approach" (Schaffner 1967, 145).

This first step is just a warmup. The second step is the crux. Schaffner writes, "Different and nonreducible (at least to one another) physical theories can have the same formal structure—e.g., the theory of heat and hydrodynamics—and yet one would not wish to claim that any reduction could be constructed here" (1967, 145). This is the "too weak to be adequate" challenge. Suppes's set-theoretic condition on reduction obtains between actual theories that are not genuine reduction pairs. The account cannot rule out some cases where no reduction obtains, and so is inadequate as a general theory of reduction. Isomorphism between related models is at best a necessary condition, but not a sufficient condition, on genuine reduction.

Schaffner did not completely dismiss Suppes's approach within a broader study of reduction in science. He saw it as useful toward articulating the *methodology* of scientific reduction, instead of its "logic." He argued that perusal of scientific writings reveals that finding isomorphisms between models of potential reduction pairs is something scientists do when trying to *demonstrate* that some reduction holds or is in the works. Schaffner even discusses in some detail the reduction of Mendelian genetics to microbiology to defend this claim (1967, 142–144).

Why is Schaffner's criticism of Suppes's account of reduction relevant to this chapter? The conditions on p stated in the previous section go well beyond the conditions on an isomorphism.[15] Nevertheless, these additional conditions do not amount to a solution to Schaffner's "too weak to be adequate" challenge. Schaffner's challenge generalizes beyond its initial target. One structuralist, C. U. Moulines, has explicitly noticed this worry (apparently independent of Schaffner's work, since Moulines does not mention or cite Schaffner when articulating the problem[16]). Concerning structuralist accounts of reduction of the sort I have developed so far, Moulines has this to say:

There is at least one further aspect of reduction that is overlooked.... This is what I would like to call "the ontological aspect." I wish to argue that, for a complete picture of a reductive relationship between two theories, one has to take into account some sort of relation between the respective domains. *Otherwise, when confronted with a particular example of a reductive pair, we would feel that all we have is an ad hoc mathematical relationship between two sets of structures, perhaps by chance having the mathematical properties we require of reduction but not really telling us something about "the world."* We could have a reductive relationship between two theories that are completely alien to each other. The possibility that we find a formally appropriate p just by chance or by constructing it in an *ad hoc* way cannot be ruled out in general. (1984, 55; my emphasis)

Notice that Moulines is urging exactly the criticism that Schaffner raises against Suppes's paradigm with his heat-to-hydrodynamics example. The formal conditions on p obtain in cases that aren't genuine reduction pairs. Hence even with the added conditions beyond mere isomorphism, and although these added conditions amount to some well-known conditions on reduction, structuralist reduction remains inadequately weak. Isomorphism is too weak, as Schaffner explicitly proved, but so are the stronger set-theoretic conditions structuralists have built into their accounts. The latter point is the Schaffner-*inspired* challenge.[17]

The source of this problem for structuralist reduction is different than its source for Suppes. According to Moulines (1984), it is the *global* character of structuralist concepts that is the culprit, the fact that p is a relation on whole theory elements as sets of potential models. As he notes, the ρs I have presented so far "do not specify any particular kind of link between the respective base sets upon which the relations and functions of both theories are constructed. And we should expect of a 'real' reduction that it connects some of the respective base sets at least—though not necessarily by means of 'coordinating definitions' or 'bridge laws,' as Nagel would have it" (1984, 56). The base sets of a theory's potential models provide the theory's ontology. This diagnosis suggests a strategy for overcoming the Schaffner-inspired challenge. Construe the global reduction relation ρ, on sets of potential models, as constructed out of "local" links between the elements making up the ρ-related potential models of the respective theory elements. That is, construe ρ as an *ontological reductive link* (ORL).[18]

To understand ORLs, we need to further specify the composition of potential models M_p of a theory element T. Any $x \in M_p(\text{T})$ is an ordered $(n + m + p)$-tuple of the form

$$x = \langle D_1, \ldots, D_n, A_1, \ldots, A_m, r_1, \ldots, r_p \rangle,$$

where the D_i are the "real" or "empirical" base sets, the A_i are the "auxiliary" base sets (mathematical or other formal spaces), and the r_i are the theory's fundamental relations *typified* by the base sets.[19] In the CCM example presented above, each potential model contains two empirical base sets ($D_1 = P$, the set of particles in intended empirical applications; $D_2 = T$, the set of time instances), one auxiliary base set ($A_1 = \Re$), and two fundamental relations typified over the base sets ($r_1 = v$, the velocity relation, with $v \in \mathscr{P}((P \times T) \times (\Re \times \Re \times \Re))$; $r_2 = m$, the mass relation, with $m \in \mathscr{P}(P \times \Re^+)$ where $\mathscr{P}$ denotes the power set and $\Re$ denotes the real numbers).

Suppose now that we have some $\rho : M_p(\text{T}_B) \rightarrow M_p(\text{T}_R)$ meeting the appropriate formal conditions on a reduction relation discussed in the section just above. Following Moulines (1984, 59), I will say that ρ is an *ontological reductive link* (ORL) if in addition ρ (partly) consists of relations between each of the empirical base sets of reduced T_R and some element or elements of the potential models of reducing T_B: either empirical base sets of T_B, singularly or in combination, or empirical and auxiliary base sets along with fundamental relations typified over them.

Intuitively, ORLs consist of links between the empirical base sets of the reduced theory's potential models and p-related elements of the reducing theory's potential models. The intended empirical applications of the respective theories induce these links.

As Moulines points out, there are three kinds of ORLs. *Homogeneous* ORLs consist entirely of partial or total identity relations between individual empirical base sets of T_R and T_B (total when some D_i of T_R's potential models $=$ some D'_j of T_B's p-related potential models [in the extensional, set-theoretic sense of identity, where $D_i \subseteq D'_j$ and $D'_j \subseteq D_i$]; partial when the $D_i \subset$ some D'_j). For example, the reduction of classical collision mechanics (**CCM**) to Newtonian particle mechanics (**NPM**) (Balzer, Moulines, and Sneed 1987, 255–267) involves a completely homogeneous ORL. The reduction (i.e., the ordered pairs of possible models comprising p) identifies all empirical base sets of potential models of **CCM** (P, the set of particles, and T, the set of time instances) with either a base set of the p-related possible model of **NPM** or with a subset of a base set.

Heterogeneous ORLs, on the other hand, consist of relations that pair empirical base sets of the reduced T_R to components of p-related potential models of the reducing T_B in a way that does not imply total or partial identification of the sets. The notion of a heterogeneous ORL is more difficult to specify formally, owing to the variety of ways to pair a D_i of the reduced T_R with combinations of elements of the potential models of the reducing T_B. For example, a D_i can be related via a heterogeneous ORL to empirical base sets (D_j) of the p-related potential model of T_B, either singularly or in combination, or to any combination of D_js, A_js (auxiliary base sets of the potential models of the reducing theory), and r_js (fundamental relations), depending on how the ontologies of the two theories relate. However, the basic idea of a heterogeneous ORL is straightforward. The reduction of T_R to T_B reveals that the empirical base sets of the former's potential models, the features of the way the reduced theory carves up the world, get related to components of the latter's way of carving up the world in such a way that the intended empirical applications significantly overlap. That is, the same "real world" systems, described in different theoretical vocabularies, are among the intended empirical applications of both—a result guaranteed by (part of) BMS-inspired condition (2) on p. At the same time, however, there is no set inclusion between the relevant components of the potential models of reduced and reducing theories (the empirical base sets).

Moulines (1984, 63–67) provides formal definitions of homogeneous ORLs and varieties of heterogeneous ORLs. I won't repeat them here. He admits that "in formal philosophy of science ... you can never rule out someone coming up with a contrived, non-intended example that fits the scheme though nobody would like to have it inside" (1984, 55). In other words, purely formal specifications alone will never solve a version of the too-weak-to-be-adequate challenge, which resorts to "*contrived nonintended examples.*" Yet his counterpoint is still instructive. The existence of contrived, nonintended examples "does not rule out the possibility of enriching our previous concept [of reduction, in this case] through appropriate modifications so as to keep outside it as many of the unwanted cases as possible. If this is possible, it should be done" (1984, 55). The additional ORL condition is an attempt to do this. If it succeeds in ruling out all *actual* cases of scientific theories that stand in the reduction relation previously specified but that are not genuine reduction pairs, why worry about contrived nonintended *imaginary* examples (especially if we adopt the general perspective on the philosophy of science suggested in note 12 of chapter 1)?

Despite their formal complexity, heterogeneous ORLs can consist of two basic types of relations (though Moulines [1984] does not note this). First, there are those that relate an empirical base set of T_R to empirical base set(s) of T_B, either singularly or in combination (but without any partial or total set inclusion obtaining). An example is the relation obtaining between the empirical base set of phlogiston elements and the base set of chemical elements in the theory of oxidation reactions within modern elemental chemistry. The set of phlogiston elements, distinguished within phlogiston chemistry as a separate empirical base set because only phlogiston can get assigned a negative value by the atomic-weight relation, gets related via an ORL to the empirical base set of chemical elements containing oxygen. The latter set fails to include phlogiston.[20] Second, a heterogeneous ORL can link an empirical base set of T_R with combinations or sequences of empirical base sets, auxiliary base sets, and/or fundamental relations of T_B. An example might be the ORL between the empirical base sets of genes on a structuralist reconstruction of Mendelian (or transmission) genetics and the combination and sequence of elements of the potential models of molecular biology relevant to the reduction. These combinations and sequences include not only empirical base sets of molecular biology (e.g., DNA segments) but also fundamental relations involving elements of the base sets and even sequences of events involving these relations (e.g., ordered events within the biosynthetic pathways and further relations between ordered sets of proteins and ordered sets of macroscopically observable phenotypic characteristics).

Notice finally that an ORL can be both homogeneous and heterogeneous. Some empirical base sets of the reduced theory are partially or totally identified with empirical base sets of the ρ-related potential models of the reducing theory, while others get linked to components of the potential models of the reducing theory in heterogeneous fashion. Moulines dubs these reductive links "mixed ORLs" and points out that they are typical in actual science. Examples are readily available. The reductions of both rigid body mechanics (**RBM**) to **NPM** and of **NPM** to special relativity theory (**SR**) reconstructed in structuralist fashion involve mixed ORLs. **RBM**-to-**NPM** reduction is mixed because the empirical base set B consisting of one or more rigid bodies in the intended empirical applications of **RBM** gets related via ρ to the empirical base set P of Newtonian particles of **NPM**. B is neither identical to nor a proper subset of P in any pair of ρ-related potential models. The fact that the two theories stand in the structuralist reduction relation ρ and the fact that ρ is an ORL reveals that rigid bodies *consist* of Newtonian particles. So the reduction reveals that a given rigid body, an element of empirical base set B in some potential model of **RBM**, is identical to an empirical base set P of particles (or a subset of P) in the ρ-related potential model of **NPM**. But an element of B is *not itself* an element of P. It is a rigid body as part of how **RBM** carves up the world, not as an element of any set of Newtonian particles. Hence the ORL composing ρ between **RBM** and **NPM** relates empirical base sets B and P of ρ-related potential models without (partly or totally) identifying a set B with a set P. This component of the ORL is heterogeneous. (For a careful structuralist reconstruction of the **RBM**-to-**NPM** reduction that does not explicitly employ ORLs, see Balzer, Moulines, and Sneed 1987, 267–275.) Similarly, the **NPM**-to-**SR** reduction involves a mixed ORL because the separate empirical base sets of space points S and time instances T of potential models of **NPM** get related via the ORL composing ρ to a single Minkowski space of ρ-related potential models of **SR**. For reasons similar to those just stated, neither S nor T is a subset of the latter.

Armed with ORLs, we can now state the full conditions on a set-theoretic model of reduction adequate to overcome the too-weak-to-be-adequate challenge. The reduction relation ρ must meet the appropriate formal conditions (i.e., of the sort detailed in the section just above), and *ρ must also be an ORL.* That is, it must be constructed out of local links obtaining between all of the empirical base sets of the reduced theory and elements of the potential models of the reducing theory in a way that respects how the two theories each carve up the world. This additional condition will rule out unwanted cases of reduction (involving actual theories, at least) like heat to hydrodynamics and exchange economics to thermodynamics. This is because even if the global relation obtaining between these pairs meet the formal conditions on ρ, the ρs obtaining do not consist of appropriate local links between the components of the ρ-related potential models to make the ρs genuine ORLs. With the ORL condition on a genuine reduction added, such cases will no longer trouble set-theoretic models of reduction, and we meet the Schaffner-inspired too-weak-to-be-adequate challenge.

The reason that these problematic cases fail to meet the ORL condition is that the ontologies of the two theories, as expressed in the base sets and fundamental relations making up their confirmed and postulated intended empirical applications (which are, recall, a special subset of the set of potential models) enjoy no links to one another. No empirical base set in the intended empirical applications of the theory of heat gets ontologically linked to components of the potential models of the theory of hydrodynamics. Furthermore, and this is the key to the argument, *any attempt to artificially fashion the ρs in these cases as ORLs will alter one or both of the theories' sets of intended empirical applications, which serve as part of the identity conditions on the two theories.* The intended empirical ("real world") applications of, e.g., exchange economics, differ completely from those of thermodynamics. The real-world systems depicted by the two theories make up distinct sets (at least concerning aspects relevant to applications of the two theories, as determined by the structure of their models).[21] A theory's intended empirical applications determine the ORLs it can have with other theories, since the other theories' identities are also partly determined by their intended empirical applications. Thus to artificially contrive ORLs in an ad hoc fashion to make the problematic cases fit our extended set of conditions (including the ORL condition) for a genuine reduction *would inappropriately alter the very identities of the two theories in question.*

Furthermore, such an attempt would also violate the fact that ORLs are *ontological* links *composed of* these local relations between components of the potential models. We *discover* that the rigid bodies of **RBM** get heterogeneously linked to sets of particles of **NPM** by *learning* that the intended empirical applications of the two theories overlap. Likewise, we *discover* that the empirical base set J of pure exchange economics (**PEE**), the set of persons or stable groups of persons in the intended empirical applications of **PEE**, bears no ontological link, homogeneous or heterogeneous, to components of the potential models of simple equilibrium thermodynamics (**SETH**), despite the quirky fact that $M_p(\textbf{SETH})$ and $M_p(\textbf{PEE})$ meet the other conditions on ρ.[22] We make this discovery in the same way as discussed above, namely, by investigating the overlap (or lack thereof) of the intended empirical applications of the two theories, the "real world" systems hypothesized or already confirmed to be actual models of the theories. These local links comprising the global relation ρ in genuine reductions meeting the ORL condition are not a matter of mere contrivance. They depend on the real-world systems that (partly) give the identity of the theories involved. The ρs obtaining in the cases motivating the Schaffner-inspired worry are simply not ORLs, so they fail to meet the additional ORL condition on the genuine reduction relation. These cases are not counterexamples to my set-theoretic model of reduction supplemented with this additional ORL condition. Thus by adding the ORL condition to the conditions on ρ provided in the previous section, we bypass the Schaffner-inspired "too weak to be adequate" challenge.

4   Blurs on ρ: Significantly Corrective Reductions

The need to account for "corrective" reductions goes well beyond a few important historical cases. All interesting reductions in the history of science imply some nontrivial correction to the reduced theory. Take, for instance, a relatively smooth reduction by any measure: physical optics (the wave theory of light) to (a portion of) electromagnetism. This reduction implies only minor corrections to the laws of physical optics. For example, physical optics fails to correctly predict an exponentially attenuated penetrating wave at reflection. Yet just this small difference, when introduced as a condition to separate T_R^* from the rest of (reducing) electromagnetic theory, will leave empty a theoretically important part of the intersection of T_R^* and the actual models of electromagnetic theory (which contain a lawlike condition that correctly describes the penetrating wave). Thus any adequate theory of reduction must include some resources enabling it to handle the sort(s) of approximation involved in (all?) progressive theory shifts in the history of science.

One nice feature of the structuralist program is the advance it has made in developing precise notions of both intra- and intertheoretic approximation. Several notions exist, sharing a variety of features (see Balzer, Moulines, and Sneed 1987, 330, for a list and references). In what follows, I will borrow Balzer, Moulines, and Sneed's (1987, chap. 7) notion of a *blur*. However, owing to the differences between my structuralist-inspired rendition of Hooker's insight concerning what gets deduced in a reduction and Balzer, Moulines, and Sneed's account of direct reduction, I'll need to apply their blurs to different constituents of the reduced and reducing theories to handle corrective reductions. I will then use blurs to shed light on the spectrum of intertheoretic reductions and the distinction between significantly corrective yet still genuine reductions and mere historical theory changes (and in the next chapter, reductions involving multiply reduced concepts in the reduced theory). These are issues that structuralists have never addressed. They are of paramount importance for my defense of new-wave reductionism.

Balzer, Moulines, and Sneed build their notion of blur on that of *uniform structure* (or *uniformity*), familiar from topology. In the case of *intra*theoretical approximation concerning the application of a theory to empirical ("real world") systems, one defines a uniform structure on classes of potential models. *Application approximation* is only one kind of approximation important for my theory of corrective *inter*theoretic reduction, and *not* the most important kind. It is the simplest kind, however, and so it nicely introduces Balzer, Moulines, and Sneed's notion of a blur. (It is also the notion that they develop first in presenting their general theory of approximation in science, in chapter 7 of their 1987 work.) However, I will later have to alter the notion of blur I am about to explain in order to apply it to the specific structures I need to blur to handle significantly corrective intertheoretic reductions.

A uniformity imposes a topology on an otherwise unstructured set. One initially characterizes a blur as an element of a uniformity on the potential models of a theory element, that is, as a set of ordered pairs of potential models from a given theory element such that if a pair $\langle x, y \rangle$ is an element of blur u (where $x, y \in M_p(T)$), then x and y approximate each other at least to the degree given by u. For the real numbers (or any other set displaying a standard metric, where the absolute value of the difference of elements is meaningful), each blur is determined by a particular ε:

$$u_\varepsilon = \{\langle a, b \rangle : |a - b| < \varepsilon\}$$

However, the general definition of uniformity, and hence of blur, does not depend on a standard metric.

Following Balzer, Moulines, and Sneed (1987, 331–332), I introduce the following notational conventions to present the formal definition of a uniformity on potential models of a theory. If Σ is a set, then $\Delta(\Sigma)$ is its "diagonal," the class of all (ordered) pairs of identical elements of Σ. If u is a set of ordered pairs, then u^{-1} is the set of ordered pairs in which the order of u's elements is reversed (i.e., $u^{-1} = \{\langle y, x \rangle : \langle x, y \rangle \in u\}$). Finally, if u and u' are sets of ordered pairs, then $u \circ u'$ is their set-theoretic product (i.e., $u \circ u' = \{\langle x, y \rangle : \exists z(\langle x, z \rangle \in u \ \& \ \langle z, y \rangle \in u')\}$). I then define a uniformity on potential models as follows (Balzer, Moulines, and Sneed 1987, 332):

U is a *uniformity on* $M_p(T)$ iff

(1) $\varnothing \neq U \subseteq \mathscr{P}(M_p(T) \times M_p(T))$

(2)   for all u, u', if $u \in U$ and $u \subseteq u'$, then $u' \in U$

(3)   for all u, u', if $u \in U$ and $u' \in U$, then $u \cap u' \in U$

(4)   for all $u \in U$, $\Delta(M_p(T)) \subseteq u$

(5)   for all $u \in U$, $u^{-1} \in U$

(6)   for all $u \in U$, there is a $u' \in U$ such that $u' \circ u' \subseteq u$

(In English, U is not empty and is a set drawn from the power set of pairs of potential models of the theory. If an element of U is a subset of some other set, then the other set is an element of U. The intersection of two elements of U is also an element of U. Every element of a uniformity contains the diagonal of the theory's potential models. The reverse of an element of a uniformity is an element of the uniformity. For every element of a uniformity, there is another element of the uniformity such that the set-theoretic product of the other element and itself is a subset of the first.)

Blurs are defined as elements of U; formally, as dyadic relations on $M_p(T)$. Uniformities U are sets of sets of ordered pairs of potential models. If we understand a uniformity intuitively as a way to immunize a theory against troubles in its application, each $u \in U$ will represent a particular degree of immunization. The bigger the u allowed, the more ordered pairs of potential models it contains and the greater the immunization. This means that the more approximation in the application of the theory we are willing to tolerate, the more divergence from the expected potential model we are willing to allow. As Balzer, Moulines, and Sneed put one example illustrating this point, "Given a system S, we make some theoretical calculations using T and predict that S will have the mathematical form described by potential model x. But then, after some 'empirical observations,' we come to the conclusion that S should better be described by potential model y, with $x \neq y$. If $\langle x, y \rangle \in u$, then we are satisfied, at least for the time being.... The more pairs $\langle x, y \rangle$, you let in u, the safer you are; and, of course, the less you can really do with the theory" (1987, 333).

Using this intuitive understanding of a uniformity, I interpret the specific conditions as follows. Condition (2) states that if a theory is immunized by a blur u, then it will also be immunized by any bigger blur u' that contains u. Condition (3) says that if a theory is immunized by u and by u', then it is also immunized by the elements they share in common. Condition (4) states that if we are satisfied by the immunization provided by blur u, then we will also be satisfied by exact application, should this occur. Condition (5) states that the order of the potential models in a blur has no bearing on the immunization the blur provides. Condition (6) is the interesting axiom. It says that for any blur immunizing a theory, a sharper blur exists that still immunizes it; specifically, a blur at least twice as sharp as the original exists. This guarantees the formal possibility of applying the theory with ever increasing exactness. As Balzer, Moulines, and Sneed put this point, (6) "represents an idealization of actual scientific practice, because it implies the possibility of making ever sharper applications of the theory" (1987, 334).

Blurs, however, are still not enough to understand approximate applications of a theory. We must rule out blurs that are too big, because they make the theory useless. The size of the blur—the number of ordered pairs it contains—is a crucial consideration, but other context-dependent and mostly pragmatic considerations figure into determining admissible blurs. These include the particular application at issue (e.g., we are willing to accept bigger blurs in applying the law of gravitation to planetary motions than to objects near the earth's surface using delicate measuring instruments), the stage of scientific and technical evolution, and so on.

Can we state any general conditions for determining an acceptable class A of admissible blurs? According to Balzer, Moulines, and Sneed (1987, 343 ff.), there are at least some weak necessary conditions. Obviously, A must be a proper subclass of U. Furthermore, one can state some semiformal conditions on a notion of *strong resemblance* between empirical base sets of a theory T's potential models. We first need some special terminology (Balzer, Moulines, and Sneed 1987, 345). An object a belonging to empirical base set D_i of potential model x of theory element T belonging to the intended empirical applications $I(T)$ (denoted as $a \in D_i^x$) is a *significant object for* T iff for all potential models x^* identical with x up to the condition that $D_i^{x^*} = D_i^x - \{a\}$, necessarily $x^* \notin I(T)$. In other words, stripping only a from D_i^x would necessarily remove x from the intended empirical applications of T. When a scientific community using T applies some more or less well-determined criteria to decide whether two descriptions expressed in the language of the community are very similar to each other, we say that they employ *very similar descriptions of objects*. Finally, when D and D' are two empirical base sets of two potential models of T, then $R \subset D \times D'$ is a *quasi bijection between D and D' relative to Q_D and $Q_{D'}$* iff $Q_D \subseteq D$ and $Q_{D'} \subseteq D'$, $\|Q_D\| \gg \|D - Q_D\|$ and $\|Q_{D'}\| \gg \|D' - Q_{D'}\|$, and $R : Q_D \to Q_{D'}$ is bijective (where $\|A\|$ denotes the cardinality of A, $\gg$ receives its natural [and imprecise] scientific reading of "significantly greater than," and a bijection is a 1-1 function onto its range). (In English, a relation from one empirical base set to another is a quasi bijection just in case its domain is a significant portion of the first empirical base set, its range is a significant portion of the second empirical base set, and the function is 1-1, where every element of the range is related to some element of the domain.) If we let $\sim$ denote the relation of *strong similarity*, where $\sim$ is both reflexive and symmetric, then the necessary conditions on $D_i^x \sim D_i^{x'}$ for potential models x and x' of **T** are these. There are Q_i and Q_i' such that $\sim$ is a quasi bijection between D_i^x and $D_i^{x'}$ relative to Q_i and Q_i', $D_i^x - Q_i$ and $D_i^{x'} - Q_i'$ contains no significant objects for **T**, and the description of every element of Q_i is very similar to the description of its similar correspondents in Q_i' (Balzer, Moulines, and Sneed 1987, 345–346). For a given $a \in Q_i$, we denote its similarity image in Q_i' as $\tilde{}a$ (and conversely for the similarity image of each $a' \in Q_i'$). *Admissible approximations A* for the application of a theory element **T** are thus blurs admissible with respect to a strong similarity relation between whatever empirical base sets of the potential models are relevant to the given case. For example, for kinematics it is the empirical base set P (the particles) for which strong similarity must obtain for a blur to be admissible. Both the location and the acceleration of the similar correspondents in potential model y of elements of P of intended empirical application x must be less than some previously agreed value for y to be an element of the admissible blurs for x.

Finally, we can define the notion of an *upper bound* of admissibility. Intuitively, this means that beyond a degree of inaccuracy at or above the upper bound, application approximation becomes unacceptable. Following Balzer, Moulines, and Sneed (1987, 347), I define the set of boundaries of all admissible blurs A of a given uniformity U on potential models of a theory element **T** as follows. Bound$(A) = \{u : u \in U$, and for all $u' \in U$, if $u \subseteq u'$ then $u' \notin A$, and if $u' \subset u$ then $u' \in A\}$. (In English, the upper bound of an admissible blur is the set of elements of a uniformity such that for all other elements of the uniformity if the former is a subset of the latter then the latter is not an admissible blur, while if the latter is a proper subset of the former then the latter is an admissible blur.) A straightforward corollary of this definition is that if $u \in U$ is an element of Bound(A), then $u \notin A$. Bound(A) is thus the upper bound of admissibility, in the sense of being just too much to be an admissible blur on the application of T.

So far, I've provided definitions of blur and admissible blur sufficient to handle *intra*theoretical approximation, i.e., the application of a theory to real-world models. However, my principal interest is *inter*theoretical approximation, specifically approximative or corrective *inter*theoretic reduction, where the reduced theory only approximates the reducing theory even in the former's principal domain of application. We thus need to extend the notion of blurs and admissible blurs to other components of theory elements besides potential models. Which components of T_B, T_R^*, and/or T_R require blurring to enable my relation ρ to obtain in this important class of intertheoretic reductions?

Consider again the features of T_R^* and T_R causing problems for the conditions on ρ in the reduction from thermodynamics to kinetic theory (our exemplar of a significantly corrective intertheoretic reduction). The first shortcoming is that the counterfactual assumptions necessary to carve off T_R^* from T_B, so that the former is strongly analogous in structure to T_R, left empty the intersection of T_R^* and the actual models $M(T_B)$, including the important *confirmed* intended empirical applications $I_C(T_B)$ ($\in M(T_B) \cap I(T_B)$). Second, the "corrections" to T_R implied by these counterfactual assumptions in T_B amount to the claim that none of the intended empirical applications $I(T_R)$ related by ρ to counterpart intended empirical applications $I(T_B)$ are confirmed. At best, real-world models to which the simple thermodynamics of gases is intended to apply meet only approximately the lawlike conditions on actual models (since the lawlike conditions of the simple thermodynamics of gases are *never* exactly realized in the real world). Figure 3.7 illustrates these problems. It resembles figure 3.2, but the counterfactual assumptions required to generate T_R^* influence every element of it instead of just some (as occurs in, e.g., the less significantly corrective reduction from physical optics to electromagnetism, where the counterfactual assumption is only relevant in some cases). These shortcomings brought on by significantly corrective reductions collectively render BMS-inspired conditions (1) and (2) on ρ (section 2 of this chapter) trivially true by virtue of false

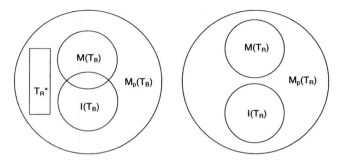

Figure 3.7
The structure of reducing (T_B) and reduced (T_R) theories in reductions implying significant correction to the reduced theory, i.e., where the assumptions necessary to separate all elements of T_R^* from the rest of $M_p(T_B)$ are counterfactual (as in the reduction of simple thermodynamics of gases to kinetic theory and statistical mechanics). Notice that the corrections imply that none of the intended empirical applications of the reduced theory $I(T_R)$ are actual models: $M(T_R) \cap I(T_R)$ is empty.

antecedents. They render Mayr-inspired condition (3) false by virtue of a false conjunct.

With the help of blurs, we easily resolve this second shortcoming. It requires an *intra*theoretical approximation, something I've already developed. Via admissible blurs, we need to "add members" to the (empty) class of confirmed intended empirical applications of T_R. To achieve this, we blur the intersection between the intended empirical applications of the reduced theory $I(T_R)$ and the actual models $M(T_R)$ by blurring the class of actual models further into the class of intended empirical applications (see T_R in figure 3.8). The additional members in the range of this blur aren't actual models of T_R. They are only potential models. They don't actually obey the empirical laws of T_R. However, they are close enough approximations to count as confirmed intended empirical applications (as elements of the intersection of $M(T_R)$ and $I(T_R)$) for the purposes of an approximative (significantly corrective) intertheoretic reduction.

Notice that there are other ways of blurring the intersection of $I(T_R)$ and $M(T_R)$. We could blur $I(T_R)$ deeper into $M(T_R)$. Or we could blur $I(T_R)$ and $M(T_R)$ until they overlapped. For the purposes of

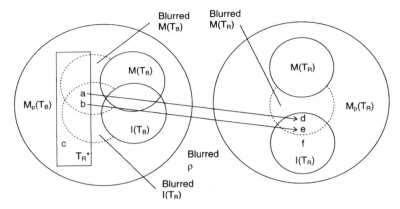

Figure 3.8
Blurring the actual models of the reduced theory $M(T_R)$ into the intended empirical applications $I(T_R)$, and the models $M(T_B)$ and the intended empirical applications $I(T_B)$ of the reducing theory into T_R^*, which permits a nontrivial way of meeting BMS-inspired condition (2) (or a way of meeting Mayr-inspired condition (3)). The intersections of T_R^*, blurred $M(T_B)$, and blurred $I(T_B)$, and of $I(T_R)$ and blurred $M(T_R)$ will be nonempty. The blurs must be big enough so that every element in the intersection of $I(T_R)$ and blurred $M(T_R)$ is related by ρ to some element in the intersection of T_R^* and blurred $I_C(T_B)$ (where blurred $I_C(T_B) =$ blurred $M(T_B) \cap$ blurred $I(T_B)$).

approximative reduction, however, neither alternative is appropriate. A corrective intertheoretic reduction doesn't imply correction to the *intended* empirical applications of the reduced theory. That set remains as originally specified. In light of the corrections, we might change the set $I(T_R)$. But this constitutes replacing the original theory with some successor, since $I(T_R)$ is a part of the theory's identity conditions. Instead, corrective reductions teach us (in part) that the intended empirical applications of the reduced theory—the original set that in part defines the reduced theory—don't contain any actual models, since nothing in the real world answers exactly to the reduced theory's empirical laws. Thus it is the set of actual models of the reduced theory that we need to blur into the intended empirical applications to capture this feature.

Balzer, Moulines, and Sneed (1987) provide us with a way to blur a set of potential models. How can we extend their account to blur a special subset of potential models, the set of actual models, to resolve this shortcoming? The adaptation is straightforward. Using the notational convention for a similarity image characterized above and letting $\sim_A$ mean "is approximately (the set of admissible approximations) A," we blur $M(T_R)$ (in symbols, $\sim M(T_R)$) into $I(T_R)$ by asserting that there is an $X \in \mathscr{P}(M_p(T_R))$ such that $X \sim_A M(T_R)$ and for all $x \in X$, $x \in I(T_R)$. In other words, X is a set of first elements of admissible blurs on models of T_R such that for each $\langle x, y \rangle \in A$, $x \in X$ and $y \in M(T_R)$. The size of an acceptable Bound(A), however, depends on some other blurs required to meet BMS-inspired condition (2) and Mayr-inspired condition (3).

What now of the first shortcoming listed above: the empty intersection between T_R^*, $M(T_B)$, and $I(T_B)$ (see again figure 3.7)? This requires two intratheoretical blurs in T_B, with the size of each (the size of an acceptable Bound(A)) depending on the blur on $M(T_R)$. First, we must blur the confirmed intended empirical applications of reducing T_B. Since the intersection of $I_C(T_B)$ and T_R^* is empty, there are no elements in this intersection for ρ to relate to elements of the blurred confirmed intended empirical applications of T_R ($\in I(T_R) \cap \sim M(T_R)$), as required to meet BMS-inspired condition (2). This blur on $I_C(T_B)$, along with the size of Bound(A) on the blur on $M(T_R)$ into $I(T_R)$, must be big enough to insure that there is some element in blurred $I_C(T_B)$ related by ρ for each element in the intersection of blurred $M(T_R)$ and $I(T_R)$ (see the blurs induced on T_B, the leftmost circle in figure 3.8). Second, since the counterfactual assumptions necessary to carve off the analog structure T_R^* from T_B render the intersection of T_R^* and the models of the reducing theory $M(T_B)$ empty, making BMS-inspired condition (1) on ρ trivially true in corrective reductions by virtue of a false antecedent, we also need to blur $M(T_B)$ far enough into T_R^* until condition (1) obtains nontrivially: until ρ relates members of the intersection of T_R^* and the admissible blurs of $M(T_B)$ to but only to elements of the (blurred) actual models of the reduced theory $M(T_R)$ (see figure 3.9). Again, elements of these blurred intersections are neither confirmed intended empirical applications nor actual models of T_B. They will be close enough approximations of confirmed intended empirical applications and actual models, however, so that besides meeting the counterfactual conditions placing them in T_R^*, they also count toward meeting the additional conditions on ρ in significantly corrective intertheoretic reductions.

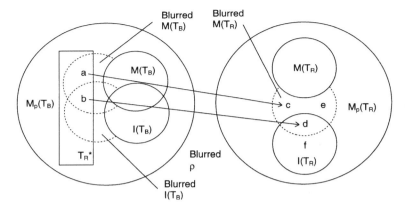

Figure 3.9
Blurs on $M(T_B)$ and $I(T_B)$ into T_R^* to meet BMS-inspired condition (1) in a non-trivial fashion. When Dom(blurred ρ) is restricted to the intersection of T_R^* and blurred $M(T_B)$, Rng(blurred ρ) must include only elements of blurred actual models $M(T_R)$.

We adapt the conditions on an admissible blur to the actual models $M(T_B)$ in an obvious fashion. Using the notational conventions adopted two paragraphs above (and the definitions of uniformity and admissible blurs introduced earlier in this section), we blur $M(T_B)$ (in symbols, $\sim M(T_B)$) into T_R^* by asserting that there is an $\mathbf{X} \in \mathscr{P}(M_p(T_B))$ such that $\mathbf{X} \sim_A M(T_B)$ and for all $x \in \mathbf{X}$, $x \in T_R^*$. We blur $M(T_B)$ in this fashion up to some Bound(A) until this intersection between T_R^* and blurred $M(T_B)$ includes all potential models $M_p(T_B)$ in T_R^* related by ρ to elements of the blurred models of the reduced theory $M(T_R)$. This disallows the trivial way to meet BMS-inspired condition (1). There will now be elements in the blurred intersection, so (1) won't be true by virtue of a false antecedent. The second conjunct of the definition carves off the blurs of $M(T_B)$ induced by admissible approximations A, these blurs being the ones relevant for approximative reduction, namely the one illustrated in figure 3.9 above.

Blurring the confirmed intended empirical applications $I_C(T_B)$ goes as follows. Adopting the same notational conventions as above, we blur $I(T_B)$ (in symbols, $\sim I(T_B)$) into T_R^* and (blurred) $\sim M(T_B)$ by asserting that there is an $\mathbf{X} \in \mathscr{P}(M_p(T_B))$ such that $\mathbf{X} \sim_A I(T_B)$ and for all $x \in \mathbf{X}$,

$x \in T_R^* \cap {}^\sim M(T_B)$. We blur $I(T_B)$ in this fashion up to a Bound(A) in which all of the potential models of T_B in T_R^* related by ρ to elements of the intersection of the intended empirical applications and the blurred models of reduced theory T_R are in the intersection of (already) blurred $M(T_B)$ and blurred $I(T_B)$. (The elements of ρ will have already been established prior to these blurrings.) Since this will render the blurred confirmed intended empirical applications ${}^\sim I_C(T_B)$ nonempty, it disallows the trivial way of rendering BMS-inspired condition (2) true and Mayr-inspired condition (3) false in significantly corrective intertheoretic reductions. The second conjunct of the definition carves off the blurs of $M(T_B)$ and $I(T_B)$ induced by admissible approximations A to the ones relevant to approximative intertheoretic reduction, namely, the ones illustrated in figure 3.8 above. Combining figures 3.8 and 3.9 yields the full account of approximative intertheoretic reduction that can handle significantly corrective reductions.

When introducing the appropriate blurs on T_R, I argued that blurring $I(T_R)$ to handle the relevant shortcoming is inappropriate, since corrective intertheoretic reductions don't alter the intended empirical applications of the reduced theory. Yet to handle the other shortcoming, I've advocated blurring the intended empirical applications of the reducing theory. Is there an inconsistency here? There is not. In significantly corrective reductions, we must somehow accommodate the falsity of the reduced theory in the reducing complex (reducing theory plus counterfactual assumptions required to mimic the structure of the reduced theory). It isn't really the reducing theory that mimics the structure of the reduced theory in these cases. It is a *falsified version* of the former, with a different set of models and intended empirical applications. That's why these blurs on T_B are appropriate.

Of course, in actual cases not any old blurrings of $M(T_B)$ and $I(T_B)$ into T_R^* and $M(T_R)$ into $I(T_R)$ will do. Details of the appropriate blurrings depend on the particular corrective reduction at issue: on the nature of the specific counterfactual assumptions required to separate T_R^* from the rest of the potential models $M_p(T_B)$ and on the specific corrections implied to T_R. In the reduction of thermodynamics to kinetic theory, for example, the two crucial counterfactual assumptions for the latter to mimic the ideal gas law are that there are no attractive forces among the molecules composing a gas to affect the motion of a given molecule, and that the volume of gas molecules is zero. These assumptions are not quite correct. In real gases there are weak attractive forces among the molecules (which increase as the molecules are closer together), and the volume of the molecules is very small but not zero. The importance of the first simplifying assumption is that when a real gas molecule is about to strike a wall of the container, there is a net backwards pull on it from the weak attractive forces of other gas molecules. The molecule thus does not strike the wall with full force, and so its contribution to the pressure is less than predicted by the kinetic theory armed with this simplification. A small extra quantity of pressure P_x must be added to the actual measured pressure P, so the ideal pressure P_i as figures in the ideal gas law is the sum $P + P_x$. Furthermore, this quantity depends on the number of molecules close to the colliding molecule, which varies with the density of the gas.[23]

The very small but actual volume of the molecules in a real gas has a second effect on the relationship between the kinetic theory and the simple thermodynamics of gases. As pressure is added to a quantity of gas, by Boyle's Law (chapter 2, sec. 2, above) volume decreases steadily toward zero. In real gases, when volume decreases to the point where the molecules eventually make virtual contact, no more decrease in volume is possible even with increasing pressure. Thus the ideal volume available for contraction V_i is the measured volume of the gas $V - b$, where b represents the volume of the molecules.[24]

These features lead to the following blurrings on $M(T_B)$ and $M(T_R)$ in the reduction of simple thermodynamics of gases to kinetic theory. On the side of the reduced theory, thermodynamics, suppose that we think of a potential model as a set of *states* S undergoing a *process*, with states assigned values for P, V, and T (these constants denoting theoretical functions for thermodynamics). Then we need to blur $M(T_R)$ (the potential models, sets of states, that also meet the various gas laws) into $I(T_R)$ by an admissible blur A such that for each $\langle S, S' \rangle \in A$, S is an empirical base set of an actual model of thermodynamics and S' is the empirical base set of the members of the intended empirical applications not included in the actual models of thermodynamics, where the values for P_x (i.e., of a/V^2) and for b (for the particular gas in question) determine A.[25] (By the definition of A, $S \sim_A S'$ for all elements of the admissible blur.) The potential models to which the S's belong will not be actual models of thermodynamics. They will be close approximations of actual models, however. In particular, they will be the close approximations relative to the increases in pressure owing to the existence of weak attractive forces in real gases and the decreases in volume owing to the small but finite volumes of real gas molecules needed to account for the corrections implied to the ideal gas law by the kinetic theory.

What now about the blurring required on the side of the reducing theory, the kinetic theory of gases? Consider again the counterfactual assumptions that separate the analog structure from the rest of the potential models. How can we blur the models and the intended empirical applications into the analog structure so that every element of the latter related by ρ to an element of the blurred actual models of thermodynamics is an element of the appropriate intersection with the blurred models and blurred intended empirical applications of kinetic theory? The counterfactual assumptions, of course, yield the relevant blurring. We want to include among the blurred models and blurred intended empirical applications those structures for which the force function assigns 0 attractive forces to elements of the empirical base set of molecules and for which the volume function assigns 0 volume to the molecules. These structures will be neither actual models nor actual intended empirical applications (e.g., real-world systems) of kinetic theory. They will not obey actual laws governing real aggregates of molecules. But for the purposes of relating the kinetic theory to thermodynamics, they will separate an analog structure mimicking the ideal gas law of the simple thermodynamics of gases. The conditions on ρ, and also the ORL condition that makes ρ a genuine reduction relation, will obtain on this subset of potential models of the kinetic theory.

Here I need to address an important worry about this reduction from the philosophy of science. Lawrence Sklar is the philosopher who has most carefully explored the interrelations between thermodynamics, statistical mechanics, and kinetic theory. Some of what he concludes seems at odds with the result just offered. For example, most recently he has written, "The alleged reduction of thermodynamics to statistical mechanics is another one of those cases where the more you explore the details of what actually goes on, the more convinced you become that *no simple, general account of reduction can do justice to all the special cases in mind*" (1993, 334; my emphasis). Is my argument at odds with Sklar's thorough analysis?

I don't think so. First, by "simple, general account," Sklar (1993, 333–344) has in mind versions of Kemeny and Oppenheim's "positivist" account or Nagel "derivational" account. I've stressed throughout the last two chapters that Hooker's insights and work in the structuralist program takes as its fundamental point of departure worries about these simpler accounts of reduction. The worries I cite at the beginning of chapter 2 above are closely akin to the worries Sklar himself cites for those "simple" accounts of reduction (1993, 333–344). A similar point holds for Sklar's skepticism about using approximation to skirt these worries. He writes, "The complex of 'taking a limit' type of operations that characterize the interrelations of the theories in important cases ... are far too subtle and formally complex for any *simple* notion of 'approximation' to cover the relationship between the theories" (1993, 336; my emphasis). Here again I agree. But the notion of approximation borrowed from the structuralist program and further developed and applied above is certainly not what Sklar has in mind. Finally, if one reads Sklar's general remarks carefully, one finds claims quite similar to new-wave reductionism. Reflecting on the reduction of thermodynamics to statistical mechanics plus kinetic theory, Sklar has recently claimed that while "simple derivation of the former from the latter seems out of the question, ... other subtler relations surely hold" (1993, 344). In light of the story I've just told about one important aspect of this case, I propose new-wave reductionism as a promising account of such a "subtler relation." (In chapters 4 and 6 below, I'll have more to say about how some of Sklar's specific conclusions about how the reduction of thermodynamics to statistical mechanics and kinetic theory comports with new-wave reductionist claims.)

5   The Intertheoretic-Reduction Spectrum and the Distinction between Genuine Albeit Bumpy Reductions and Mere Historical Theory Successions

With my notion of approximative reduction now specified and illustrated by the reduction of simple thermodynamics of gases to kinetic theory, I turn to some of its additional suggestive features. What about the spectrum of intertheoretic reduction, the idea that reductions line up on a spectrum ranging from smooth to bumpy, depending intuitively on the amount of correction implied to the reduced theory (as illustrated by the top arrow of figure 2.1)? This is an important aspect of Hooker's theory of reduction, though as we saw in the quote at the end of the previous chapter, Hooker finds no precise way to quantify it. Blurs provide a suggestive resource, for blurs have size. Being elements of uniformities, and hence sets of ordered pairs, each blur will have a cardinality determined by its bound. Bigger blurs have greater cardinality. They contain more ordered pairs. This feature provides a natural measure of smoothness of a reduction. Smoother reductions require smaller blurs on $M(T_R)$, $M(T_B)$, and $I(T_B)$ to meet the conditions on ρ (in something other than the trivial fashion that blurs disallow). Bumpier intertheoretic reductions require bigger blurs. Referring back to the top arrow of figure 2.1, we can say that location of a given case on the intertheoretic-reduction spectrum depends on the size of the bounds on the blurs required to meet non-trivially the conditions on ρ.

In light of some representative scientific reductions, this idea seems sound. The blurs one must induce on physical optics to allow reduction to Maxwell's electrodynamics are small. In many cases (i.e., those not involving penetrating waves at reflection), one need not introduce any blurrings at all. The analog structure T_R^* in Maxwell's electrodynamics has a nonempty intersection with the models and the confirmed intended empirical applications of that theory (see again figure 3.2). The reduction relation ρ relates all of the actual models of physical optics, those real-world systems that exactly meet the lawlike axioms of that theory, to actual models of Maxwell's electrodynamics. There are some intended empirical applications of physical optics not contained in the actual models of that theory that ρ relates to elements of the analog structure T_R^* of Maxwell's electrodynamics not included in $M(T_B)$ or $I(T_B)$ (and ipso facto not in $I_C(T_B)$). These are the cases where the former fail to correctly predict a penetrating wave at reflection. But these potential models of physical optics closely approximate actual models of the theory. We need to include in the blur capturing them only a relatively small number of ordered pairs, at least compared to the blurs required to get thermodynamics to reduce to kinetic theory. Similarly, the blurrings we need in order to induce the models of Maxwell's electrodynamics into the analog structure to meet BMS-inspired conditions (1) and (2) (or, correspondingly, Mayr-inspired condition (3)) in a nontrivial fashion are relatively small. Again, for some elements of the analog structure, we require no blurring at all. The reduction relation ρ already relates only elements in the intersection of the analog structure and the actual models of Maxwell's electrodynamics to actual models of physical optics (i.e., those cases not involving penetrating waves at reflection). In the cases requiring some blurring, we need to blur only the models where the empirical base set of electromagnetic waves gets assigned mathematical properties that match the (incorrect) predictions for penetrating waves at reflection offered by ρ-related potential models in the intersection of the intended empirical applications and the blurred models of physical optics. Since the only difference pertains to the exponential value of the attenuated wave, the cardinality of the blur capturing this approximation is relatively small (as compared with the cardinality of the blurs required for less smooth reductions). Blurs, at least partly, quantitatively capture our intuitions of approximation. Since their cardinality is the central component of this measure, approximative reductions can be ranked on a scale of the cardinality of the blurs, the size of the requisite bounds, required to meet the conditions on ρ. Location on the intertheoretic-reduction spectrum (top arrow of figure 2.1) seems potentially amendable to quantitative analysis after all.

Second, we can use the size of the blur, along with the nature of the ORLs, to distinguish genuine but bumpy reductions from mere historical successions of theory. This is a worry that many have stressed, at least in conversation, about the new-wave account of reduction. For example, in counting the transition from phlogiston chemistry to oxygen chemistry as an instance of genuine (albeit bumpy) reduction, new-wave reductionists seem to be playing fast and loose with actual scientific practice. I myself am not sure about the factual basis of this worry. Would scientists count these "bumpy reductions" as genuine reductions? I don't know, but I'll yield on this point for the sake of argument. If the ORLs in a particular reduction are mostly heterogeneous (if ORLs relate empirical base sets of reduced theory to elements of the potential models of the reducing theory that do not contain those base sets) *and* if the reduction is bumpy (if the blurs required are relatively large), then the case can be considered a mere historical succession from one theory to an incommensurate successor (although the ρ must still be a genuine ORL). These cases fall well out toward the bumpy endpoint of the top arrow of figure 2.1. I suppose that a case could count as a mere historical succession also if the intended empirical applications of the two theories overlapped significantly (that is, they are intended to apply to the same real-world systems), even though no ORLs obtain or the conditions on reduction (BMS-inspired (1) and (2) or Mayr-inspired (3)) can't be met.

Intuitively, the transition from a caloric heat theory to the kinetic theory and from phlogiston chemistry to oxidation seem more like mere historical successions than genuine (although bumpy) intertheoretic reductions. The ORLs mapping empirical base sets of the replaced theory to elements of the potential models of the replacing theory are obviously heterogeneous. However, they are genuine ORLs. The intended empirical applications significantly overlap, while caloric fluid pressure is linked to mean molecular kinetic energy and phlogiston is linked to oxygen. Here we don't have a case like the so-called "reduction" of exchange economics to thermodynamics, where ρ meets the abstract mathematical conditions but no ontological ties obtain between the their intended empirical applications (which makes this neither a case of genuine albeit bumpy reduction nor one of historical theory succession). Also, the sizes of the required blurs to meet the conditions on ρ in these cases of theory succession are relatively large. In "reducing" caloric fluid to kinetic theory, for example, one must blur the models of the kinetic theory to include structures that violate conservation laws of physics. This is because in cases involving objects meeting frictional resistance, the total amount of mean molecular kinetic energy must increase in potential models of the kinetic theory related by ρ to intended empirical applications of caloric-fluid theory. Both the moving object and the resisting object get hotter. According to caloric theory this can only obtain via an increase in caloric-fluid pressure in both, this being the commodity related via ORLs to increases in mean molecular kinetic energy. Obviously, these ρ-related potential models lie a long way from the actual models and intended empirical applications of kinetic theory, which are limited to real-world cases in which the basic laws of physics obtain. A similarly huge blur is required on the side of the caloric-fluid theory to blur its models into the intended empirical applications (see again figure 3.7). (In these even more extreme cases of approximative reduction, when a uniformity induces a topology on the potential models of T_B and T_R, the T_R^* is even farther away from $M(T_B)$ and $I(T_B)$, as is $M(T_R)$ from $I(T_R)$, than in the reduction of simple thermodynamics of gases to kinetic theory. They thus require blurs with significantly bigger bounds to meet the conditions on ρ.) The analog structure is so far removed from the models of kinetic theory, and intended empirical applications are so far removed from the actual models of caloric-fluid theory (and the confirmed intended empirical applications of caloric-fluid theory are empty, containing no real-world systems), that the blurs required to meet the conditions on ρ in a nontrivial fashion have comparatively huge bounds. Hence we classify them as mere historical theory successions, despite the fact that conditions on genuine reduction obtain.

On the other hand, even when ORLs are heterogeneous, if the blurs required are relatively small, the cases seem better classified as genuine reductions (although bumpy) than as mere historical theory successions. The reduction of thermodynamics to kinetic theory seems to be a case of this sort. The states of gases in a potential model of thermodynamics is not a subset of any empirical base sets of ρ-related potential models of kinetic theory. Included in the latter are base sets consisting of molecules, containers, and those required by mechanics. The ORL linking states of gases to collections of molecules with various properties in ρ-related potential models obviously are heterogeneous. But the blurs are not relatively large, though they are significant. The analog structure in kinetic theory has an empty intersection with the actual models (owing to the required counterfactual assumptions) and the intended empirical applications of thermodynamics has an empty intersection with the actual models (as no real-world systems exactly obey the ideal gas law). Topologically, the relevant structures are closer than in cases of mere theory succession, so the requisite blurs are smaller. Referring again back to the top arrow of figure 2.1, we can say that genuine but bumpy reductions stop somewhere short of the "limit bumpiness" endpoint. Beyond that stopping point lie cases of mere historical theory succession.

It is ridiculously optimistic to hope that we find some bound value on the cardinality of the required blurs separating blurs small enough to count as genuine reduction from blurs big enough to count as mere historical theory succession and applicable to every historical case. The quantitative features of blurs are devices for separating the two notions in a precise although necessarily abstract fashion. I only intend this discussion to show that I can make quantitative sense of "amount of correction" that locates reductions on the smooth-to-bumpy spectrum. To hope for more—for instance, to hope for some quantitative value applicable to all fully reconstructed historical cases to determine a theory transition as either an actual but bumpy reduction or a mere historical theory succession—strikes me as too strong a demand to place on formalistic philosophy of science. I haven't purported to provide *that sort* of resource here. This doesn't bother me, because no one has ever come close to providing any such thing, and the hope for it seems to me a tilt at a windmill. I've at least provided quantitative guidelines that can aid our judgments about particular cases.

The purpose of this chapter is foundational. I sought to capture the insights I find in Clifford Hooker's work on reduction within a framework that provides resources to take us beyond where Hooker leaves off. I find those resources implicit in the work of the structuralist program, though they must be developed in ways that structuralists have not attempted. I also sought to make precise some features of intertheoretic reduction that will figure heavily in the arguments to follow, where I will try to show that new-wave reductionism does not founder on the rocks sinking classical reductionism. I claim to have done all of this using standards of precision and formalization beyond those typically recognized in current philosophy of science. I now feel confident in using these features of intertheoretic reduction in good faith. With all the pieces in place, I have three issues to address. First, how does new-wave reductionism avoid the well-known problems sinking classical reductionism? Second, are there any reductions of genuinely cognitive psychological theories to neuroscience looming on the horizon, and can we even begin to formulate theories from the cognitive and brain sciences in structuralist-inspired fashion? Third, where on the intertheoretic reduction spectrum are potential reductions headed? Each issue receives separate treatment in the final three chapters.

4

The Irrelevance of Arguments against Classical Reduction

The purpose of this chapter is to show how new-wave reductionism side-steps the principal arguments that classical reductionism is superfluous or false. First up are two "conceptual" arguments, one based on Donald Davidson's famous principle of the anomalousness of the mental, the other on Hilary Putnam's and Jerry Fodor's equally famous appeal to multiple realizability. I call these arguments "conceptual" because they do not appeal to current or projected developments in the cognitive and brain sciences. Instead, both focus on features of the mental thought sufficient to sink reductionism independent of future empirical discoveries. After these I'll consider some "empirical" arguments against classical reduction, based on results from, and methodological consequences for, "special" sciences like psychology.

1   Antireductionist Arguments Based on Davidson's Principle of the Anomalousness of the Mental

Donald Davidson presented one of the first influential critiques of reductionism from within the physicalist camp. It still has many sympathizers, at least as a challenge that any reductionism must address. For example, in a critical notice of Patricia Churchland's *Neurophilosophy* (1986), John Bishop raises Davidson's worry for Churchland's claim that psychological phenomena are predictable in principle from "purely neurobiological information." His reasoning is that "such a prediction would require the resources of a psychophysical theory, and, following David-son, ... such a theory is impossible. Given this, it would have been useful for Churchland to have explained why she thinks that the Davidsonian arguments for psychophysical anomaly don't succeed—or to have argued (as I believe can be justified) that the kind of reduction to which her naturalism commits her does not rest on the possibility of psychophysics" (1988, 384).

In this section, I will argue that Bishop's final conjecture is correct, at least as pertains to new-wave reductionism. The account of reduction developed in the previous two chapters does not require the resources of psychophysics, at least not the sort that Davidson's principle challenges. New-wave reductionism is thus immune from Davidson's argument against reduction on the basis of the nonexistence of psychophysical laws. Even if Davidson is right about the anomalousness of the mental, his principle is irrelevant to the potential new-wave reducibility of psychological theories to physical theories.[1] I will also argue that supervenience and other nonreductive relations cannot serve as grounds for physicalism. I will have dismissed Davidson's motivations for adopting supervenience, motivations that remain standard in the current literature. Finally, I will show how new-wave reductionists can answer a Davidson-inspired challenge raised by Terence Horgan and James Woodward (1985) against Paul Churchland's (1981) argument for eliminative materialism. Although new-wave reductionism has not yet committed to any particular solution to the reformulated mind-body problem and is not in the business of defending Churchland against his critics, Horgan and Woodward's challenge targets an aspect of Churchland's eliminativism shared by new-wave reductionism. Responding to this final challenge also illustrates where new-wave reductionism might locate Davidson's philosophy of psychology around the intertheoretic-reduction spectrum.

I begin by reviewing Davidson's principle of the anomalousness of the mental and why it is troubling for classical reductionism. In his seminal essay "Mental Events" (1970), Davidson offers a theory of the mental dubbed "anomalous monism" to dissipate the apparent contradiction arising from jointly accepting the following three principles:

(1) *The principle of causal interaction*   Some mental events interact causally with physical events.

(2) *The principle of the nomological character of causality*   Events related as cause and effect have descriptions that fall under a strict deterministic law.

(3)   *The principle of the anomalousness of the mental*   There are no strict deterministic laws from which mental events can be predicted and explained.

The apparent inconsistency is that (1) and (2), conjoined with some plausible assumptions, seem to imply that there are strict deterministic laws from which we can predict and explain some mental events, while (3) denies that there are such laws. Since Davidson accepts all three principles, he needs to show that this apparent contradiction is not actual. His "Kantian" strategy describes a view of the mental and the physical that is internally consistent and entails all three principles. That this view turns out to be a version of the mind-brain identity theory makes it especially interesting. Davidson writes, "If the argument is a good one, it should lay to rest the view, common to many friends and some foes of identity theories, that support for such theories can come only from the discovery of psychophysical laws" (1973, 246). The truth of this conditional is obvious, since principle (3) alone denies the existence of such laws.

Davidson's argument for the "minimal" physicalist thesis is novel. He begins by showing how the three principles are consistent. Causality is a relation obtaining between individual events, no matter how they are described (and even regardless of whether they are described at all). But laws are *statements*—linguistic items—and so events fall under laws only under particular descriptions. Thus principle (1), dealing with events in extension, is blind to the physical/mental dichotomy, which is purely descriptive. Principle (3), on the other hand, speaks only of events *described as mental*. It states that there are no strict deterministic *laws* (linguistic items) by which events *described as mental* can be predicted and explained. Thus principle (2) is the key. According to Davidson, it "must be read carefully: It says that when events are related as cause and effect, they have descriptions that instantiate a law. It does not say that every true singular statement of causality instantiates a law" (1970, 215). In other words, when an event described as mental interacts causally with an event described as physical, there are descriptions of both events— nonmental descriptions, as required by principle (3)—that fall under a strict law, as required by principle (2).

From this the thesis of "minimal" physicalism follows, with the help of a few assumptions. Suppose m is a mental event that interacts causally with some physical event p. According to principle (2), there is some description of m and p that falls under a strict law. But according to principle (3), there are no strict laws containing mental predicates, including psychophysical laws. So the strict law under which the descriptions of m and p fall must be a physical law, i.e., a lawful statement containing only physical predicates. But if m falls under a physical law, then it has a physical description. Any event that has a physical description is a physical event. So m is a physical event.

Why did Davidson advertise his anomalous monism as a *nonreductive* physicalism? This question gets to the crux of my concern. I claim that Davidson did so because his anomalous monism is an alternative to a reductionism *built on the orthodox logical-empiricist (e.g., Nagelian) account of intertheoretic reduction*, the classical reductionism prevalent at the time he was developing his philosophy of psychology (1970–1974). (For the fundamentals of Nagel's account, see chapter 1, sec. 1, above.) Defending this claim will require some textual exegesis. Davidson never explicitly mentions Nagel's account of reduction in his philosophy-of-psychology writings. But consider the case I can make from the prevalence of Nagel's account among philosophers of mind in the early 1970s—psychoneural reductionists had already begun appealing explicitly to it in developing and defending their positions—and more important, from what Davidson does and doesn't *argue for* in the relevant essays. A curious feature of those essays, particularly his essays of 1970 and 1973, is the structure of the main arguments. Davidson offers many detailed, explicit arguments in favor of principle (3), the anomalousness of the mental. But once he takes that principle as established, he offers the antireductionist conclusion *without any additional premises*. Consider this passage from "Mental Events": "The thesis is ... that the mental is nomologically irreducible; there may be true general statements relating the mental to the physical, statements that have the logical form of a law; but they are not lawlike" (1970, 216). The natural reading is as a self-contained argument whose conclusion is the statement prior to the first semicolon, and whose premise is what follows. On this reading, the conclusion is the antireductionist claim, and the sole premise is the principle of the anomalousness of the mental.

More telling textual evidence is found in the following passage from "The Material Mind": "We are not committed to the view ... that psychological events can be reduced to physical events.... For I have not assumed, nor does anything I have assumed entail, that we can effectively correlate important open classes of events described in physical terms with classes of events described in psychological terms" (1973, 249). In the paragraph that follows, Davidson makes clear that the kind of "effective correlation" he has in mind (the kind he is "not assuming") is "nomological correlation": lawlike connections supported by their instances, correlations of the sort "science is interested in." Again, the natural reading of this passage is that the denial of such "effective correlations"—exactly what the principle of the anomalousness of the mental amounts to—is alone a sufficient reason for denying reduction, even if anomalous monism entails the minimal physicalist thesis.

This curious feature of Davidson's writings, his assumed direct inference from mental anomalousness to the irreducibility of psychological theory, suggests a hypothetico-deductive argument for my claim that he is implicitly assuming a Nagelian account of reduction. If he is, and if he further assumes that the required connecting principles in heterogeneous cases must be laws, then the irreducibility of psychological theories to physical (e.g., neurobiological) theories does follow from principle (3) alone. (The additional assumption here was quite common circa the early 1970s. One popular term for the required connecting principles was "bridge laws.") If mental predicates can figure in no laws, then ipso facto there can be no psychophysical laws. If there can be no psychophysical laws to bridge the heterogeneous descriptive vocabularies of the mental and the physical, then there can be no nontrivial logical derivations of psychological theories from (heterogeneous) neurobiological theories, and hence no Nagelian reductions. Mental anomalousness, conjoined with a common assumption about the lawful status of the connecting principles, undercuts a reductionism built on Nagel's account. No other premises are required.[2]

This analysis sets the stage for dismissing Davidson's principle as irrelevant to new-wave reductionism. Recall (from chapter 2, sec. 1, above) that one key difference between Nagel's and Hooker's theories of reduction is their accounts of what gets deduced. For Hooker, it is never the reduced theory T_R (as Nagel insists that it always is). Rather, it is the analog structure T_R^*, *already specified within the vocabulary of the reducing theory* T_B. One consequence of this difference, noted in chapter 2, is that connecting principles, lawlike or otherwise, are not required to effect the derivation. There are no disparate vocabularies to connect between premises (T_B and C_R) and conclusion (T_R^*). We saw above that this consequence enables Hooker's account to avoid troublesome (fatal?) questions about the logical status of connecting principles when radically false theories with nonexistent ontologies reduce to (presumed) true ones. Now we can see another advantage to a reductionism incorporating Hooker's insight. Davidson's challenge, based upon the impossibility of *psychophysical* (bridge) laws, is entirely without force. If the deductive part of a reduction has no gap to bridge between the language or the ontology of premise and conclusion, then the nonexistence of lawlike connections between reduced and reducing concepts or kinds is of no consequence. Since it incorporates Hooker's insight, new-wave reductionism nowhere requires connecting principles of the sort that Davidson's principle nixes. Bishop's conjecture at the end of the quote cited at the beginning of this section is correct for new-wave reductionism. The "kind of reduction" at issue does not depend on the "kind of psychophysics" rejected by Davidson's principle of the anomalousness of the mental.

From this conclusion, I can quickly undercut Davidson's reason for adopting supervenience as a nonreductive relation to ground physicalism. Davidson's legacy in philosophy of mind lives on primarily in his being the first to apply supervenience (and/or determination) explicitly to relating psychological and physical kinds and theories (see especially Davidson 1970, 214, and 1973, 253). However, the argument I just gave sweeps away Davidson's principal motivation for replacing reduction with supervenience and determination: that the latter provides an account of the one-way dependency of the mental on the physical required by the minimal physicalism without violating the principle of the anomalousness of the mental, as (classical) reduction does. A quote from "The Material Mind" shows that Davidson's principal motivation for adopting supervenience and determination is the untenability of reduction: "Although, as I am urging, psychological characteristics *cannot be reduced* to [physical characteristics], nevertheless they may be (and I think are) strongly dependent on them. Indeed, there is a sense in which the physical characteristics of an event (or object or state) determine the psychological characteristics; in G. E. Moore's view, psychological concepts are supervenient on physical concepts" (1973, 253; my emphasis). That Davidson's challenge to reductionism fails to challenge the new-wave variety thus undercuts *his reason* for adopting supervenience and determination. From here we can generalize. Davidson's motivation remains a (the?) principal motivation for seeking out nonreductive alternatives. By disabusing people of the notion that mental anomalousness is inconsistent with reducibility, I've take a step toward showing the lack of a need for such a search.

While still on the subject of Davidson's principle of the anomalousness of the mental, I can address one final potential challenge to new-wave reductionism. I say "potential" because the specific target of this challenge is Paul Churchland's (1981) argument for eliminative materialism. So far new-wave reductionism is not committed to any particular solution to the mind-body problem. (This will come in chapter 6, where, incidentally, I reject strong Churchland-style eliminativism.) Furthermore, my concern here has nothing to do with defending Churchland against his critics. But since Churchland's eliminativist arguments presuppose a reformulation of the mind-body problem very much in the spirit of new-wave reductionism, and since that is the feature this argument challenges, with a little tinkering it applies to the latter.

The challenge comes from Terence Horgan and James Woodward (1985, sec. 2). Unlike many of Churchland's critics, Horgan and Woodward have no gripe with some of his controversial premises. They don't challenge his arguments for the conclusions that folk psychology is an empirical theory, that folk psychology purports to provide genuine causal explanations, and that it might turn out incompatible with a developed and more comprehensive scientific theory of behavior. They question instead the strength of the "meshing" Churchland requires between folk psychology and some scientific successor to achieve an integration that would "save" our ordinary mentalistic vocabulary. The meshing in question is intertheoretic reduction. They seek to show that Churchland "employs an implausibly stringent conception of how FP [folk psychology] would have to mesh with lower-level theories in order to be compatible with them" (1985, 198). Again, since this meshing and the resulting IR reformulation of the mind-body problem (chapter 2, secs. 3 and 4, above) are features that Churchland's eliminativist arguments share with new-wave reductionism, Horgan and Woodward's challenge carries over. What, then, is their argument?

They find fallacious Churchland's "third, and most fundamental argument" for eliminative materialism (in his 1981 essay), the probable incommensurability of the categories and principles of folk psychology with a developed scientific successor. They argue by counterexample. One can assume the truth of Churchland's premises. Smooth intertheoretic reduction to some future scientific account of human behavior is one way to salvage the ontology of folk psychology, and for a variety of reasons, folk psychology will probably not smoothly reduce to some future scientific successor.[3] Yet the eliminativist conclusion can still be false, because a noneliminativist mind-body theory is consistent with the truth of the following premises:

Even if FP cannot be reduced the lower-level theories, and even if lower-level theories can themselves provide a marvelous account of the nature and behavior of *homo sapiens*, it simply does not follow that FP is radically false, or that humans do not undergo the intentional events it posits. Churchland's eliminative materialism is not the only viable naturalistic alternative to reductive materialism. Another important alternative is the *non-reductive, non-eliminative materialism of Donald Davidson....* The availability of anomalous monism as an alternative to reductive materialism makes it clear that even if FP is not reducible to neuroscience, nevertheless the token mental events posited by FP might well exist, and might well bear all the causal relations to each other, to sensations, and to behavior which FP says they do. (1985, 203–204; my emphasis)

So Churchland's eliminativist argument is fallacious because it ignores this alternative consistent with its premises. Notice how this challenge extends beyond Churchland's eliminativism to new-wave reduction in general. Davidson's alternative materialism, anomalous monism, apparently denies the possibility of an ideal intertheoretic reduction of (folk) psychology to the natural sciences. But it also insists that this impossibility is consistent with the former's ontological integrity. If this is true, then Davidson's anomalous monism strikes at a central claim of new-wave reductionism: that ontological consequences are secondary to and entirely depend on the answer to the logically prior issue of *intertheoretic reduction* between the theories promulgating the ontologies in question.

One can express the same critical point in slightly different fashion. If Davidson's anomalous monism is as advertised—a nonreductive, noneliminative physicalism—then where can we locate his account on the new wave's intertheoretic-reduction spectrum (figure 2.1, top arrow)? No answer suggests itself. There seems to be no room for this alternative. If Davidson's account is a physicalism, then according to new-wave reductionism, the affiliated intertheoretic reduction must be located somewhere on the spectrum. If the reduction is bumpy, then it must lie out toward the "replacement" endpoint, which implies, contrary to Davidson's claim, an elimination (or significant conceptual revision) of our ordinary psychological concepts. This failure of Davidson's alternative to fit anywhere on the intertheoretic reduction spectrum yet still be a physicalism seems to imply the inadequacy of new-wave reductionism's reformulation of the mind-body problem. It apparently can't find a place for a legitimate physicalist alternative. The crucial question for new-wave reductionism is thus whether Davidson's anomalous monism presents a genuine alternative—a nonreductive, noneliminative physicalism. Reformulated in new-wave terms, this amounts to whether the physical sciences will in principle displace intentional psychology in its explanatory and predictive roles.

This is a tricky question for Davidson exegesis, since he never explicitly addresses it and some offhand comments he makes suggest conflicting answers. In a *nonreductive, noneliminative* but also *nonphysicalist* vein, he sometimes suggests that the physical sciences *could never* offer adequate explanations of "higher cognitive behavior," as compared to those from intentional psychology. For example, when discussing the specific problems involved in explaining linguistic behavior, he claims that the conditions on accepting one "system of interpretation" over another "include criteria of consistency and rationality, and can no doubt be sharpened and made more objective. *But I see no reason to think that they can be stated in a purely physicalistic vocabulary*" (1973, 259; my emphasis). This sounds like a remark aimed at the *explanatory autonomy* of at least some of intentional psychology, that part addressing linguistic behavior. From the perspective of new-wave reductionism, this remark is tantamount to *dualism,* not physicalism. Davidson would have us remain committed to the autonomous existence of the entities and/or properties of our best explanatory psychological theories. Davidson's resulting dualism is clearly not of the substantive, Cartesian kind. But the quote above suggests that at least certain *properties* of the mental are forever beyond physical explanation (see again chapter 1, sec. 2).

This (property-)dualistic interpretation of Davidson's anomalous monism is not unique to new-wave reductionism. Jaegwon Kim (1985) has offered it, for reasons quite similar to mine (although from within a very different philosophical framework). Kim writes, "It undoubtedly will strike many readers as at best paradoxical to characterize Davidson as a dualist. I believe, however, that in spite of his anomalous monism, *dualism in the form of a commitment to the mental as an autonomous domain* is a nonnegotiable premise of Davidson's overall position in 'Mental Events'" (1985, 385; my emphasis). From the quote from Davidson offered just above, it also seems a nonnegotiable premise of "The Material Mind" (1973). If we understand "autonomous domain" as "postulates of an autonomous theoretical framework for explaining some domain of phenomena," then Kim is offering the same argument for Davidson's being a dualist as a new-wave reductionist might offer.

Yet there are also other passages in Davidson's writings that suggest a *reductive, noneliminative, physicalist* view of the potential explanatory power of the physical sciences. Again in "The Material Mind," he insists, "In saying an agent performed a single intentional action, we attribute a very complex system of states and events to him.... *I am not of course arguing that there is not a corresponding physical description—I am sure there is*" (1973, 255; my emphasis). In "Psychology as Philosophy" he claims, "The nomological irreducibility of the psychological ... does not mean that there are any events that are in themselves undetermined or unpredictable; it is only events as described in the vocabulary of thought and action that resist incorporation into a closed deterministic system. *These same events, described in appropriate physical terms, are as amendable to prediction and explanation as any*" (1972, 230; my emphasis). Quotes like these, especially conjoined with Davidson's ubiquitous claim to accept a "minimal physicalism," suggest that, when translated into new-wave reductionist terms, we best construe his anomalous monism as a version of smoothly reductive physicalism. This means that the derived T_R^* will be a closely equipotent isomorphic image of the syntactic structure of the psychological theory in question (as reflected in Davidson's use of terms like *"corresponding* physical description" and "same events described in *appropriate* physical terms"), and its derivation within the counterpart theory from the appropriate physical science will not require numerous and wildly counterfactual limiting assumptions and boundary conditions (C_R). So in several passages Davidson seems to suggest (from the new-wave reductionist's perspective) that a physical science could smoothly displace intentional psychology (at least in principle, if not in practice), with the character of this displacement fitting the description of a smooth new-wave reduction.

Finally, and perhaps most surprisingly, some of Davidson's fundamental ideas sound like new-wave reformulated *eliminativism.* Anomalousness itself implies nothing about the explanatory power of intentional psychology compared with physical science. According to Davidson, neurobiological theories might prove to have complete explanatory and displacement potential (especially in light of the quotes provided in the paragraph above). But then the "deep structural differences" between intentional psychology and the physical sciences entailed by the anomalousness of the mental would require substantial correction, in the form of numerous counterfactual C_R conditions (realized in the fashion described in the previous chapter), in order to derive a T_R^* in a "nomolous" neurobiology strongly analogous (again, in the sense described in the previous chapter) to intentional psychology. Thus these reductions will fall significantly out toward the bumpy endpoint of the intertheoretic-reduction spectrum (top arrow of figure 2.1). This in turn justifies an eliminativist ontological conclusion for intentional psychology.

Once again, this unorthodox interpretation of Davidson's anomalous monism is not unique to new-wave reductionism. Kim (1989a) (in a paper different from the one cited above in connection with the dualistic interpretation of Davidson's anomalous monism) argues that Davidson's principle of the anomalousness of the mental leads to eliminativism. But Kim there distinguishes irreducibility from bumpy reduction, so his argument is a little different from the one I just suggested.

Textual evidence is ambiguous on the proper treatment of Davidson's anomalous monism from the IR-reformulation perspective of new-wave reductionism. But one point is clear, whichever interpretation one favors. None of them provide a reason for thinking that Davidson offers a *nonreductive, noneliminative physicalism*. Each of the three interpretations denies one of these three characteristics. But applying Horgan and Woodward's (1985) argument against Churchland's eliminative materialism to new-wave reductionism requires Davidson's anomalous monism to have all three characteristics. Hence a final Davidson-inspired argument fails.[4]

2 Fodor's Conceptual Argument from Multiple Realizability

In the rest of this chapter I consider the most pervasive and convincing arguments against classical reductionism. The key to these arguments is the *multiple realizability* of psychological kinds on physical kinds. For more than three decades antireductionists have argued that radically different physical systems could realize identical mental kinds, and that for a variety of reasons this fact is inconsistent with reductionism. They often defend the premise of multiple realizability with thought experiments involving silicon-based extraterrestrials, computers, androids, robots, and other brainless yet sentient fictional beings. But one doesn't need science fiction to defend the key premise. Terrestrial biology provides many creatures with quite different nervous anatomies that nonetheless seem to share psychological processes like pain.

It is difficult to overestimate how widely philosophers continue to reject reduction because of multiple-realizability arguments. In one sense, their reason is sound. Multiple realizability is telling against classical reduction. But it can be handled within new-wave reduction. To show this, I will start by explaining the fundamental problems multiple realizability poses for classical reduction, using as a springboard the probably still most cited essay in this literature: Jerry Fodor's 1974 essay "Special Sciences." Then I will show how new-wave reductionism avoids these problems. This will require a number of sections, since Fodor offers both conceptual and empirical (methodological) arguments.[5] All have been further developed by Fodor and others since that essay.

At the outset, notice that ρ's being a *relation* from $M_p(T_B)$ into $M_p(T_R)$, and not a 1-1 function, permits *many* potential models of T_B to be related to a *single* potential model of T_R. Hence the new-wave account of intertheoretic reduction allows into the fold cases involving reduced theories multiply realized in the reducing theory. The reduction relation ρ can relate many token potential models of the reducing theory to a single potential model of the reduced theory. This alone is an interesting knock against the applicability of multiple realizability arguments against new-wave reductionism. But resting my case against the most influential antireductionist argument on this logical point seems disingenuous. What else can I say about multiple realizability from the perspective of new-wave reduction?

First, it is useful to point out that multiple realizability has troubled philosophers of mind about the possibility of reduction much more than philosophers of science. The latter have recognized that multiple realizability is a common phenomenon throughout science, with no important consequences for claims about reducibility (though, of course, with important consequences for how to explicate the reduction relation). Clifford Hooker, for example, writes the following:

It is often argued that, e.g., cognitive psychology cannot be reduced to neurophysiology because the former cross-classifies the latter; any number of different systems (from brains to machines to leprechauns passing notes) could realize the same functional or computational theory. It helps to remove the intellectual dazzle of this fact to realize that this is true of *any* functionally characterized system. The same cross-classifications turn up *within* such prosaic fields as electrical engineering (cf. "is an amplifier of gain *A*" *vis-à-vis* particular circuit diagrams) and physics (cf. "is a high energy electron source" *vis-à-vis* quantum specification). In these cases the issue is not whether reduction is possible, but how it goes. The same applies, I hold, between theoretical domains as well. (1981, 505)

Lawrence Sklar makes a similar point with regard to a case that has figured and will continue to figure heavily in my arguments:

Temperature shares with intentional cognitive states in functionalist theories of mind the property of "multiple realizability." ... The microscopic feature of a system associated with its temperature can, then, vary from system to system depending on its constitution.... But even sticking to "temperature" as referring to a property of an individual system, does the variation in microscopic correlate from system to system make an assertion of identity of temperature with any microscopic feature impossible? It would seem not. To be sure, the temperature of one kind of system is "identical with" one feature for one kind of system and with a different feature for some other kind of system. But this hardly precludes our saying that in each case the temperature of the system is identical to its relevant microscopic feature. (1993, 352)

Notice that Sklar here characterizes temperature as a *property* of individual systems! While these remarks hardly settle the issue of whether multiple realizability spells doom for psychoneural reduction, the fact that philosophers of science generally aren't concerned with its consequences for reduction should make us curious as to why antireductionist philosophers of mind have rested so much weight upon it.

First up are the conceptual versions of the argument. Jerry Fodor was not the first philosopher to emphasize the multiple realizability of psychological kinds on physical kinds, or the problem it poses for classical reduction. That accolade probably goes to Hilary Putnam (1960), although the well-known thought experiments mentioned above didn't start populating Putnam's writings until his 1964 essay. On one occasion, Putnam writes,

Consider what the brain-state theorist [classical reductionist] has to do to make good his claims. He has to specify a physical-chemical state such that *any* organism (not just a mammal) is in pain if and only if (a) it possesses a brain of suitable physical-chemical structure; and (b) its brain is in that physical-chemical state. This means that the physical-chemical state in question must be a possible state of a mammalian brain, a reptilian brain, a mollusc's brain (octopuses are mollusca, and certainly feel pain), etc. (1967, 436)

I'll call this type of multiple realizability "realizability across structure types," since it claims that distinct *types* of higher nervous systems (distinct *types* of neural structures) can realize identical psychological phenomena in different ways. This claim not only accords with intuitions, as the thought experiments show. The biological fact of "corticalization of function" also counts empirically in its favor. As cortex mass increases as we move up the evolutionary scale, the cortex assumes a greater role in carrying out cognitive processes, particularly sensory processes. Thus merely in terms of the anatomy involved, the brain state realizing my seeing a red object is very different than a rat's, and the rat's brain state in turn is very different from an octopus's. If, as Putnam tells us, the classical reductionist insists that *every* psychological state is identical to some physical-chemical state, the antireductionist needs to find only one psychological predicate that is applicable to all these creatures but whose physical-chemical correlates differ. According to Putnam (1967, 437), it is "overwhelmingly likely" that such a predicate can be found.

In "Special Sciences" (1974) Jerry Fodor continues Putnam's thread. He seeks to show that reductionism imposes too strong a constraint on acceptable theories in the special sciences, and that for any reasonable purpose, *token physicalism* is sufficient. Token physicalism claims that "all events that the sciences talk about are physical events" (Fodor 1974, 130). It is weaker than *reductionism*, which is "the conjunction of token physicalism with the assumption that there are natural kind predicates in an ideally completed physics which correspond to each natural kind predicate in any ideally completed science" (Fodor 1974, 131). It is the second conjunct that Fodor attacks.

Fodor acknowledged that the literature circa 1974 contained various notions of reduction. To his credit, he gave the reductionists' most developed account: in essence, Nagel's (see again chapter 1, sec. 1, above). Let the S_i's stand for descriptive predicates in some theory of the special science S. Let the P_i's stand for predicates from some theory of physics (or, more generally, from some lower-level science relative to S). And read $\rightarrow$ as "brings about" or "causes" and $\rightleftarrows$ (for now) as "bridges with." Then a necessary and sufficient condition on reduction is that for all the laws of S like

(1) $S_1x \rightarrow S_2x,$

there exists laws of the form

(2) $S_1x \rightleftarrows P_1x$

and

(3) $S_2x \rightleftarrows P_2x$

and a law of P like

(4) $P_1x \rightarrow P_2x$

such that (1) is a deductively valid consequence of (2) & (3) & (4).

How should we interpret the connective $\rightleftarrows$? According to Fodor, if reductionism is to provide a defense of physicalism, then nothing less than "contingent event identity" will do. Thus laws like (2) and (3) must be read "Every event which consists of x's satisfying S_i is identical to some event which consists of x's satisfying P_i, and vice versa" (1974, 130). Coupling this interpretation of $\rightleftarrows$ with the thesis that every event falling under a (proper) law of some special science S also falls under a law like (2) or (3) yields (classical) reductionism. Why, then, is reductionism "too strong"? Fodor draws out its problematic consequence thus: "If reductionism is true, then *every* kind is, or is coextensive with, a physical kind.... This follows immediately from the reductionist premise that every predicate which appears as the antecedent or consequent of a law of a special science must appear as one of the reduced predicates in some bridge law, together with the assumption that the kind predicates are the ones whose terms are the bound variables in proper laws" (1974, 132–133). Multiple realizability directly contradicts this consequence. If distinct kinds of the basic science realize one kind from some special science, then one-to-one mappings of predicates in laws like (2) and (3) will not obtain. At best, wildly disjunctive "laws" will obtain, "laws" like (2′):

(2′) $S_1 x \rightleftarrows P_1 x \lor P_2 x \lor \cdots \lor P_n x$

To use Putnam's example, such a (2′) might be "Every event consisting of x's being in pain state p is identical to x's being in brain state B_1 for humans or to x's being in brain state B_2 for octopuses or to x's being in electronic state E for T-2700 series androids or to x's being in green slime state G for the silicon-based aliens or to...." All of this sets up Fodor's critical thesis. The disjunctive component of (2′) is not a kind predicate, and the entire expression is not a law, of any physical science P. This is Fodor's conceptual argument from multiple realizability. Multiple realizability *alone* implies consequences that conflict with reduction, no matter what future brain and behavioral science might turn up.

Fodor provides two examples to illustrate his point: one from economics (the concept of monetary exchange) in contrast with physics, and one from psychology in contrast with neurophysiology. Concerning the latter, he urges, "It is entirely possible that the nervous system of higher organisms characteristically achieves a given psychological end by a wide variety of neurological means" (1974, 135). Put this way, "multiple realizability" is ambiguous. There is a stronger and a weaker reading. Besides

Putnam's weaker sense of "across structure types," Fodor might intend a stronger sense, which I'll call the "same individual across times" sense. A *token* higher nervous system might realize the same psychological state or process in different physical states at different times. Notice that on this stronger reading, the disjunctive component of statements like (2′) expands significantly. For every *token psychological being* there will be a disjunction of physical predicates related by $\rightleftarrows$ to a single psychological predicate.

One final observation before I address Fodor's conceptual argument using multiple realizability. I pointed out that Fodor explicitly attacks a reductionism built upon the orthodox empiricist model (Nagel's). Implicitly, however, the reach of his argument is much broader. In note 2 of his 1974 essay he claims, "I suspect (though I shan't try to prove it) that many of the liberalized versions of reductionism suffer from the same basic defect as what I shall take to be the classical form of the doctrine," namely, inconsistency with multiple realizability. My purpose now is to show that Fodor's argument does not reach new-wave reductionism.

For two reasons, I begin by clearing away the "across structure types" argument. First, a response to it already exists that is compatible with new-wave reductionism as developed so far. Second, the obvious counter against my response to the stronger "across individuals at times" argument just collapses that argument into a weaker "across structure types" version. If I've already got a response to the latter in place, such a counter won't cut any ice.

A number of reductionist responses to Putnam's "across structure types" argument have emerged over the past three decades. Paul Churchland (1982), for example, recommends descending from the level of neuroscience and seeking reductive "unifying natural integrity" for the class of cognizers at some lower level of physical science. He suggests nonequilibrium thermodynamics as a potential candidate. Finding reductive unity there is more than a bare logical possibility. Churchland notes some parallels between biological activity, whose multiple realizations do find a unifying theme in that lower science, and cognitive activity (particularly learning), whose reductive potential is at issue.

Robert Richardson (1979) offers a more direct challenge. His conclusion is bold: "Contrary to the claims of Hilary Putnam and Jerry

Fodor, there is no inconsistency between computational models and classical reductionism: neither plurality of physical realization nor plurality of function is inconsistent with reductionism as defended by Ernest Nagel" (1979, 533). This is because Putnam and Fodor attribute to Nagel a view of reduction that he did not hold, namely, that reduction (in heterogeneous cases) requires *biconditional* bridge laws. Logically, the mappings between theoretical expressions demanded by Nagel's "condition of connectivity" (1961, 353–354) need only hold from reducing to reduced terms. Merely *sufficient* conditions at the reducing level are enough to effect a derivation of reduced from reducing laws. While Nagel's own examples of scientific reduction all use biconditional bridge laws, Richardson even quotes from Nagel an explicit claim that conditional bridge laws are logically sufficient: "The linkage between A [a term from the reduced theory] and B [a term from the reducing theory] is not necessarily biconditional in form, and may for example be only a one-way conditional: If B, then A" (Nagel 1961, 355 n.; quoted in Richardson 1979, 548–549). That "If C, then A," "If D, then A," ... are also true (where C, D, ... are the realization of A in other structure types) is irrelevant to a *Nagelian* reduction of, e.g., psychology to *human* neurophysiology (to octopi neurophysiology, to T-2700 series android electronics, ...) when one-way conditional bridge laws are enough. Observant as Richardson's point is, however, it probably isn't enough for new-wave reductionism. Merely conditional connecting principles seem insufficient to serve the aim of ontological unification via intertheoretic reduction. This consequence probably mattered little to Nagel, wedded as he was to logical empiricism and its aversion to ontological issues. But Fodor's point above about reductionism as a defense of physicalism might not be met by Richardson's response.

However, the most telling response to the argument from multiple realizability across structure types, and the one most consonant with new-wave reductionism, remains the oldest one, first voiced by David Lewis in a reply to Putnam. Lewis writes, "[Putnam] imagines the brain-state theorist [reductionist] to claim that all organisms in pain—be they mollusks, Martians, machines, or what have you—are in some single common nondisjunctive physical-chemical brain state. Given the diversity of organisms, this claim is incredible. But the [reductionist] who makes it is a straw man. A reasonable [reductionist] would anticipate that pain might well be one brain state in the case of men, and some other brain (or nonbrain) state in the case of mollusks. It might even be one brain state in the case of Putnam, another in the case of Lewis" (1969, 24–25). Lewis provides a commonsense example to illuminate the ubiquity of his point. Consider the following triad of claims:

(1)   There is only one winning lottery number.

(2)   The winning lottery number is 03.

(3)   The winning lottery number is 61.

These three claims seem inconsistent, in the same way as these three:

(1′)   *The reductionist's thesis*   There is only one physical-chemical realization of a given psychological kind.

(2′)   The physical-chemical realization of pain p is resonance pattern r in neural pathway n.

(3′)   The physical-chemical realization of pain p is . . . (something else entirely).

As Lewis points out, there is no mystery in reconciling (1) through (3). One just needs to note their "tacit relativity to context" (1969, 25). Append "per week" to (1), "last week" to (2), and "this week" to (3), and the inconsistency evaporates. Similarly, append "per structure type" to (1′), "in a human" to (2′) and "in a mollusk" to (3′), and the inconsistency again evaporates. Lewis's point, put simply, is that reductive identities, and hence the intertheoretic reductions that ground them, are *specific to a domain (structure-type)*.

Several authors have adopted Lewis's point, at least implicitly. Some have strengthened it by showing that domain specificity of this sort is commonplace in some "textbook" examples of scientific reduction. Berent Enç (1983) appeals to a favorite illustration of scientific reduction: classical thermodynamics to statistical mechanics.[6] It is common to assert that the identification of temperature with mean molecular kinetic energy is an ontological consequence of this intertheoretic reduction. But the identity holds only for gases. Temperature in a solid is a different statistical mechanical kind: mean *maximal* molecular kinetic energy, since the molecules of a solid are bound up tightly in lattice structures and hence are limited to a range of vibratory motions. Temperature in a plasma is something else again, since the "molecules" have been ripped into their atomic parts. Even a vacuum can have a ("blackbody") temperature, depending upon the electromagnetic waves coursing through it, although it contains no molecular components. Temperature is a multiply realized property across types of physical states. Yet its affiliated theory, classical equilibrium thermodynamics, is a paradigm reduced theory. Multiple realizability across structure types, and hence domain-specific reduction, is not unique to psychology. These are common features throughout all of science.

Implicitly employing Lewis's insight, Jaegwon Kim (1989b) shows that an account of reduction restricted to biconditional connecting principles can handle multiple realizability across structure types. This sort of multiple realizability is consistent with what Kim dubs "species-specific strong connectivity," meaning biconditional bridge laws conditional on structure types. Such laws have the form $S_i x \supset (Mx \equiv P_i x)$, where S_i denotes a determinate type of physical structure (narrower than a biological species when psychological kinds are at issue, according to Kim), M denotes some mental-state type, and P_i denotes the physical realization of M for S_i's. Psychophysical laws of this sort read, "If x is of structure type S_i, then x is in M just in case x is in P_i." Creatures belonging to different structure types can have expressions denoting different physical-state types in the P_i position of their species-specific bridge law for mental state M.

Kim argues that the consistency of structure-specific strong connectivity with multiple realizability across structure types is sufficient to block any antireduction conclusion, since "these laws will buy us a series of *species-specific* or *local* reductions. If we had a law of this form for each psychological state-type for humans, we would have a physical reduction for human psychology; this reduction would tell us how human psychology is physically implemented, how the causal connection between our psychological events and processes work at the physical-biological level, what biological subsystems subserve our cognitive capacities, and so forth. This is reduction, in the full-blown sense, except that it is limited to individuals sharing a certain physical-biological structure" (1989b, 39). Since local reductions "are the rule rather than the exception in all of science, not just in psychology" (1989b, 39), we should not demand more of any reducing theory. As Kim puts it, local reductions are "reductions enough," both by "any reasonable scientific standard and in their philosophical implications" (1989b, 39). Physicalism, for example, would be vindicated by a series of local reductions of psychological theories to the physiologies of all of the structure types to which they apply.[7]

Thus regardless of one's views on intertheoretic reduction—whether Nagelian or otherwise—the reductionist's recipe for handling multiple realizability across structure types is straightforward: restrict reductions to specific structure types, that is, treat reductions as domain-specific. This move is conceptually impeccable and has plenty of precedent from actual scientific practice. This move is not enough, however, to dismiss Fodor's conceptual argument from multiple realizability. The reductionist must still say something about multiple realizability in the same individual across times. This is a harder problem. It is also the feature that recent antireductionists have championed. As Terence Horgan puts it, concern with multiple realizability across structure types "tends to obscure the full extent to which intentional mental concepts are strongly realization-neutral. Multiple realizability might well begin at home. For all we now know, ... the intentional mental states we attribute to one another might turn out to be radically multiply realizable, at the neurobiological level of description, even in humans; indeed, even in *individual* human beings; indeed, *even in an individual human given the structure of his central nervous system at a single moment of his life*" (1993b, 308; my emphasis). This italicized sort of multiple realizability is more troubling for reductionists, because a Lewis-inspired response won't work against it.

In Lewis's example, to handle this second sort of multiple realizability, claims (1′) to (3′) must be restricted to whatever physical-chemical state happens to realize the psychological state *in the individual subject at a given time*. Hence we must restate the reductionist's thesis (1′) as follows:

(1″) There is only one physical-chemical realization of a given psychological kind *in a token individual (of a given structure type) at time t*.

Relativizing psychophysical reductions to specific domains now involves relativizing them to physical-chemical states of individuals at times. Any general identities (e.g., that the same neurobiological state realizes both Alfred's and Alonzo's belief at time t that water is wet, or that the same neurobiological state realizes Alonzo's belief at time t and time t' that water is wet) are purely accidental. Thus we must also restrict the scope of the "theories" to which psychological theories will reduce in domain-specific fashion to token systems at times. Surely this much domain-specificity is inconsistent with the assumed generality of science.

As one would expect, this problem infects Kim's elaboration of Lewis's strategy. On Kim's account, the structure-type predicates before the biconditional in connecting principles will now denote only individuals at times, e.g., "For Alonzo at time t, M just in case P_i." The criticism above applies. This much specificity for structure types is inconsistent with the generality of science. A series of "local reductions" of psychological theories to theories of Alonzo's physiology at time t, Alfred's at t, Kurt's at $t, \ldots$, Alonzo at t', Alfred's at $t', \ldots$ does not deserve the label of "a reduction of psychology to *human* neurophysiology."

How can a reductionist handle this more radical sort of multiple realizability? In Bickle 1992b, I suggested (and sketched) the following strategy. Find a textbook case of reduction from the history of science that involves this stronger sort of multiple realizability. This by itself is sufficient to show that even multiple realizability in the strong sense *by itself* does not block reducibility, and so it undercuts the key premise of the conceptual argument from multiple realizability. Then, to defend *new-wave* reductionism, show how the account of intertheoretic reduction on which the program rests can handle this case.[8]

We've already got a case ready to hand: the reduction of the simple thermodynamics of gases to microphysics (the kinetic theory) and statistical mechanics. We saw in chapters 2 and 3 how Hooker's insights and the full new-wave account of intertheoretic reduction handles key features of this case. What does that have to do with the conceptual argument from multiple realizability? We here have a demonstrably genuine case of reduction that exhibits the radical "same individual across times" sense of multiple realization. The case shows that multiple realizability in the strong sense of across individuals at times by itself is not sufficient to block a new-wave intertheoretic reduction. Consider temperature (as a thermodynamic kind). For any aggregate of molecules, there are an *indefinite* number of realizations of the kinetic-theory analog, *mean molecular kinetic energy*, in terms of the *microcanonical ensemble*, the finest specification of a gas's microphysical state in which the location and the momentum (and thus the kinetic energy) of each constituent molecule are individually fixed. Obviously, indefinitely many distinct microcanonical ensembles of a fixed volume of gas can produce the same *mean* molecular kinetic energy. Thus at the lowest level of microphysical description, temperature is vastly multiply realizable in the same aggregate of molecules at different times. Yet this reduction is a textbook example of intertheoretic reduction, reconstructable within the new-wave account.

A simple schematic illustrates this argument. Consider the two "volumes" of gas illustrated in figure 4.1. Each represents the microcanonical ensemble of a single "volume" of gas at different times. The vectors indicate direction and speed. The mean molecular kinetic energy of the two "volumes" are identical, while the microcanonical ensembles differ. Hence different microphysical states of the same token volume of gas at different times can realize the same temperature. Yet the theory

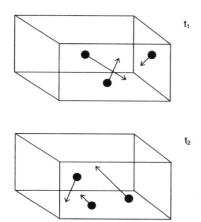

Figure 4.1
The same "volume of gas" at different times, with identical mean molecular kinetic energy but completely different microcanonical ensembles.

to which the latter, multiply realized notion belongs (the simple thermodynamics of gases) reduces to the theory to which the former belongs
(statistical mechanics and the kinetic theory). I have even accomplished a
part of this reduction within the new-wave account (chapter 3).

I conclude that multiple realizability *alone* is no barrier to potential
(new wave) reducibility, even in the radical sense of same individual
across times. Its being an obstacle is the key premise of the conceptual
argument from multiple realizability. But that premise is false, so the
argument is unsound.

3   The Obvious Objection to the "Across Individuals at Times" Counter

To the argument above, I often hear the following objection. In the
reduction of the simple thermodynamics of gases to statistical mechanics
and kinetic theory (microphysics), there is an underlying commonality
for temperature as a thermodynamic (reduced) kind, namely mean molecular kinetic energy. The latter is an underlying necessary and sufficient
condition for a given thermodynamic temperature, present in every
volume of gas at a given time. However, the point of the worry about
psychophysical multiple realizability is that there may not be such a
commonality for psychological kinds. That is, we may not find the analog of mean molecular kinetic energy relating intentional-psychological
kinds to neurobiological "microcanonical ensembles." So while it is correct to say that multiple realizability alone doesn't block the conceptual
possibility of reduction, the case cited in defense of this claim contains
an element—the intervening notion of mean molecular kinetic energy—
whose very existence is in doubt in the alleged reduction of psychology
to physical science.[9]

Here is another way to frame this worry.[10] Within statistical mechanics, temperature is not multiply realized. Rather, it is uniquely realized
by a particular mathematical construct, mean molecular kinetic energy.
Multiple realizability across token systems at times is then explained
simply by the fact that temperature as a thermodynamic kind is uniquely
realized by a statistical construct, in particular, a mean. Obviously, different microcanonical descriptions of a system can instantiate the same

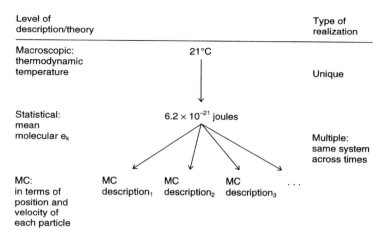

Figure 4.2
Multiple realizability in the same individual across times in the reduction of the simple thermodynamics of gases to kinetic theory and microphysics. Multiple realizability at the microcanonical (MC) level obtains via a unique realization of temperature in terms of a statistical construct (mean molecular kinetic energy, e_k).

mean (see figure 4.2). Yet we can imagine, and very well expect, to find no psychophysical analog to mean molecular kinetic energy. That is, in the psychophysical case, we might have multiple realizability at both levels, rather than just from the intervening level to the neurobiological microcanonical level (see figure 4.3). Hence the response based on the reduction of thermodynamics to statistical mechanics and microphysics contains an important potential disanalogy to the case at issue.

Here we must be careful. There is a way for the above counter to collapse into an argument based on an "across structure types" sense of multiple realizability, and hence to fail on the domain-specific point stressed above. In fact, the illustration of the counter in figure 4.3 shows exactly this. Once we relativize reductions to specific domains (that is, to specific structure types), it is not enough to argue that the nonexistence of a unique realizer for all the specific domains blocks the possibility of reduction or even the analogy with the reduction of thermodynamics to statistical mechanics and the kinetic theory. That same point holds for the latter case (see again figure 4.2). Mean molecular kinetic energy uniquely realizes thermodynamic temperature *only in ideal gases*. As I

Level of description/theory			Type of realization

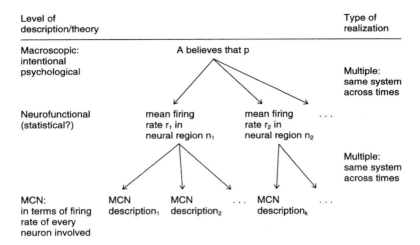

Figure 4.3
A more radical possibility for the realization of an intentional psychological kind. A given psychological state might be multiply realized at both the neurofunctional and "microcanonical neurobiological" (MCN) levels of description/theory.

pointed out earlier in the chapter, many reductionists have noted that there is no unique realization of thermodynamic temperature over all physical states. Rather, for the disanalogy between the compared cases to go through, the antireductionist must assert a more radical claim. *Within a given domain* (a given structure type, e.g., across human beings with our characteristic nervous systems), we must be unable to find a unique realization of a given intentional-psychological kind at any intervening level down to microcanonical neurobiology. Relative to humans (or some other subtype of cognizer sharing our characteristic nervous system), the belief, e.g., that there is beer in the cooler must enjoy no unique realizing neurofunctional concept, analogous to mean molecular kinetic energy. It is not enough to simply find a type of cognizer capable of entertaining the belief but with a very different physical mechanism for doing so. To that example we can respond with the domain-relative point urged against the weaker "across structure types" kind of multiple realizability. That is all this objection would amount to. The objection would then be akin to arguing against the reduction of the thermodynamics of gases to statistical mechanics and the kinetic theory because temperature in a solid isn't mean molecular kinetic energy. The proponent of this stronger sense of multiple realizability needs to argue that no neurofunctional kind will play a role analogous to mean molecular kinetic energy in the subtype of cognizers to which humans belong, e.g., to creatures with nervous systems like ours. Is this stronger claim plausible?

I contend that the only reason that it will seem plausible is if we stick with statistical ideas like "mean firing rate r of neurons in brain region n" about neurofunctional kinds. A given belief in an individual human can surely be realized by distinct firing rates in different brain regions at different times. For example, Alonzo's belief that there is beer in the cooler might be realized by some mean firing rate r by neurons in brain region n on one occasion, by a different mean firing pattern r' by neurons in n on another (since the rest of his brain is occupied by different tasks at the two times), by mean firing rate r in a different region n' on another, and so on. This seems empirically possible, even plausible perhaps, and is certainly consistent with everything we now know about localization of neural function. The problem with this move, however, is that it is far too limited a view of neurofunctional resources, even at the present time. In fact, one increasingly popular approach within current computational neuroscience yields a picture of the relationship between the intentional-psychological, neurofunctional, and canonical neurobiological levels exactly analogous to the thermodynamics of gases, statistical mechanics, and microcanonical levels: unique realization of the first by the second, multiple realizability (of the strong "across token systems at times" type) of the second on the third. The approach I have in mind uses the notion of high-dimensional vector spaces, which has come to computational neuroscience from "connectionist" ("parallel distributed processing" or "PDP," "neural network") artificial intelligence (AI).[11]

What follows is not an entry in the battle over whether connectionist cognitive science in general offers reductive potential to neuroscience. Some connectionists think that it does (e.g., Paul Churchland [1989], Patricia Churchland [1986, chap. 10], Churchland and Sejnowski [1991]); others are more cautious (e.g., Smolensky [1988, chap. 4], Rumelhart et al. [1986, chap. 4]). At least one serious obstacle faces those who argue for the general reducibility of connectionist cognitive science to neuroscience. The learning strategies and algorithms for read-justing connection weights during training used in many results deemed cognitively significant are "supervised." Weight changes to minimize the error percentage in the network's output to a particular input are derived by subtracting actual network output from the target output. This is the first step in both learning by "backpropagation of error messages" and "Boltzmann" learning—the strategies employed in connectionist parade results, including Rosenberg and Sejnowski's (1987) NETtalk (which transforms written English text into audible speech), Gorman and Sejnowski's (1988) rock-mine sonar-echo detector, and Lehky and Sejnowski's (1988) pattern extractor (which extracts 3-D shapes from 2-D shading). These learning algorithms make use not only of resources not known to exist in real nervous systems but also of others that seem downright biologically implausible. Real brains (presumably) lack storage of and access to target output vectors, and the external "teachers" of brains lack direct access to the plastic microstructure of synapses. This worry about biological plausibility doesn't concern me here. I'm only going to show how the connectionist account of the structure of cognitive representations carries over into computational neuroscience. The features of connectionist nets that make this account of representation fruitful are exactly the features these nets share (in extremely simplified form) with real brains. Learning—the account of how these trained representations are acquired—has nothing to do with the applicability of this part of connectionist theory to neuroscience.

The connectionist theory of cognitive representation to follow utilizes the mathematics of dynamic systems. This treatment has been common in connectionist modeling and analysis for almost a decade (Smolensky 1988, Horgan and Tienson 1992). Consider an extremely simple PDP network (figure 4.4). Suppose we wish to teach a small network like this to make a binary classification ("A" or "B") of input vectors.[12] The network is three-layered and densely connected, with every unit at a lower layer enjoying an active connection with every unit at the next layer up. The network is entirely feedforward, having neither intralayer nor backward connections. It also has no connections that skip a layer. There are m units at the lowest (input) layer, n units at the middle (hidden) layer, and 2 units at the topmost (output) layer, for $(m \cdot n) + (n \cdot 2)$ total con-

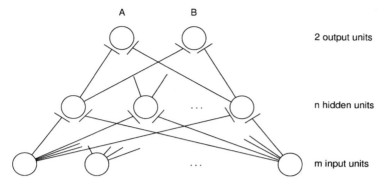

Figure 4.4
A schematic simple connectionist network. (Adapted from Bickle 1995a.)

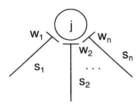

Figure 4.5
Total input to a connectionist unit j. Here $s_i =$ signal strength on input line i; $w_i =$ connection weight on line i; $E_j =$ total input to unit j; and $\Theta_j =$ threshold value of unit j: Thus $E_j = -\Theta_j + \sum_i w_i \cdot s_i$. (Adapted from Bickle 1995a.)

nections. Assume that for each unit there is some constant minimum and maximum activation value, respectively min and max. Scales with min and max as lower and upper bounds may be either continuous or discrete. The activation value reached in a given unit during processing is an arithmetical function of the total input to the unit—in real connectionist modeling, typically a quasi-linear logistic (S-shaped) function. Total input to a unit above the input layer is the sum of the strength of the signals from the units below multiplied by the weights of the connections (see figure 4.5). Input units are simply activated to a particular value to represent the input to the system (as explained in the next paragraph). Connection weights too can be continuous or discrete values between a min_{cw} and a max_{cw}. Assume that some training strategy has been used so that a set of connection weights permits the network to identify elements of its training set (the inputs over which learning is accomplished) correctly as *A*s or *B*s. For each input vector in the training set (these being *m*-ary vectors, with the *j*th constituent of each reflecting the activation value induced in the *j*th unit of the input layer), the network correctly responds with an output sufficiently close to ⟨max, min⟩ for each *A* input of the set and an output sufficiently close to ⟨min, max⟩ for each *B* input (where "sufficiently close" makes use of some previously set standard of error).[13]

An intriguing feature of even very simple connectionist nets is that when (quite minimal) conditions obtain on the size and variety of the training set and the number of hidden units, networks possess the capacity to generalize their output capabilities well beyond the members of their training sets. To use our schematic network as an illustration, when we present the trained network with a novel-*A* input (one not included in its training set), it will respond with an output near ⟨max, min⟩. Prompted by a learning algorithm directing it to find higher-order relational features among the training input vectors grouped together, the network evolves a set of connection weights that embody general knowledge of the desired distinction. At the cognitive level of description, what the trained network has acquired are *representations* of the classificational features distinguishing *A* inputs from *B* inputs. As Paul Churchland puts this point, "Upon repeated presentation of various real world examples of the several features to be learned (*F*, *G*, *H*, etc.), and under the steady pressure of a learning algorithm that makes small adjustments to the network's synaptic connections, the network slowly but spontaneously generates *a set of internal representations*, one for each of the several features it is required to recognize" (1989, 123; my emphasis).

How can we best describe the structure of these representations? One very influential answer borrows from the mathematics of dynamic systems. We can think of a network's behavior after training in terms of a *hidden-unit activation-vector state space*, where each axis (dimension) represents the activation value produced in one hidden unit during processing (see figure 4.6). An activation-vector space is nothing more than a geometrical representation of the activation values produced in the units in question. We represent the activity in each unit on a separate dimension. A point in the space thus represents the entire set of activation

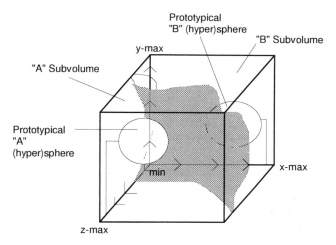

Figure 4.6
Hidden-unit activation-state space for the simple network described in the text.
(Adapted from Bickle 1995a. Originally adapted from P. M. Churchland 1989.)

values produced in every unit of the hidden layer during the processing of
a given input.

To illustrate this notion, consider again our schematic network. Suppose that it has only three hidden units (i.e., $n = 3$). Geometrically, we
can represent its hidden-unit activation-state space as a Euclidean cube,
with the x axis representing the activation value of hidden unit 1, the y
axis that of hidden unit 2, and the z axis that of hidden unit 3. Values
along each axis will range from min to max (see again figure 4.6). Under
this characterization, training up the network partitions the subvolume
of its hidden-unit activation-vector state space (the cube) that groups
together the hidden-unit activation values produced by the A inputs of
the training set from a disjoint subvolume grouping together those produced by the B units. The center point (or set of points or path) within
each disjoint subvolume represents the *prototypical* or *exemplary* As and
Bs (relative to the members of the training set). Thus, when a novel input
gets processed by the trained network, it is judged as an A or a B
depending on whether the set of activation values it produces in the
hidden units falls within the A or B subvolume and the extent to which
this point lies geometrically near the center of that subvolume.

Paul Churchland nicely phrases this connectionist theory of the structure of cognitive representations: "According to the style of theory we have here been exploring, it is *activity vectors* that form the most important kind of *representation* within the brain. And it is *vector-to-vector transformations* that form the most important kind of *computation*" (1987, 165; my emphases). This account of the structure of representational states and processes conflicts sharply with the classical theory of languagelike representations and logiclike computations over their contents embodied in symbolic cognitive science.[14] Churchland also stresses the similarities between this connectionist theory of representation and "prototype" models of concept representation developed by psychologists. He argues that some mathematical resources mobilized by connectionists can help to address some sticky questions that have plagued prototype theories (1989, chap. 6, sec. 2).

For ease of exposition, I have described a simple network limited to a binary-decision problem. However, connectionists have constructed networks with many more output and hidden units, which can draw numerous distinctions. One much discussed example, Charles Rosenberg and Terence Sejnowski's (1987) NETtalk, learns to pronounce written English text. NETtalk contains 26 output units. It encodes English phonemes using 21 features of human articulation, with the remaining 5 output units encoding stress and syllable boundaries. NETtalk contains 80 hidden units and 18,629 connections. It is trained using a 7-character window as input, where each character represents a letter of written English. The middle (fourth from left) character represents the pronunciation target during a single processing step. During training, its pronunciation (an activation vector across the 26 output units) is compared to the target output, and weights are adjusted (using backpropagation). With its output hooked up to a sound synthesizer, the trained network transforms written English words (of 7 letters or less) into audible English speech. NETtalk has also displayed impressive generalization capacities. Shavlik et al. (1991) trained NETtalk on just 500 randomly chosen words and found that it could pronounce correctly about 60 percent of randomly selected novel words.[15]

The activation-vector-space theory of representation nicely accounts for the performance of complex nets like NETtalk. During training, the evolving set of connection weights partition NETtalk's 80-dimensional hidden-unit activation-vector state space into 79 distinct subvolumes, one for each English transformation from letter to phoneme and stress. Using the differences between the center points of these subvolumes as a measure, Rosenberg and Sejnowski (1987) also discovered that NET-talk's representations reflected the hierarchical organization of the phonetic structure of English speech. Partitions representing phonemes that sound more alike (e.g., k-k and c-k, as compared to c-k and c-s) were located closer to one another in activation-state space (see Rosenberg and Sejnowski 1987, figure 8).

The applicability of this account of cognitive representation to computational *neuro*science follows from the biological plausibility of its three key features. These are the layered arrangement of processing units, which distinguishes hidden from input and output units; the connection weight values, which partition activation-vector space into informationally rich subvolumes according to the nature of the training set; and the dynamic system properties of the activity of trained nets in performance mode after input activation. These three features are shared by artificial connectionist networks and real brains. So the activation-vector-space theory of cognitive representations is directly applicable to *computational-neuroscientific* theorizing. But now imagine the staggering increase in representational power in real brains, with their multitide of layers and vast increases in numbers of units (neurons) and connection weights (synapses), over currently existing "tinker toy" artificial nets. As Paul Churchland puts this point, "A network the size of a human brain . . . can be expected, in the course of growing up, to partition its internal vector spaces into many billions of functionally relevant subdivisions, each responsive to a broad but proprietary range of highly complex stimuli" (1989, 178).[16] If the activation-vector-space theory of representations illuminates how an artificial neural net of a few more than 300 simplified "neurons" and 18,000 simplified "synapses" can come to pronounce written English text (Rosenberg and Sejnowski's [1987] NET-talk), think of the light this theory can shed on the capacities of systems as massive and connectionistically complex as human brains, with their multiple layers, 100 billion neurons, 100 trillion synapses (excitatory, inhibitory, modulatory), and massive recurrency ("feedback" connections).

Applying this connectionist theory of the structure of cognitive representations directly to neuroscientific theorizing promises some real understanding of how a finite physical brain could produce the richness, sophistication, and complexity of human cognition and behavior. Small wonder that it has become common currency in one influential branch of computational neuroscience.

But what does all this have to do with multiple realizability? The following. First, *representations construed as partitions in activation-vector-spaces are vastly multiply realized at the "microcanonical" neurobiological level of description*, in which the firing rate and frequency of each neuron of the relevant layer are individually specified.[17] Activation vectors are ordered *n*-tuples of activation values, and on the activation-vector-space model of cognitive representation, *distinct n-ary vectors get grouped together in a given partitioned subvolume as realizing the same representational content.* Connectionist activation-vector-space representations are multiply realized in events at the microcanonical neurobiological level (in the same token system over time). Second, at least relative to the domain of cognizers sharing humanlike brains, a given intentional psychological content is *uniquely realized* at the neurofunctional level of activation-vector-space partitions. This situation is diagrammed in figure 4.7. Notice that this figure is directly analogous to figure 4.2, which illustrates the reduction of thermodynamics to statistical mechanics and microphysics.

We can illustrate these features with our simple connectionist net. Consider again figure 4.6, but now imagine each axis divided into ten discrete units representing possible activation values for each unit (so min $= 0$ and max $= 10$ along each axis). Notice that the activation vector $\langle 1, 8, 9 \rangle$ falls within the prototypic region of the A subvolume. So does $\langle 2, 7, 8 \rangle$, along with many other ordered triples of activation values in hidden units 1, 2, and 3. Each of these triples is thus a representation of a prototypic A. Yet at the microcanonical neurobiological level of description, these two states are completely distinct. They share *nothing* (of relevance) in common, since no unit is firing at the same rate across the two states. (This was exactly the point illustrated in figure 4.1 above, for the simple thermodynamics of gases when reduced to microphysics.)

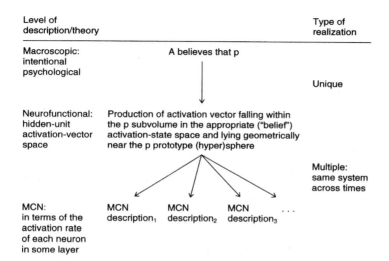

Level of description/theory		Type of realization
Macroscopic: intentional psychological	A believes that p	
		Unique
Neurofunctional: hidden-unit activation-vector space	Production of activation vector falling within the p subvolume in the appropriate ("belief") activation-state space and lying geometrically near the p prototype (hyper)sphere	
		Multiple: same system across times
MCN: in terms of the activation rate of each neuron in some layer	MCN MCN MCN . . . description₁ description₂ description₃	

Figure 4.7
Intentional psychology is uniquely realized at the intervening neurofunctional level of description and multiply realized at the microcanonical neurobiological (MCN) level in the same individual across times. Compare with figure 4.2, and contrast with figure 4.3.

So in any single system over time, distinct microcanonical neurobiological states can realize the same representation, when we characterize the latter as a partition of activation-vector space. This is multiple realizability of the radical "within a token system across times" variety stressed by recent antireductionists. Yet if this representation of A as a partition of activation-vector space were embedded in a system of such representations that enabled it to play a computational role akin to human representations (and clearly neither my simple network nor even Sejnowski and Rosenberg's NETtalk provide that), then the system's belief that (input) x is an A would be uniquely realized at the neurofunctional level in terms of that partition (see again figure 4.7). Again, this is exactly the combination of relations obtaining in textbook scientific reductions. Hence the analogy between the potential psychoneural case and that case is restored, and with it the possibility of reduction despite multiple realizability, even in the strong sense of "across token systems at times."

To round out this discussion, I should also point out that even my sketch of a neurofunctional theory built on high-dimensional geometry is extremely oversimplistic. Brains are *dynamic systems*. They constantly evolve new partitions of high-dimensional vector spaces over time. Hence any adequate neurofunctional framework for brain science must also employ the full mathematics and geometry of dynamic systems. Neural realizations of contents and neurocomputational processes over them will have to be described in terms of trajectories through state spaces, attractors, their basins and boundaries (some chaotic), and the like. This additional required complexity further strengthens my response to the supposed disanalogy between the reduction of thermodynamics to statistical mechanics and kinetic theory and the potential reduction of intentional-psychological theories to microcanonical neurobiology by way of some neurofunctional analog of statistical mechanics. The case for unique realizability between the intentional-psychological and (domain-specific) neurofunctional levels is enhanced when we consider the resources current computational neuroscience has to play with.

The time has come for antireductionists to give up the conceptual argument based on multiple realizability. It is outdated by both the general philosophy of science and developments in the brain and behavioral sciences. So is it now time to fight the issue of reduction on the grounds where it really belongs, namely, on a case-by-case examination of the scientific details of potential reductive pairs from the cognitive and brain sciences? That is, is it time to take on the "put up or shut up challenge"? Not quite. New-wave reductionism must still confront some methodological worries based on multiple realizability. We find hints of most of these in Fodor 1974, although others have added some interesting twists.

4   Three Methodological Caveats and the Mistakes They Rest Upon

The methodological caveats are worries about how reduction will constrain and restrict theory choice and development in special sciences like psychology.[18] These arguments are empirical. If reductionism imposes constraints on theory choice and development that stunt scientific progress, then so much the worse for reductionism. But each of these criticisms rests on mistakes about the methodological implications of new-wave reduction. At center stage in new-wave responses is the view of reduction as an empirically based prediction about the relationship to expect between developed scientific theories. I claim that the methodological implications of new-wave reductionism are both weaker and fewer than what critics of classical reductionism target, and that the actual methodological implications of new-wave reductionism are reasonable. New-wave reductionism has its house in order concerning acceptable methodology in the special, to-be-reduced sciences.[19]

Methodological caveat no. 1: reduction imposes stultifying constraints on theory choice in special sciences

Terence Horgan (1993b) eloquently states this first methodological criticism. After quoting two widely cited passages from Jerry Fodor (1974) concerning the wildly disjunctive nature of all possible physical realizations of monetary exchange, Horgan insists, "In my view, the line of argument in these passages constitutes a very convincing case against the appropriateness of *imposing* classical reducibility *as a constraint* on interlevel fit among theories or explanatory frameworks" (1993b, 306–307; my emphases).[20] Fodor himself is explicit about this constraining feature of reductionist methodology when he writes,

Though reductionism is an empirical doctrine, it is intended to play a *regulative role in scientific practice*. Reducibility to physics is taken to be *a constraint upon the acceptability of theories in the special sciences*. (1974, 128–129; my emphases)

Fodor's statement is particularly instructive, since it points out *how* reductionist methodology is supposed to constrain theory choice. Reduction requires that theories in the special sciences, to be allowed to survive and develop, must both successfully explain the relevant "higher level" data and show reductive potential to accepted lower-level ("basic") theories. The second conjunct carries methodological implications. Given two theories in some special science that are equally explanatory, one will be preferred to and chosen over the other if the former displays reductive potential and the latter does not. On some versions of reductionism, this methodological implication is even stronger. We might choose a theory with *less* explanatory power over another because the former displays reductive potential while the latter does not.

The problem with this imposed constraint, according to Fodor, Horgan, and other champions of "the autonomyof psychology," is that it will probably inhibit theory development in the special sciences. It is overwhelmingly likely, the autonomists contend, that we will thereby miss generalizations discoverable by a special science that is allowed to develop its own explanatory principles and concepts, independent of how they relate to lower explanatory levels. Zenon Pylyshyn clearly emphasizes the deleterious potential of this methodological principle: "There are many reasons for maintaining that explanations of behavior must involve cognitive terms in a way that does not serve merely as a heuristic or as something we do while waiting for neurophysiological theories to progress. One of the principal reasons involves showing that there are regularities and generalizations which can be captured using cognitive terms that could not be captured in descriptions using behavioral or physical (neurophysiological) terms" (1984, 6–7). Since science is in the business of capturing all such regularities, we must reject reductionism on this empirical-cum-methodological ground.

The key premise of this first methodological criticism is simply mistaken about the methodology required by reductionism. The new-wave reductionist will remind the autonomist that intertheoretic reduction is a relation that obtains between *developed* theories, which are currently few in both cognitive psychology and cognitive neuroscience. So the new-wave construal of the reductionist thesis is a *prediction* that as successful development occurs within psychology and the neurosciences, psychological theories will increasingly come to be reduced (in the new-wave sense) to counterpart neuroscientific theories. The evidence for this prediction is current developments in the relevant sciences and projected future developments of approaches now gaining steam. Notice that Fodor acknowledges the empirical status of reductionism in the passage cited two paragraphs ago. But he fails to see that someone offering this empirical prediction need not *impose* anything as a methodological *constraint* on theory development and especially on theory *choice* in the special, to-be-reduced sciences.

I choose carefully the words "impose," "constraint," and "theory choice." Below I will argue that new-wave reductionism connects smoothly with a "coevolutionary" research methodology (Hooker 1981;

P. S. Churchland 1986, chap. 9). This latter conclusion is consistent with the argument just presented. Coevolution is not a methodological *imposition* but rather a *recommendation*, itself justified only by broadly empirical considerations, e.g., by its results in more developed cross-level cases of scientific reductions generally and its promise for a reduction of psychology to neuroscience in particular. Coevolution is not offered as a *constraint* on theory *choice*, as a prescription for *ruling out* theories and suggestions in the special sciences that fail to display reductive potential. Instead, it is a principle for *keeping alive* certain nascent theoretical suggestions, to give them a chance to display explanatory potential because they comport with the reductionist's prediction, a prediction, again, whose justification rests on independent empirical grounds. I direct the argument above at antireductionists who see reduction as imposing constraints of the "ruling out" sort. The new-wave reductionist commits to none of these, beyond general constraints on theory development and choice imposed by science itself.

A similar response is available to a second argument of Horgan's (1993b), which concludes that imposing reductionism on psychology violates the *autonomous epistemic warrantability* of its generalizations: "Generalizations in the special sciences, and statements attributing to individuals the properties that figure in these generalizations, can possess—and often do possess—a high degree of epistemic warrant, quite independently of whether or not those higher-level properties are multiply realizable. . . . To insist on [evidence for unique realizability] would be to shackle the special sciences (and folk psychology) with an epistemic demand that is incommensurate with the strong realization-neutrality of their concepts. . . . The integrity of the special sciences just doesn't require their ultimate reducibility to physics" (1993b, 308). Unfortunately, Horgan expresses this methodological criticism against a reductionism committed to the unique realizability of the reduced theory's kinds in the reducing theory's kinds. As we've seen, new-wave reductionism is not so committed. It had better not be, given that multiple realizability is a common feature of cross-level reductions in science generally.

Let us put this problem aside, however, since Horgan's methodological worry is also unfounded. For the reasons cited the in previous argument (three paragraphs above), new-wave reductionism does not "shackle" the special sciences with any special epistemic demands beyond those of general scientific methodology. By construing reductionism as an empirically based prediction about the relationship to expect between future psychological and neuroscientific theories, new-wave reductionism can comfortably agree with Horgan that generalizations in the special sciences (as generalizations in the special sciences) can have a high degree of epistemic warrant independently of how theories in these sciences relate at a given time to those at lower explanatory/theoretical levels.

Two considerations should cinch this point. First, since new-wave reductionism draws inspiration from all of science, it must accommodate Horgan's point. Cases from the history of science reveal that successful theories often develop initially with only a cursory acknowledgment of how they relate to counterpart theories both below and above them. Reductionists must acknowledge that there are methodological prescriptions other than potential reducibility that can take precedent in guiding development in the special sciences. Otherwise, reductionism is wrong about cross-level intertheoretic relations across the board in science, not just in cases specific to psychology and neuroscience. New-wave reductionism acknowledges Horgan's point by emphasizing the *predictive* nature of the reductionist thesis about the relation to expect between mature theories.

Second, when we conceive of the reductionist thesis in this fashion, it *must* be compatible with the autonomous epistemic warrantability of generalizations in the special sciences. If reduction is at bottom a two-place relation between developed theories, then there must be developed theories *at both a higher and lower level* for reduction to obtain. The special sciences *must provide developed theories* to stand in the reduction relation. If verifiable higher-level theories independent of lower-level theories don't exist, the predicted reduction relation won't obtain. It will lack one component of the binary relation.

At this point one might wonder whether new-wave reductionism gives away too much to accommodate this first methodological criticism. For example, one might insist that even before psychology and neuroscience progress to the point of having "developed" theories, evidence favoring psychological theories with reductive potential might be strong enough to rule out the rationality of pursuing alternatives (or, conversely, too weak to support theories displaying reduction potential). Perhaps what the new-wave reductionist should be saying here is not that its methodology imposes *no* special constraints but rather that it imposes special constraints *if* (and only if?) certain empirical conditions are fulfilled.

The new-wave reductionist can easily accommodate this possibility. Remember, the new-wave reductionist insists that reductionism as an empirically based prediction imposes no special constraints on theory choice and development in the special sciences *beyond those imposed by general scientific methodology*. Surely it is a principle of general scientific methodology that when, in a given discipline, evidence strongly favors one theoretical approach, the pursuit of that approach supersedes the pursuit of alternatives (independently of whether the winning approach is reductionist or not). In such a case, the "imposed" constraints aren't "special" to reductionist methodology.[21]

Methodological caveat no. 2: reduction implies the disappearance of the reduced theory

This second methodological criticism also has its genesis in Fodor 1974. The quote from Fodor cited in the first paragraph of caveat no. 1 finishes as follows, "Reducibility of physics is taken to be a constraint upon the acceptability of theories in the special sciences, *with the curious consequence that the more the special sciences succeed, the more they ought to disappear*" (1974, 128; my emphasis). In the first paragraph of the same essay, Fodor insists, "The development of science has witnessed the proliferation of specialized disciplines at least as often as it has witnessed their *elimination*, so the widespread enthusiasm for the view that *there will eventually be only physics* can hardly be a mere induction over past *reductionist successes*" (1974, 127; my emphases). The natural reading of these passages is that successful reductions imply the disappearance or elimination of the reduced theory not only from ontology but also from the practice of science. Since this methodological implication contradicts the fact that explanatory levels appear in scientific practice as regularly as they disappear, reductionists lose again on broadly empirical grounds.

Again, the key premise of this methodological criticism is inapplicable to new-wave reductionism. For nearly three decades philosophers of science have acknowledged that historical cases of intertheoretic reduction line up on a spectrum (figure 2.1, top arrow). Cases range from relatively smooth or retentive cases at one endpoint, where the theoretical posits of the reduced theory are mostly preserved by the reducing theory via cross-theoretic identities, to bumpy or replacement cases at the other, where the posits of the reduced theory suffer elimination from our scientific ontology. This feature of a spectrum of historical cases is a centerpiece of Hooker's (1981) and Paul Churchland's (1979) initial account of reduction. We even saw in chapter 3 above how new-wave reductionism can analyze the source of a given case's location on this spectrum in a way that goes far beyond what Hooker or Churchland provides. The point about the spectrum that I wish to stress now is that the location occupied by a given case on the intertheoretic reduction spectrum carries *methodological* as well as ontological consequences. Refer back to figure 2.1 in chapter 1 and the discussion concerning it. Cursory investigation of the intertheoretic-reduction spectrum (top arrow of figure 2.1) reveals that besides preserving the ontology of the reduced theory via cross-theoretic identities, more smoothly reduced theories also retain more currency in subsequent scientific practice. Practicing scientists still use physical optics and equilibrium thermodynamics more often than phlogiston chemistry. These theories continue to be used and developed along dimensions suggested by the additional successes of the reducing theory, especially within their principal domain of application. There is a very good methodological reason for this. Reducing theories are typically more general in their scope of application than reduced ones, and so are often much more unwieldy to use in actual scientific practice. So a projected smooth reduction is by itself a good reason to continue using the reduced theory in scientific practice and technological application and to further develop it along lines suggested by the reducing theory. There is nothing unnatural about being a new-wave reductionist and still recommending that psychology retain a place in scientific practice, rather than "disappear" in the way Fodor bemoans. If future reductions appear at least as smooth as equilibrium thermodynamics to microphysics via statistical mechanics, there is a very good methodological reason for so recommending.[22]

Methodological caveat no. 3: the ontology of a reduction implies the uselessness of psychology

This third methodological criticism is more difficult to find explicitly in print. Starkly stated, it runs like this. Reductionism is, at bottom, a thesis about the ontological nature of psychological kinds. It asserts that psychological states, properties, and events are physical states, properties, and events—"are" in the sense of contingent identity, with the relevant physical states, etc., being neural states, etc., for us. But if one holds this thesis, then it seems pointless to give psychological theorizing any sort of autonomy from neuroscience, even now (prior, that is, to detailed theoretical development). If our mental states (events, properties) are nothing over and above our brain states (events, properties)—a claim that any reductionist, new-wave or otherwise, seems committed to—then behavioral science ought to be brain science. This is a methodology doomed to failure, for familiar reasons. Behavioral science will thereby miss true generalizations we can find only at the psychological level of theory and explanation.

We find hints of this argument in Fodor 1985, although given the larger context from which I take it, Fodor's terminology doesn't quite match mine:

Viewed from a neuroscientist's [read "reductionist's"] perspective ... functionalism [read "antireductionism"] may appear to be merely a rationale for making do with bad psychology. A picture many neuroscientists have is that, if there really are beliefs and desires (or memories, or percepts, or mental images, or whatever else the psychologist may have in his grab bag), it ought to be possible to "find" them in the brain.... Functionalism just *is* the doctrine that the psychologist's theoretical taxonomy doesn't need to look "natural" from the point of view of any lower-level science. This seems to some neuroscientists, and to some of their philosopher friends, like letting psychologists get away with murder. (1985, 82)

Fodor's point is that the reductionist's ("neuroscientist's") ontology—that mind *is* brain, for humans at least—implies this dim view of a psychology seeking autonomous explanatory resources. Whatever one's brand, new-wave or otherwise, no reductionist can wiggle out of this ontological commitment. So again, if one holds methodological qualms about constraining psychological theorizing from below, then one cannot accept psychophysical reduction, new-wave or otherwise.

The mistake here about reductionism's methodological requirements is quite subtle. All reductionists must commit to this ontological thesis. However, it is crucial to emphasize that for new-wave reductionism this ontological thesis *follows from*, and hence *depends on*, answers to two prior questions. First, is it reasonable to expect inter*theoretic* reduction (construed in new-wave fashion) to obtain between developed psychological and counterpart neuroscientific theories? Second, if so, where on the intertheoretic-reduction spectrum (the top arrow of figure 2.1) do these cases appear to be heading? As I argued in chapter 2 above, nothing less than *a reformulation of the mind-body problem* lies at the heart of new-wave reductionism: away from exclusive concentration on the phenomena and their relations (away, that is, from questions like "What are mental *states*?" and "Are mental *states* identical to physical *states*?"), and instead toward a focus, first and foremost, on the relationships obtaining between the *theories* promulgating these ontologies. From the new-wave perspective, the ontological thesis is a consequence following from affirmative answers (predictions at this stage of the game) to the two questions above. As Paul Churchland puts this very point, "It is smooth intertheoretic reductions that motivate and sustain statements of cross-theoretic identity, not the other way around" (1985, 50).

Appreciating this direction of fit—ontological consequences are secondary to and dependent on the prior issue of intertheoretic reduction—is crucial for dismissing this criticism of reductionist methodology. This criticism is impotent against new-wave reductionism because it gets the dependency between ontology and the predicted future reductions of theory *exactly backwards*. It sees the ontology of reductionism guiding its methodology, with the latter then guiding theory construction and development and hence ultimately intertheoretic relations between psychology and neuroscience. But on the new-wave picture, ontological conclusions depend on the outcome of theory reduction, while the latter depend upon future developments in the relevant sciences. In terms of justification, developments in the relevant sciences come first. New-wave reductionism is an empirically informed guess about where current developments appear headed. Since its ontology is logically posterior to its prediction about future intertheoretic reductions, the latter carries methodological implications. As we've seen in the previous two subsections, however, these methodological implications are benign.

It is interesting to note again (see note 19) that one need not accept new-wave reductionism's specific theory of intertheoretic reduction to adopt this response to this methodological criticism. One can accept another theory of intertheoretic reduction, explicitly reformulate the mind-body question as first and foremost a question of intertheoretic reduction, and use this response (although this possibility is blunted somewhat by the inability of orthodox logical empiricists to take onto-logical unification seriously as an aim of intertheoretic reduction, owing to their epistemic attachment to observation [Hooker 1981, 38–39], and the fact that most classical work on intertheoretic reduction occurred within the orthodox logical empiricist tradition). Philosophers of mind debating classical psychophysical reduction seem not to have noticed this possible reformulation of the mind-body problem. Patricia Churchland accurately describes how philosophers of mind often misunderstand reductionism when she writes, "When we raise the question of whether mental states are reducible to brain states, the question must be posed first in terms of whether some theory concerning the nature of mental states is reducible to a theory describing how neuronal ensembles work.... A good deal of muddle concerning reduction can be avoided with this initial clarification regarding reductive relations" (1986, 279). This muddle is reflected, e.g., in the fact that antireductionists raised, and classical reductionists felt compelled to answer, questions on how in-credulous it seemed to identify thoughts (as mental *phenomena*) with C-fiber firings, and on how nonsense results when mental predicates are applied to physical terms.[23] This debate still brewed long after logical empiricism had focused discussions of reduction in the philosophy of science on relations between theories. So even if classical reductionists could have availed themselves of the intertheoretic-reduction reformula-tion of the mind-body problem, many did not. It is the philosophy of mind's traditional primary emphasis on ontological questions that opens the gate for this methodological criticism. New-wave reductionism, in putting this reformulation of the mind-body problem at the top of its agenda, breaks with classical reductionism *as the latter is typically formulated*. This reformulation closes the gate on the third methodological criticism.

Throughout this section I have tried to show how benign new-wave reductionism is concerning methodological impositions that might blunt theory development in special sciences like psychology. However, new-wave reductionists adhere to one explicit methodological prescription. Following Clifford Hooker (1981, part 3) and Patricia Churchland (1986, chap. 9), I'll dub this *the principle of mutual coevolutionary feedback*. Patricia Churchland states this principle as follows: "Categories at any level specifying the fundamental *kinds* may need to be revised, and the revisionary rationales may come from research at any level.... Discoveries at one level often provoke further experiments and further corrections at the other level, which in turn provoke questions, corrections, and ideas for new explorations" (1986, 362–364). A methodological upshot of this principle is obvious. Be on the lookout for suggestive influences from any level of theory and explanation above or below that of the theory on which you are working.

This methodological prescription is hardly unique to new-wave reductionism. It is probably best construed as a principle of general scientific methodology, in view of the influence it has exerted throughout science generally (Hooker 1981, part 1; P. S. Churchland 1986, 362–373). This principle is not a *constraint* on theory choice and development in psychology, in the sense of a prescription for *ruling out* certain theories because they fail to display reductive potential. Quite the contrary. Notice that as stated, it is directed more toward *increasing* the number of theoretical alternatives alive in special sciences, especially during the early years of theory development. Also, this principle is not implied by more fundamental theses of new-wave reductionism, but it does connect quite smoothly with the picture of the structure of science underlying the new-wave program: a hierarchy of explanatory/theoretical levels, tied together by chains of intertheoretic reductions. This levels picture of science, with the accompanying theme of intertheoretic reduction as the relation tying the levels together, is most closely associated with Oppenheim and Putnam (1958), but its explicit statement goes back at least to the Vienna Circle. New-wave reductionism seeks to advance beyond these historical views by putting forth a more adequate general theory of intertheoretic reduction and reformulating the traditional direction of fit between ontology and intertheoretic reduction. Objections to the "unity of science" hypothesis are usually objections to the particular account of reduction employed, rather than to the levels picture of the structure of science. New-wave reductionism seeks to blunt the edge of these criticisms by building into the levels picture a more adequate account of intertheoretic reduction. The result *sanctions* cross-level influences via a coevolutionary research methodology without *imposing* special bottom-up methodological constraints that *limit* theory choice, beyond the general canons of scientific methodology.

However, there is another way in which new-wave reductionism might be sneaking in more methodological constraints than I am admitting. Might new-wave reductionism become so well confirmed a thesis *in science generally* that it becomes irrational to pursue nonreductive theories in less developed special sciences like psychology? (This is the constraining possibility I mentioned and set aside in note 21.) This possibility need not trouble the new-wave reductionist. Should it obtain, reduction would still be the outcome of broadly empirical developments. This is in keeping with the new-wave stricture to put empirical developments prior to ontological conclusions. In addition, the new-wave reductionist can point out that as of now, actual examples of achieved reductions come from fairly low levels in the scientific hierarchy: typically from within branches of physics itself (as illustrated by the paradigm examples of reduction in figure 2.1). It will take instances of actual reductions of theories from levels much higher on the scientific hierarchy before anyone should feel secure (or worried) that new-wave reductionism in science is generally on its way toward empirical confirmation. I think that we do already have some reductions of higher-level theories in place, and I will argue for this in the next chapter. But we surely don't have enough to rule out nonreductive alternatives *now* in higher special sciences! For now, the new-wave reductionist need not worry about imposing reductionism as a constraint on theorizing in levels of science as high as psychology on the grounds just suggested. Any attempt to do so would be extremely premature.

Clifford Hooker has probably best articulated the methodological importance of employing cross-level identities as "working hypotheses" in both potentially reduced and reducing theories. So it is appropriate to let him close the book on the methodological criticisms articulated so far. Reflecting on a historical reduction by now familiar to readers of this book to illustrate his general point, Hooker has this to say:

The thermodynamics-to-statistical-mechanics case displays another widespread and important feature: mutual co-evolutionary feedback between reduced and reducing theories. First, the mathematical development of statistical mechanics has been heavily influenced precisely by the attempt to construct a basis for the corresponding thermodynamical properties and laws. E.g., it was the discrepancies between the Boltzmann entropy and thermodynamic entropy that led to the development of the ergodic theory. Conversely, however, thermodynamics is itself undergoing a process of enrichment through the injection "back" into it of statistical mechanical constructs, e.g., the various entropies can be injected "back" into thermodynamics, the differences among them forming a basis for the solution of the Gibbs paradox. More generally, work is now afoot to transform thermodynamics into a generally statistical theory, while retaining its traditional conceptual apparatus and there is some hope that this may eventually allow its proper extension to non-equilibrium and irreversible processes as well (to which statistical mechanics already applies, but where the traditional thermodynamical concepts are, strictly speaking, inapplicable). (1981, 48–49)

This sort of mutual coevolutionary feedback—*not* unidirectional, i.e., exclusively bottom-up—is a feature common to many historical reductions in science and has proven beneficial to the continuing development of both reduced and reducing theories.[24] So instead of imposing methodological constraints and shackles on theory development and choice in special sciences like psychology, new-wave reductionism connects smoothly with a "communitarian" research strategy.

5   From Multiple Realizability to a Final Methodological Caveat and the Introduction of Token-Token Reduction to Address It

We aren't yet finished with methodological criticisms and multiple realizability. For there is a way of combining these two concerns into a final worry about new-wave reductionism. Nothing I've introduced so far in this chapter will completely remove this final worry. Indeed, responding to it requires an addition to the new-wave account of intertheoretic reduction.

The reader might have noticed that my responses to the methodological criticisms in the previous section of this chapter—in particular, my responses to the first and third criticisms—left unchallenged one premise in those arguments. I'll call this the premise of missing available generalizations. It asserts that reductionist methodology will miss out on generalizations available to a psychology that seeks its own explanatory resources, independent of how these resources relate to the brain. Ignoring this premise wasn't a problem for my responses to those antireductionist arguments, because other premises were faulty. However, one can construct a separate argument against reduction from this premise. Zenon Pylyshyn (1984, chaps. 1 and 2) is perhaps the most eloquent spokesperson for this argument, although it goes back to Fodor (1974). In brief, the argument runs like this. Science is in the business of capturing generalizations. That's what explanation accomplishes. But generalizations depend upon the theoretical vocabulary in which scientists describe phenomena. Particular descriptions require a particular theoretical vocabulary. When we describe phenomena in a particular way, even coextensive terminology can be insufficient to capture the relevant generalization. When human behavior *described in the vocabulary of actions* is at issue, many generalizations there for the capturing can only be captured using the *intentional* vocabulary of *cognitive* theory. In particular, neuroscientific theory is often insufficient, because of a consequence of multiple realizability. Neuroscience *cross classifies* psychological kinds. Hence embracing reductionism (of any variety) embraces a methodology that limits our ability to capture generalizations capturable by autonomous cognitive-level theorizing. We must therefore reject reductionism for a methodological reason grounded on a goal of science, namely, to capture all capturable generalizations.

Pylyshyn (1984, 2–3) uses a simple example to illustrate this consequence of cross-classification. A pedestrian, after visually witnessing an automobile accident, rushes to a telephone booth on the nearest streetcorner and dials the numbers 9 and 1. Why did the pedestrian *run to the phone booth*? What will he *do* next, what *action* will he *perform*, and why? The answers seem obvious. He *recognized* that an emergency occurred, he *knows* the emergency telephone number, and he is *dialing that number*. The next thing he will do, with overwhelmingly high probability, is dial another 1. Why? Because when one recognizes that an emergency has occurred, one typically wants to communicate that information to those who can help the victims. One way to communicate such information efficiently is to use the emergency telephone number. Most adults in our culture know that the emergency telephone number is 911. So when a person knows that he has successfully dialed 9 and 1 in this situation, he will intend to dial another 1. When it comes to telephone dialing, people tend to dial the number they intend to dial. The connection between *the perceived situation* and *the action* is systematic. There is a generalization between perceived situation and action here for the capturing, and this generalization extends beyond merely this situation to the equivalence class of all situations involving collections of beliefs and desires whose contents are similarly related.

We won't discover this generalization, however, if we attempt to predict the next behavior from a physiological account of the pedestrian's nervous and muscular systems. Pylyshyn doesn't mean here that biological (and ultimately physical) laws don't govern muscular movements during this process. They do, and so future muscular movements are predictable from current neurophysiological and physical states. Instead, his point is that the demand for a prediction on this basis is inappropriate. Most important, it is too weak, "for it does not—indeed, *cannot*—tell us that the minute sequence of movements *corresponds to the act of dialing a 'one,'* which is what we really want to know in this situation" (Pylyshyn 1984, 10; his emphases). The reason is that there are many situations in which we can predict correctly that the person will perform an action like "dialing a 1," although the precise way in which the person does it "lies outside a uniform set of regularities covered by the [physiological] theory" (Pylyshyn 1984, 10). Physiological explanations in particular "provide a distinctly different causal account linking each of a potentially unlimited number of ways of learning the emergency phone number, each of a potentially unlimited number of ways of coming to know that a state of emergency exists, to each of a potentially unlimited number of sequences of muscular movements that correspond to dialing 911" (Pylyshyn 1984, 11). However, there may be—and in this simple example surely is—an important systematic generalization we can state in psychological terms, ranging over this neurophysiological variety.

That is, there seems to be a level of theory that unites all of this neuro-physiological variety into equivalence classes, and hence enables us to find systematic generalizations concerning this class of events. However, each instance of this class would count as a different sequence when described neurophysiologically. In other words, there is a generalization there for the capturing, but only if we recognize a higher level of description and explanation than the neurophysiological.[25]

So far, so good. But next comes the antireductionist conclusion. Concerning special sciences in general, "every science other than basic physics," Pylyshyn insists, "In each case, generalizations from each science are statable only over their own special vocabulary; consequently, the lawlike generalizations of these sciences *are not reducible* to some finite combination of physical law" (Pylyshyn 1984, 21; my emphasis).[26] Because of multiple realizability, the generalizations of the relevant higher and lower disciplines *cross-classify* one another. Categories of the former map onto an indefinite number of categories of the latter, with those of the latter only arbitrarily related to one another from the point of view of the lower-level theory. Consequently, reductionism violates one of science's fundamental methodological prescripts: capture all of the generalizations there for the capturing. In this fashion, multiple realizability produces a final methodological criticism of reduction.

How can the new-wave reductionist respond to this combination of multiple realizability and a methodological criticism? First, I sense in it a conflation between claiming an intertheoretic reduction and relying exclusively upon *reductive explanations*. One can predict an intertheoretic reduction without tying one's methodological practices to reductive explanations. Reductive *explanations* seek to explain *phenomena* described in a higher-level vocabulary as explananda by exclusive appeal to lower-level kinds and laws as explanans. Pylyshyn's upshot of the point his pedestrian example illustrates lends credence to my charge that he has reductive explanation rather than intertheoretic reduction in his sights. He writes, "All I am suggesting in this informal example is that some *phenomena* seems to demand *explanations* couched in a certain vocabulary" (1984, 5; my emphases).

An inter*theoretic* reductionist can agree wholeheartedly with this methodological point. He need have no commitment to the exclusive use of reductive explanation. As I've already pointed out (in response to Horgan's second version of the first methodological criticism, in section 4 of this chapter), there is a very good reason for a reductionist to want mature, developed higher-level theories. They are one relatum of a necessarily two-place relation of intertheoretic reduction. If we eschew higher-level theories in favor of exclusive use and development of lower-level ones, there won't be candidates for the "reduced" place in the relation. Reduction is a prediction about how candidate *theories* will comport with one another *after the fact* of maturity and development. Construed in this fashion, it can accord a high degree of independence and explanatory autonomy to higher-level theories, so long as *intertheoretic-* reductive contact ultimately gets established.

As a further parry, we can develop a response that Patricia Churchland (1986, chap. 9) once offered to this very argument. Similar to the attitude I've been expressing about the methodological criticisms in general, Churchland insists that Pylyshyn's argument shows "only that cognitive psychology is respectable. Taken as arguments for the view that cognitive psychology is worth pursuing and is a necessary, indispensable part of the enterprise of coming to understand how the mind-brain works, I think they are fair enough, and I have no quarrel. What are contentious are the much larger claims of irreducibility and autonomy, and these go beyond what the premises can support" (1986, 381). One key to seeing this, according to Churchland, is to recognize that neuroscience itself can offer neuro*functional* theories: a level of theory inserted *between* cognitive psychology and "structural" neuroscience. (We even saw an example of this, drawn from computational neuroscience, earlier in this chapter.) As she puts it, "At the appropriate *neurofunctional* level, therefore, psychological states of a given type may be found to have a common neurofunctional property" (1986, 382). The result will be "an explanation of macrolevel effects in terms of microlevel machinations, of macrolevel categories in terms of microlevel business" (1986, 382.) And if the *scope* of the macrolevel theory doesn't extend beyond that of its micro-*functional*-level counterpart—if there are no events in principle explainable by the former but not by the latter—then, according to Churchland, "reductive integration will have been achieved" (1986, 382).

Churchland's remarks contain the germ of a telling response to this argument that combines multiple realizability with a methodological criticism. Unfortunately, she leaves completely undeveloped one necessary aspect of a full response. She does seek to substantiate the premise that neuroscience can supply functional theories in its own terms, in chapter 10 of *Neurophilosophy* (1986) and more completely throughout her and Terry Sejnowski's *Computational Brain* (1991). What she doesn't do, however, is to explain why such a result is sufficient for "achieving reductive integration." Thus I need to show how the basic account of reduction underwriting the new-wave program can accommodate the existence of a micro*functional* level of theory between the macro- and microstructural levels in a fashion that allows the cross-classifications between the higher and lower levels to be functionally integrated.

Fortunately, Clifford Hooker (1981, part 3) once again provides the initial insight. I need to build this insight into the full new-wave account of intertheoretic reduction. As part of his general theory of reduction, Hooker seeks to extend his basic account to "cases of would-be reduction which seem torn between two conflicting intuitions. On the one side there is a strong intuition that reduction *is* involved, and a strongly retentive reduction at that. On the other side it seems that the concepts at one level *cross-classify* those at the other level, so that there is no way to identify properties at one level with those at the other" (1981, 496). The key component of Hooker's extension is his distinction between *relatively type* reduction and *relatively token* reductions.[27]

The basic species of cross-categorical reductions relevant to psychology-to-neuroscience reduction is the reduction of functional to structural theories.[28] The fundamental element of Hooker's analysis is a reduction of function to structure and dynamics. This involves three distinct levels of theory (1981, 503). L_1 is the pure input-output level, characterized by predicates denoting the performance of particular "observational" operations. L_2 is the operational-mechanisms level, characterized by predicates denoting sequences of operations described in terms of the kind of operation involved. L_3 is the level of basic physical theory, in which derivative laws governing the behavior of the system advert to system constitution and structure (what Hooker calls the "engineering-systems descriptions"). Predicates at each of these levels cross-classify those at the other two levels. To use an illustration from psychology, a form of behavior specified at the L_1 level might be "obtains a food reward," while at L_2 it might be "turns left in a T-maze," and at L_3 it would be in terms of the physiological (neural and muscular) events producing the movement.

As Hooker emphasizes, level L_2 must not be confused with the specification of *machine mechanisms* derived from the laws of L_3. He dubs descriptions of a system's operation in terms of its physical ("machine") mechanisms the L_3' level. Using his illustration of a simple machine that performs carpentry tasks by choosing operation sequences in a way partly determined by its recent input history, a component operation specified at L_2 might be "drills a hole," while the drilling would be specified in L_3' as the removal of material by a rotating gouge. (At L_3, the event would be described purely in terms of the physical processes governing the machine's component parts.) The existence of L_3' is essential for understanding reductions of function to structure and dynamics, for "*it is in L_3' that the functional generalizations of levels L_1 and L_2 are to be reconstructed and thus explained*" (Hooker 1981, 503). As Hooker points out, it is generally both "difficult and pragmatically inconvenient" to explicitly construct such an L_3' theory, perhaps accounting for "why it is often ignored" (1981, 503). For human behavior, for example, an appropriate L_3' would be a "functional neurophysiology" derived from an "appropriate biochemical dynamics" at level L_3. A daunting undertaking!

Despite the pragmatic difficulty, however, Hooker's theoretical point is straightforward. If we can explain the cross-classifications at the combined functional $L_1 + L_2$ level within L_3', this warrants our claiming a reduction of function $(L_1 + L_2)$ to structure (L_3) and (purely physical/machine) dynamics (L_3'). L_3' predicates denote functions of the L_3-level structural elements composing the system, and each functional $(L_1 + L_2)$ property is contingently identical with the designata of one of these predicates. The justification for this identity is that Hooker's basic account of theory reduction applies directly to such cases. Predicates at the level of physical mechanisms designate functions that mimic the nomic role each $L_1 + L_2$ predicate plays in the functional-level laws. This amounts to constructing *an analog structure* in L'_3 (recall T^*_R from Hooker's basic model of reduction) that mimics the syntactic structure of the $(L_1 + L_2)$-level theory. In reductions of function to structure and dynamics, the L'_3-level predicates will usually designate dynamic sequences of structural (L_3-level) states. These sequences will be "exceedingly complex," especially for systems whose behavior is as stimulus-free as humans, since the entire physical theory of the system mediates them. As Hooker remarks, to capture the full complexity of human behavior in terms of a functional neurophysiology derived from appropriate biochemical dynamics, an adequate L'_3 theory equipotently isomorphic to some developed $L_1 + L_2$ "functionalist" cognitive psychology "must include a full representation of the cognitive state, including future possibilities, gambles on these, the values-preferences-goals-interests complex and so on" (1981, 504). We can now provide very little of the relevant theories on any of these levels. But that is beside the point when our aim is to address the methodological criticism built upon the cross-classifications introduced by multiple realizability. We've now seen how such a reduction would go in principle: For the particular system at issue, construct an analog structure akin to T^*_R in Hooker's general model of reduction in L'_3 (human neurophysiology) that mimics the nomic role of each functional predicate at the $L_1 + L_2$ level (behavioral and cognitive psychological). If the resulting reduction is sufficiently smooth, contingently identify the properties designated by the related predicates at levels $L_1 + L_2$ and L'_3.

This account of reduction of function to structure plus dynamics is illuminating, but by itself it still does not fully address the challenge at hand. The particular L_3 system involved might be just a single element of a vast class of possible physical realizations of the functional $(L_1 + L_2)$-level theory. Furthermore, the particular story of the L'_3-level physical mechanism involved might be just a single element of a (vast?) class of possible mechanisms for even that particular type of L_3 system. (This corresponds to the distinction drawn earlier in this chapter between the "across structure types" and "in the same system across times" senses of multiple realizability.) In what sense, then, is some *particular* L'_3-level explanation of an $(L_1 + L_2)$-level theory a *reduction* of the latter to the former? In what sense can we *contingently identify* the functional properties with the physical-mechanism properties (in smooth cases)?

Hooker's answer is that such explanations provide *token-token* reductions, defined as follows. Let S be the predicate "satisfies $(L_1 + L_2)$-level functional theory F," let T be the particular class of systems to which the token system in question belongs, let S' be an appropriate predicate of some L_3'-level theory meeting the demands on a function-to-structure-plus-dynamics reduction of F, and let T^* be the class of systems at the basic physical level L_3. Then "systems of type S of class T are contingently token/token identical with systems of type S' in class T^* $=_{df}$ every instance (token) of a type S system *externally classified as in class T* is contingently identical with some instance (token) of a type S' system externally classified as in class T^*" (Hooker 1981, 504; my emphasis). (By "external classification" Hooker means the sort of cross-classification that holds across distinct determinable/determinate hierarchies. See 1981, 499.) Notice that token-token reductions don't *eliminate* classifications across levels, even when they *explain* them. But these cross-classifications can be explanatorily displaced without remainder. As Hooker puts it, token-token reduction shows that "they [the cross-classifications] are a phenomenon solely of the nonbasic level of description offered" (1981, 505). At an L_3' level derived from *some* L_3-level theory, the nomic structure of the pattern of classification across levels will be constructable *for every token system to which F applies*. Though, of course, there will not be a *single or unique* L_3-level theory that does this for all *F*s.

Hooker's account of token-token reduction will remind many of Kim's account of local reduction, rejected earlier in this chapter as inadequate to handle multiple realizability in the same system across times. But there is a crucial difference, directly relevant to the more radical sort of multiple realizability. Since token-token reduction is an extension of Hooker's general model, it makes no use of bridge laws, of either the classical variety or Kim's species-specific variety. Hooker's account can thus handle cases of radical multiple realizability without relativizing the reduction relation to overly narrow structural types. His definition of the relation builds in the token-to-token feature. Unlike Kim's local reductions, the contingent identities obtain directly between functional-state and physical-state *tokens*, not types. So Hooker's account doesn't run the risk of relativizing reductions to overly narrow *types*. This was the problem for Kim's local reductions. The *types* P_i required indexing to individuals at times. It seems plausible to say, abstractly, that every *token* cognitive system belonging to the class of human beings is contingently identical with some token neural system in which *some* sequence of neurophysiological states (derivable on human biochemical dynamics) matches the nomic roles assigned to the relevant predicates by the functional cognitive theory. That is what a claim of token-token reducibility amounts to. Similarly for other (possible) classes T and T^* of cognizers: chimps, T-2700 androids, silicon-based aliens, and whatever else nature or inventive cognizers can build. Similarly for token $L_3 + L_3'$ systems at different times. Nothing in these claims is "relativized to overly narrow *types*." Every *token* system of a particular type is contingently identical to *a token* of some structure-plus-dynamics type ($L_3 + L_3'$ type) in a fashion that preserves the nomic structure of the relevant functional-level theory in each lower-level structure-plus-dynamics account. When the former type is that of humans, the latter are human biochemical dynamics and a neurophysiology derivable from that.

Still, one might have the uneasy suspicion that this token-token addition to the reduction of function to structure plus dynamics is nothing more than an ad hoc addition tacked on merely to extend Hooker's basic account to the cases psychophysical reductionists wish to get into the reductive fold. Why otherwise would an adequate general theory of reduction need this token-token supplement? Simply because the possibility of future token-token reductions of psychological to neuroscientific theories is *not* an ad hoc stipulation tagged onto an otherwise adequate general theory just to handle these specific cases. Psychophysical reduction is instead a single member of an enormous class of token-token reductions in science. We saw some examples in the quotation from Hooker cited at the beginning of my discussion of multiple realizability. They included cross-classifications within as "prosaic" a field as electrical engineering ("is an amplifier of gain A" in particular circuit diagrams) and external cross-classifications across levels within physics ("is a high-energy electron source" in quantum specifications). Token-token reductions are the norm in all cases involving a purely functionally characterized theory vis-à-vis its reducer. Far from being merely an ad hoc add-on to bring psychology into the reductive fold, "token-token" reduction is Hooker's attempt, in a fashion consistent with his general theory of reduction, to specify how reduction goes in a broad class of scientific cases.

As I did with Hooker's general insights about intertheoretic reduction, I can also work his notion of token-token reduction into the new-wave account. Recall from chapter 3 above first that ρ is a relation from the analog structure of the reducing theory T_R^* to potential models of the reduced theory $M_p(T_R)$, with no special conditions that preclude it from being many-one (i.e., from relating distinct elements of T_R^* to a single element of $M_p(T_R)$). Recall also that the relata of ρ are *potential models* of the reducing and reduced theories. Potential models are *token systems*, either empirical ("real world") or mathematical. Many-one ρs thus indicate reductions involving multiple realizability, for the ORLs (partly) comprising ρ relate distinct constituents of the potential models of the reducing theory to a single empirical base set of the reduced theory. This amounts to multiple realizability of the "same token system across times" type, since none of the conditions on ρ preclude its relating different potential models (token systems) of the reducing theory to a single potential model of the reduced theory at different times. Structurally speaking, multiple realizability poses no problem for the new-wave account of the reduction relation ρ, as it should not, since, as I've emphasized, multiple realizability is omnipresent in all scientific reductions that cross levels of theory and explanation. Any account of reduction adequate for science generally must be able to handle it.

Furthermore, when T_R is a purely functional theory (in Hooker's sense of an $(L_1 + L_2)$-level theory), we get a sense of how its kinds become "structured through reduction." This suggestive phrase is from Moulines (1984, 67). Unfortunately, he does not develop it further. The empirical base sets of the functional theory contain elements without internal structure. These elements are merely elements of the specified base sets, standing in the theoretical relations specified by T_R. Elements of these base sets get linked via heterogeneous (though nonetheless genuine) ORLs to elements of systems composed of much internal structure. In the reduction of simple thermodynamics of gases to statistical mechanics and kinetic theory, for example, ideal gases lack any internal structure. Elements of that base set are merely assigned quantitative properties by the relational base sets of the theory (pressure, volume, temperature). However, every "real world" system meeting (approximately) the lawlike conditions gets related by ρ to a system composed of gas molecules. The ORLs link the gas as unstructured thermodynamic kind to an aggregate of gas molecules with its own set of properties and relations (specified by combinations of empirical base sets, auxiliary base sets, and theoretical relations comprising ρ-related potential models of statistical mechanics and kinetic theory). It is ORLs to elements of the kinetic theory with much internal structure—aggregates of gas molecules standing in relations enabling them to obey mechanical laws—that structure ideal gases via the reduction. A similar point holds for other reduced, "unstructured" functional kinds.

Notice also that because it is a relation (as opposed to a function), nothing precludes ρ from being one-many, i.e., from relating one element of T_R^* to distinct elements of $M_p(T_R)$. In principle, this gives the new-wave account a resource for handling an argument against classical reductionism that I haven't discussed, the "context dependency" argument. Alledgedly, the realization of mental kinds on physical kinds are context-dependent. Depending on the context of their occurrence, a number of distinct mental kinds can be realized by one and the same physical kind. (Notice that, quite literally, context dependency is the converse of multiple realizability.) Many of, e.g., Lynne Baker's (1987) critiques of physicalism rest on this feature. I haven't discussed this antireductionist line because I find it *empirically* unmotivated at present. Context-dependency arguments rest almost exclusively on "Twin Earth"-style intuitions. My doppelgänger and I, in identical physical states, can nevertheless be in psychological states with distinct content, depending on our physical, social, cultural, or linguistic surround (see Putnam 1975; Burge 1979, 1982). Hence the context dependency. However, until I see a convincing empirically based theory in *cognitive science* that clearly yields context dependency at a physical level, I am inclined to treat context dependency as a philosopher's fantasy. The only work I know of that seeks to argue for context dependency in actual science is Burge 1986. However, my being wrong about this is of no consequence for new-wave reduction. If context dependency is a genuine psychological phenomenon, the status of ρ as a relation (hence as potentially one-many from T_B to T_R) yields the suggestion just sketched for how to handle it.

So multiple realizability in either direction poses no insurmountable problem for new-wave reductionism. However, before reductionists get too comfortable about accepting the premises of the autonomists' anti-reduction arguments while rejecting their conclusion, I should note a potentially discomforting final wrinkle of Hooker's account. Sometimes reductions of function to structure plus dynamics require "resisting putative $L_1 + L_2$ semantics." Hooker illustrates this point with his example of the simple carpentry machine guided by a computer that selects sequences of operations according to a hierarchically structured set of operating principles that consider the previous recent history of input orders (e.g., maximize the number of component devices operating simultaneously, minimize the length of sequences needed to perform each operation, minimize wear of the component devices in accordance with some wear-weighting function, etc.). A history of this machine's operations might be describable by a "functional" $(L_1 + L_2)$-level predicate like "prefers to use sequence S_{xy} over sequence S_{ab}," so our first inclination will be to try to specify a semantics for this predicate in terms of some inbuilt set of preferences over sequences. But the L'_3-level machine theory, which builds in the history-dependent dimension of sequence choice, might require instead that the functional-level predicate be semantically fused with its history-dependent context. Then the analysis of "M prefers to use S_{xy} over S_{ab}" might be something like "There is some internal choice mechanism C such that C causes the ratio of outputs to total input orders performed by S_{xy} to be greater than the ratio of outputs to total input orders performed by S_{ab}," where C is fully describable at the physical-mechanisms (L'_3) level. The "inbuilt set of preferences over sequences" reading of the functional predicate, natural at the $L_1 + L_2$ level, is *explained away* at the level of physical mechanism. In such cases we conclude that the functional-level predicates fail to denote. Notice, however, that this "eliminating" analysis comes after the reduction is in place. As before, the prediction of reduction by itself carries no constraining methodological implications for theory development at the functional level. And if that's the way the ontological cards fall, so be it. (We will come back to this issue in chapter 6.)

Hooker even provides a start toward specifying an account of contingent property identity (1981, 216–221). I won't need to elaborate or incorporate his account, however, because in chapter 6 below I will argue that the potential psychology-to-neuroscience theory reductions looming on the current horizon (some of which I take up in chapter 5) will not be sufficiently smooth to warrant contingent property identities. The ontological consequences will instead be *revisionary*: neither cross-theoretic property identity nor straightforward elimination of the caloric-fluid and phlogiston variety. The reduction of simple thermodynamics of gases to statistical mechanics and kinetic theory will again provide the relevant analog. Temperature as a thermodynamic property is not contingently identical to mean molecular kinetic energy in any empirically actualized circumstances. Nor are the propositional attitudes of cognitive-psychological theories that are the current candidates for neuroscientific reduction contingently identical to any neuroscientific counterpart. (I'll argue for both of these claims in chapter 6.) Since I don't foresee any future contingent identities of psychological and neuropsychological properties, (in the strict sense), I don't owe an account of contingent property identity.

New-wave reductionism can thus reject the combination of multiple realizability and methodological criticism. The cross-classifications of psychological mechanisms on physical mechanisms show that cognitive psychology is "respectable." If we stay with science's general methodological prescription to capture all capturable generalizations, there is a genuine place for explanation and theory at the functional level. Such cross-classifications also lead us to expect only token-token reductions. But token-token reductions are reductions, with plenty of scientific precedent, and so such cross-classifications do not show that "category differences" prevent reduction. They don't even guarantee that the categories of the functional theory have genuine ontological extension (though I defer a full discussion of eliminativism until chapter 6).

Over the past two decades, the most influential criticisms of reductionism have been the multiple-realizability challenges and the methodological caveats. Because of the similarities of these two sorts of arguments, antireductionists have not always carefully specified the argument they are running. But in the end, their carelessness is moot. When we pick apart the various strands of these arguments, we find that despite their toll on classical reductionism, none of them stand up against new-wave reductionism. There exist an account of intertheoretic reduction and a reformulation of the reductionist hypothesis, *adequate for and applicable to science generally*, that render the premises of these arguments consistent with the claim of potential reducibility. With the ground now cleared of the principal reasons for rejecting reduction, it is time to do two more things. First, I must address the "put up or shut up" challenge by arguing that there exist potential intertheoretic reductions of genuinely cognitive-psychological theories to neuroscientific counterparts. Second, I need to draw out the ontological predictions from these cases on the basis of where they appear headed on the intertheoretic-reduction spectrum. Chapter 5 addresses the first of these concerns; chapter 6 the second.

5

The "Put Up or Shut Up" Challenge

The preceding chapters have sought (1) to introduce philosophers of mind and cognitive scientists to some recent insights about intertheoretic reduction in post-logical-empiricist philosophy of science, (2) to provide a rigorous foundation for (1); and (3) to show how a new-wave reductionism informed by (1) and (2) defangs popular philosophical arguments against psychoneural reduction. To stop here, however, would be to stop short of the real philosophical payoff. I haven't said enough about how this bears on the philosophical mind-body problem reformulated in intertheoretic-reduction (IR) fashion. Doing so is the purpose of the final two chapters.

This final endeavor requires several steps. First, I need to show the *empirical* plausibility of reductionism. I need to show that neuroscience is developing theories that have reducing potential for *genuinely cognitive* psychological theories. Current consensus, at least among philosophers of psychology and some prominent cognitive scientists, is that it has not and (perhaps) will not develop such theories. This is the "put up or shut up" challenge for new-wave reductionism. I intend to meet it in this chapter.

Once I establish the empirical plausibility of new-wave reductionism, I'll then return to the IR reformulation of the mind-body problem. As we saw in chapter 2, this includes reformulating the traditional solutions as empirically based *predictions* about the nature of the reduction relation that will obtain (or fail to obtain) between folk psychology and some developed neuroscientific successor. I'll return to empirical developments in the relevant sciences to defend one of these predictions: that an intermediately bumpy intertheoretic reduction of folk psychology to future neuroscience appears to be emerging midway between the smooth and bumpy endpoints of the intertheoretic-reduction spectrum (top arrow of figure 2.1). The result is a *revisionary physicalism* about our common-sense mentalistic ontology. This will be the focus of chapter 6.

The "put up or shut up" challenge to new-wave reduction is really a pair of challenges. First, it is a challenge to cite cases of potential reductive pairs in the current cognitive and brain sciences. Everything that has come before in this work is little more than an academic exercise, at least for philosophy of psychology, if there are not yet potential reductions of *genuinely cognitive* psychological theories to neuroscientific counterparts. Second, even if the first challenge can be met, there remains the question of whether theories from the cognitive and brain sciences can actually be formulated in the set-theoretic framework of the underlying account of intertheoretic reduction. If they cannot, we have a serious gap between the foundations and the applications of the underlying philosophy of science. In this chapter I'll take on these two challenges in this order.

1   Associative Learning: It's Not What You Think It Is

At the beginning of chapter 1, I noted that the standard mark of the cognitive is the need for representations and computations over their contents in psychological explanations. I now seek to show that reductions to neuroscience already exist for genuinely cognitive-psychological theories that meet this standard mark.[1] Specifically, the two planks of my argument are the following:

• Current scientific thinking about associative learning recognizes the need for cognitivist resources (representations and computations over their content) in psychological theories adequate to explain even Pavlovian conditioning, the simplest form of associative learning.
• The most widely accepted psychological theory of associative learning, which uses cognitive resources, already reduces to a purely neurophysiological theory.

The reduction of a theory from a psychology that is genuinely *cognitive*, by the standard mark of the cognitive, is already an accomplished fact. Antireductionist intuitions nurtured by armchair reflection succumb again to actual scientific advance. New-wave reductionism can meet the first part of the "put up or shut up" challenge.

I borrow the title of this section from Robert Rescorla's (1988) review essay in *American Psychologist*. In that essay, Rescorla intends to bring psychologists up to date on developments over the past twenty years in an area most assume to have been technically and conceptually completed by the methodological behaviorists. He writes, "Pavlovian conditioning is one of the oldest and most systematically studied phenomena in psychology. Outside of psychology, it is one of our best known findings. But at the same time, within psychology it is badly misunderstood and misrepresented. In the last 20 years, knowledge of the associative processes underlying Pavlovian conditioning has expanded dramatically. The result is that modern thinking about conditioning is completely different from the views psychologists held 20 years ago. Unfortunately, these changes are very poorly appreciated by psychologists at large" (1988, 151). The fundamental change has been the introduction of cognitivist resources, representations and computations over their contents, into the most widely accepted theories. Rescorla sometimes refers to these resources as "information," e.g., "It [the modern view of Pavlovian conditioning] emphasizes the *information* that one stimulus gives about another" (1988, 152; my emphasis). But in other passages he uses "representation" explicitly, e.g., "These theories emphasize the importance of a discrepancy between the actual state of the world and *the organism's representation* of that state. They see learning as a process by which the two are brought into line.... A useful shorthand is that organisms adjust their Pavlovian associations only when they are 'surprised'" (1988, 153; my emphasis).

Recognizing this need for representations and computations to explain even the simplest form of associative learning is now common among animal-learning theorists, despite widespread ignorance of this need among psychologists in general and philosophers of psychology and cognitive science.[2] In a book limited to surveying work from the late 1960s through the 1970s on animal associative learning, Anthony Dickenson remarks that the "contemporary view" is that such learning "must consist of setting up some form of *internal representation* of the relationship which exists between events in the animal's environment" (1980, 22; my emphasis). Yet names like Chomsky, Marr, and other cognitivist heroes familiar to philosophers and cognitive psychologists don't even appear in Dickenson's index.[3] These textual observations nicely illustrate that a different set of heroes forged the "cognitivist revolution" among animal-learning theorists than those championed in philosophers' and cognitive scientists' accounts of the history of cognitivism. This fact is further supported by the observation that the names of cognitivist heroes of associative-learning theory—Kamin, Rescorla, Wagner, Macintosh— *never* appear in reconstructions of the cognitivist revolution written by philosophers and cognitive psychologists.

Since current thinking about associative learning is so unfamiliar to many philosophers and cognitive scientists, I begin the first plank of my argument by discussing in detail one important result that set associative-learning theorists onto the modern track.[4] Consider Leon Kamin's (1968) demonstration of the "blocking effect." Suppose we train an animal (e.g., a rat) to respond to a conditioned stimulus (CS) (e.g., a light flash) using an aversive unconditioned stimulus (US) (e.g., a mild foot shock) until presentating the CS alone completely suppresses the trained response (e.g., pressing a bar for a food reward). Next suppose that in a second training phase, we present the animal with a compound CS consisting of the CS from the previous phase (the light flash) and a new CS (e.g., a tone), paired with the same US from the first phase (the foot shock). After a few presentations of the compound CS and the US, suppose we present the new component (the tone) alone. Will the animal respond to it (by suppressing the trained behavior)? Not nearly to the extent animals do that undergo no pretraining in the first phase to the other component of the compound CS (the light flash). Hence the name of the effect. Pretraining to one CS *blocks* any learning about the other CS and US connection during the phase-two compound-CS and US pairings (see table 5.1).

How might one explain the blocking effect? At least two proposals seemed promising, in light of the crumbling but still prevalent behaviorist methodology in experimental psychology in the late 1960s. First, the preconditioning might block the animal from *noticing, becoming aware of,* or *attending to* the new CS during the compound-CS trials. Except for the problem of explicating these concepts in behaviorist terms, this pro-

Table 5.1
The blocking effect (basic procedure)

	Phase 1 (to asymptote)	Phase 2 (several parings)	Presentation	Result
Experimental group	CS_1, US	Compound CS (CS_1 & CS_2), US	CS_2	Little suppression
Control group	None	Compound CS (CS_1 & CS_2), US	CS_2	Significant suppression

CS_1 = light flash; CS_1 = tone; US = mild foot shock.

posal seemed not to violate behaviorism's basic explanatory methodology. The second alternative was significantly more troubling. Perhaps the pretrained animals *notice* the new component of the compound CS but do not condition to it, because the new CS is *redundant*. For those animals that have undergone pretraining, the old CS already *predicts* the coming aversive US (the shock). The pretrained animals lack a necessary component for conditioning, surprise that the aversive US occurred, during phase-two training. This second proposal is more radical and unsettling for methodological behaviorism because it adverts to internal representations not only of previous environmental events but also of their predictive value for future events. These are posits of the very species that methodological behaviorists propose to do without. Countenancing attention is problem enough. But treating rats in associative-learning situations as tracking environmental regularities over time and predicting future events on the basis of the connections between current and prior (remembered) representations is to give up on methodological behaviorism.

So Kamin and his lab undertook to discover whether the pretrained animals were noticing the new CS during phase-two of the blocking procedure. (According to Kamin [1968], they were initially doing so in complete confidence that they would vindicate the "failure to notice" hypothesis, the one more in keeping with methodological behaviorism.) They divided untrained rats into two groups: experimental and control. They conditioned both groups to a noise (CS) combined with a foot shock (US) until the noise fully suppressed the target activity (pressing a

Table 5.2
Nonreinforcement experiment (the basic procedure abbreviated)

	Phase 1 (to asymptote)	Phase 2 presentation	Result
Experimental group	CS_1, US	Compound CS (CS_1 & CS_2), no US	Trial 1: less suppression than control Trial 2: statistically significantly less suppression than control
Control group	CS_1, US	CS_1, no US	

CS_1 = tone; CS_2 = light flash; US = mild foot shock.

bar for food). They then subjected the experimental group to a compound stimulus, noise and light flash, not reinforced by a US. They subjected the control group to the noise only during this second phase, also not reinforced. Their question was how these patterns of nonreinforcement affected performance of the target activity (see table 5.2).

Contra Kamin's initial expectations, the results spoke clearly in favor of the "noticing but redundant" hypothesis. On the first phase-two (nonreinforced) presentation, bar pressing behavior of the experimental group was less affected (less suppressed) than the control group, suggesting that the rats had noticed the new component of the compound stimulus. (Notice that immediately after presentation of the compound CS in the first phase-two trial, before nonreinforcement, the experimental rats have undergone the same training regime as the pretrained rats in the basic blocking procedure.) On the second presentation of the compound CS, activity was significantly less suppressed in the experimental group as compared with the control group. This shows that the experimental rats had quickly learned that the compound CS was not reinforced. To learn this, they had to notice the new component of the compound CS.

Even in light of this second experimental result, Kamin realized that behaviorists willing to countenance attention still had a response. Perhaps some gating mechanism exists, blocking attention to the new component of the compound CS, and it only becomes operative after the first transitional (phase two) trial. To test this final (and admittedly ad hoc) alter-

Table 5.3
An informative CS (the basic procedure modified)

	Phase 1 (to asymptote)	Phase 2 (several parings)	Presentation	Result
Experimental group	CS_1, mild US	Compound CS (CS_1 & CS_2), severe US	CS_2	Significant suppression
Control group 1	CS_1, mild US	Compound CS (CS_1 & CS_2), mild US	CS_2	Little suppression
Control ground 2	CS_1, severe US	Compound CS (CS_1 & CS_2), severe US	CS_2	Little suppression

CS_1 = tone; CS_2 = light flash; US = foot shock.

native to the noticing and redundancy hypothesis, Kamin (1968) reasoned as follows. If for animals given pretraining, redundancy of the new component produces blocking, then making the new CS informative should eliminate it. They divided rats into one experimental group and two control groups. They conditioned both the experimental group and the first control group to a noise (CS) coupled with a mild foot shock (1 ma.) (US) in the first phase, and they conditioned the second control group to a noise (CS) coupled with a severe foot shock (4 ma.) (US). In phase two, they conditioned the first control group to a compound CS (noise and light flash) coupled with the mild US, and they conditioned the experimental and second control group to the compound CS (noise and light flash) coupled with the severe US. Finally, they tested each group with the light flash alone. Both control groups displayed blocking. Their target activity was virtually unsuppressed upon presentation of the light flash. But the experimental group displayed virtually no blocking to the light flash. Target activity was greatly suppressed in response to it (see table 5.3). So blocking does not occur when the new component of the compound CS is informative. This is exactly the result that the noticing and redundancy explanation predicts, but it is completely mysterious on the explanation that attributes the failure to notice to a gating mechanism.

So experimental results spoke clearly in favor of the noticing and redundancy explanation of blocking, the explanation that no form of methodological behaviorism seems able to accept. Now the real question arises. *How* is the redundancy of the compound CS preventing the formation of an association between its new component CS and the US? Kamin's published answer is more in the style of Grandma than in that of a hard-nosed, behavioristically trained experimentalist from the Princeton Psychology department circa 1968: "Perhaps, for an increase in associative connection to occur, it is necessary that the US instigate some *mental work* on the part of the animal. This mental work will occur only if the US is *unpredicted*, if it in some sense *surprises* the animal" (1968, 293; my emphases). This explanation is part of a general account of associative learning, not merely an ad hoc addition tagged on to explain higher-order associative phenomena like blocking. Kamin applied it directly to ordinary Pavlovian conditioning: "In the early trials of a normal conditioning experiment, the US is an *unpredicted, surprising event* of motivational significance, and the CS-US association is formed" (1968, 293; my emphasis).

Like any good scientist, Kamin did not leave these explanations at so folksy a level. In an attempt to make these notions "more respectable, as well as more specific," he analyzed them in terms of "backward scanning of memory stores of recent stimulus input." A necessary condition for association formation is such scanning, and such scanning only occurs when the US is unpredicted and hence surprising. But Kamin realized exactly what he was proposing, even when the central notions were tidied up: "We have clearly moved some distance from the notion of attention to the CS, perhaps to enter the realm of *retrospective contemplation* of the CS" (1968, 293; my emphasis). All of this within the domain of "rat psychology"!

To make this use of cognitivist resources respectable among animal-learning theorists, a more precise (and experimentally testable) account of these representations and computations was necessary. This result came about as mathematical formulations of the folksy notions of "surprise," "expectation," etc. The most influential result is Robert Rescorla and Alan Wagner's (1972) theory of Pavlovian conditioning. Explicitly noting that "Kamin's notions concerning the 'surprisingness' of a US originally encouraged" their formulations (1972, 74), Rescorla and Wagner phrased the explanatory intuitions they were attempting to quantify in explicitly "cognitivist terms" (their expression): "Organisms only learn when events *violate their expectations*. Certain *expectations* are built up *about* the events following a stimulus complex [note the appeal to content]: *expectations* initiated by that complex and its component stimuli are then only modified when consequent events disagree with the *composite expectation*" (1972, 75; my emphases). I remind the reader that Rescorla and Wagner describe their theory as "Pavlovian conditioning." Yet as this quote illustrates, its fundamental explanatory resources are cognitivist, in a full-blooded, even folk-psychological, sense.

Rescorla and Wagner's quantification of Kamin's surprise hypothesis uses a modification of Hull's "growth of habit strength" model. They describe their formulation in terms of changes in the strength of association to stimulus i, ΔV_i. Its fundamental departure from Hull's linear model concerns the treatment of compound CS, with reinforcement (US) and nonreinforcement. Rather than treating changes in associative strength to each component of a compound CS (component A and component X) in terms of the strength of the respective components, Rescorla and Wagner take these changes to depend on the strength of the compound, V_{AX}. Letting α_i represent the learning rate (the "stimulus salience") for CS type i, β represent the stimulus salience of the US (with $0 \leq \alpha_i, \beta \leq 1$), and Λ represent the asymptote of learning (the point on the learning curve at which presentation of the CS evokes a complete response, e.g., total suppression of some trained activity for a specified length of time), they represent changes in the associative strengths of the individual components A and X comprising some compound CS (AX) as follows (1972, 76):

$$\Delta V_A = \alpha_A \beta (\Lambda - V_{AX})$$

$$\Delta V_X = \alpha_X \beta (\Lambda - V_{AX})$$

They specify the associative strength of a compound CS in terms of its components. For simplicity, Rescorla and Wagner initially assumed it to be simple summation ($V_{AX} = V_A + V_X$), although this simplifying assumption can be (and later was) altered. Finally, they assume a mapping from V values into behavior, adopting the simplifying assumption of mapping Vs into magnitudes or probabilities of conditioned responses that preserve the ordering of the latter.

In their 1972 paper Rescorla and Wagner not only articulate this mathematical model of "amount of surprise" but also apply it to experimental results from simple Pavlovian learning situations up through higher-order features of associative learning like blocking. In simple conditioning, the equations reduce to Hull's linear model. As V_A increases with repeated reinforcement of A, $\Lambda - V_A$ decreases, and the conditioned response increases. (The obvious contrary story holds for nonreinforcement.) In the blocking experiment, the pretrained animals already have near-asymptotic values for V_A on the first presentation of AX in phase-two trials, so little or no change to V_{AX} is possible. (A is the CS used in phase-one pretraining, X is the new component of the phase-two compound CS.) Animals undergoing no pretraining have no associative strength to either component when phase-two training begins, so they condition to both A and X. Rescorla and Wagner (1972) also show how their model applies to many other higher-order features of associative learning that were eluding behaviorist explanation in the late 1960s, including stimulus specificity and generalization, extinction of response and spontaneous recovery, second-order S-S conditioning, and US pre-exposure.

Their model also yields extremely precise and occasionally surprising predictions about learning rates in a variety of experimental situations. Later experiments vindicated many of these. For example, Kremer (1978) vindicated a unique prediction of Rescorla and Wagner's model: that associative strengths decrease when the summed Vs of all components of the compound stimulus exceeds Λ. In one of his experiments (1978, experiment 3), Kremer conditioned a group of animals separately to both a light flash CS and a vibratory CS during phase-one training. In phase two, the light flash and the vibration was compounded with a noise CS that was associatively neutral for the animals. Following several phase-two pairings, Kremer tested each element of the compound CS in isolation. Rescorla and Wagner's model predicts that the phase-one components will each be less excitatory after the phase-two presentations (since $V_A + V_X > \Lambda$ at the beginning of phase-two training, owing to the individual pretraining to asymptote to both during phase one). It also predicts that the noise CS, which was associatively neutral at the beginning of compound phase-two training, *will now be inhibitory*, since its V value at phase two started at 0 and all V values of the compounds during phase two decrease until their sum equals Λ. Rescorla and Wagner's model thus predicts, surprisingly, that this inhibition to conditioning will occur despite the fact that the new CS began as associatively neutral and was reliably paired with an effective US. Using a variety of controls and cleverly interspersing compound-CS presentations in phase two with pairings of light flashes with the US and vibrations with the US to keep these V values relatively constant, Kremer showed that this highly unintuitive prediction of Rescorla and Wagner's model actually obtained.

To wrap up this section concerning the current status of cognitive theories of associative learning, a quote from Dickenson is instructive: "There is no doubt that the Rescorla-Wagner theory, especially in the form elaborated by Wagner, provides a powerful explanation of many of the cardinal features of simple associative learning, and over the last decade it has become the major theory in the area" (1980, 142). Psychologists have developed competing theories in response to some problematic experimental results, but these competitors also use quantified cognitive resources.[5] That the mainstream theories in this area employ genuinely cognitivist resources will be crucial when we turn next to neurophysiological attempts to explain them.

2   Lessons for Antireductionists

We've seen that current psychological theories of associative learning explicitly advert to cognitivist resources: representations and computations over their contents. Consensus among learning theorists now deems these theories to be the best, even for what was once methodological behaviorism's explanatory forte, animal associative learning. This result establishes the first plank of my agenda. Current psychological theorizing about associative learning recognizes the need for genuinely cognitivist resources in acceptable accounts of even the simplest form of this phenomenon.

Now what about the second plank, that the best current theories of associative learning, employing cognitive resources, have been reduced to neurobiological theories? To establish this plank, I first turn to the work of neurobiologists Richard Hawkins and Eric Kandel (1984a, 1984b). They use the gill and siphon withdrawal reflex in the sea slug *Aplysia californica* as their anatomical and physiological model, primarily because the neural circuitry in *Aplysia* is well known and easily investigated (in comparison with other electroneurophysiological preparations). Their goal was to construct a neurophysiological account of the *intra*cellular processes producing the simplest forms of associative learning (habituation, sensitization, and reflexive conditioning). They then use these as the "letters" of a neurophysiological "alphabet" that in sequences and combination allowed by increasingly complex neural circuities explain more advanced types of learning.[6] Hawkins and Kandel describe their "alphabet" strategy thus: "Do the [intracellular] mechanisms so far encountered form the beginning of an elementary cellular alphabet? That is, can these units be combined to yield progressively more complex learning processes? We would like to suggest on theoretical grounds that such an alphabet exists and that certain higher-order forms of learning generally associated with cognition can be explained in cellular-connectionistic terms by combinations of a few relatively simple types of neuronal processes" (1984a, 386). I'll point out below how the results of this strategy are a special version of the reduction relation described in chapter 3.

Hawkins and Kandel's intracellular mechanisms constituting the "letters" of their neurophysiological alphabet are *presynaptic*. These mechanisms change the amount of neurotransmitter released into the synaptic junction, producing increased or decreased response by the postsynaptic cell. For example, a pairing-specific enhancement of synaptic strengths subserves simple reflexive (noncognitive) conditioning, increasing the amount of neurotransmitter released by presynaptic sensory neurons stimulated by the CS to motor neurons producing the *Aplysia* gill and siphon withdrawal reflex. Activity in interneurons (lying between sensory and motor peripheries) guides this specific facilitation. These interneurons respond to US presentation, and synapse back onto the terminal bulbs of the sensory neurons excited by the CS. Activity in these interneurons broadens the action potentials in the CS sensory neurons, producing an increase in intracellular calcium ions. This sets in motion an enzymatic process culminating in increased rates of neurotransmitter release by the sensory neurons upon subsequent CS presentations, and finally, increased postsynaptic response by the motor neurons.[7]

Hawkins and Kandel (1984a, 1984b) then neurophysiologically explain higher-order, cognitive features of associative learning like the blocking effect by *sequences and combinations* of these intracellular processes. Their explanations require two unproblematic biological assumptions. First, in the area of anatomy, sensory neurons must also synapse back onto the facilitator interneurons, whose activity serves to enhance the specific sensory-motor connections that produce the conditioned response. Owing to the dense connectivity between neural layers in higher organisms, the applicability of this anatomical assumption beyond sea slugs is not controversial. Second, in the area of physiology, the output of the facilitator interneurons must decrease under continuous stimulation. This assumption is likewise unproblematic beyond *Aplysia*, owing to omnipresent cellular processes of accommodation and recurrent inhibition. So as the synapses between sensory neurons stimulated by the CS and the interneurons become progressively strengthened during phase one of the blocking procedure, the interneurons come to fire more during CS presentations and less during the US presentations that follow. Finally, after sufficient training, the firing of these interneurons during CS presentations becomes strong enough to prevent any firing during the subsequent US presentations, and conditioning in phase one reaches the asymptote. Thus when the compound-CS presentations begin during phase two of the blocking procedure, no firing in the interneurons follows presentation of the new CS. No conditioning occurs to it because the activity in these interneurons necessary to strengthen sensory-motor neuron synapses does not occur. In addition to this explanation of blocking, Hawkins and Kandel (1984b) also explain many other higher-order cognitivist features of associative learning with combinations and sequences of their fundamental intracellular processes, coupled with reasonable anatomical and physiological assumptions. These include stimulus specificity and generalization, extinction and spontaneous recovery, second-order conditioning, and US pre-exposure effects.

Furthermore, their neurophysiological account captures exactly the mathematical regularities reflected in Rescorla and Wagner's equations. To see this, however, we must move beyond Hawkins and Kandel's purely qualitative explanations to the quantitative model developed by Hawkins (1989). Hawkins mimics in a computer-simulated neural network the structural anatomy and cellular physiology of *Aplysia* assumed by Hawkins and Kandel to be the neurophysiological "letters." Then using the postsynaptic potential of a simulated motor neuron as a behavioral measure, Hawkins shows that the learning curves of the quantitative model exactly match the learning curves, behavioral dynamics over time, and changing patterns of reinforcement predicted by Rescorla and Wagner's equations. (The quantitative measure is the firing rate over time in the simulated motor neuron, as determined by set parameters and the changing synaptic weight values among sensory, facilitator, and motor neurons.) Exactly this sort of mimicking of the important quantitative equations of the simple thermodynamics of gases within the kinetic theory is a central condition for claiming a reduction of the former to the latter (chapter 2, section 2, especially equation 1). In terms of the account of reduction in chapter 3, when we restrict the domain of organisms to those in which the presynaptic cellular mechanisms constituting Hawkins and Kandel's neurophysiological "letters" determine synaptic weight values, all the intended empirical applications of Rescorla and Wagner's theory get mapped onto intended empirical applications of Hawkins and Kandel's account. Furthermore, as illustrated by Hawkins's (1989) quantitative modeling, a key aspect of the lower-level explanations—the dynamics of action potentials in motor neurons—maps directly onto a key aspect of the higher-level explanations—the behavioral dynamics predicted by Rescorla and Wagner's equations. Hence the fundamental laws of the former fully explain those of the latter (the equations governing behavioral dynamics over time and reinforcement schedules). These are exactly the conditions captured semiformally in the account of reduction developed in chapter 3 (BMS-inspired conditions (1) and (2)).

Hawkins and Kandel's own statements of their goals and results amount to exactly the reductive claim I am urging. They state at the outset, "Our goal is to suggest how cognitive psychology *may begin to converge* with neurobiology to yield a new perspective in the study of learning" (1984a, 376; my emphasis). In conclusion, they claim, "We have tried to provide *neuronal versions of the Rescorla and Wagner models of conditioning* (1984a, 388; my emphasis). After offering their neurophysiological explanation of Kamin's blocking result, they write,

These examples illustrate that our model incorporates in very rudimentary forms the notions of *predictability* and *internal representation*. The predicted effect of CS_1 is represented internally as the strength of the synapse from CS_1 to the facilitator neuron. The actual consequences of CS_1 are compared to this prediction through the operations of accommodation and recurrent inhibition, which in effect subtract the strength of CS_1 from the strength of the US that follows it. When these two strengths become equal, CS_1 can be said to fully predict the US, which thus loses its reinforcing power, and no further learning occurs (Hawkins and Kandel 1984a, 386–387; my emphases).

Notice that these cross-theoretic ontological links hold at the level of *quite specific concepts*. Rescorla and Wagner's "predicted effect of CS_1" and "subtraction of associative strength of CS_1 from associative strength of US" get linked, respectively, with "strength of synapses from CS_1 sensory neurons to facilitator neurons" and "operations of accommodation and recurrent inhibition." Thus this case meets an ontological-unification condition (e.g., the ORL condition on the theory of reduction sketched in chapter 3). In terms of my theory of reduction, the empirical base sets of Rescorla and Wagner's theory get directly related, although heterogeneously, to base sets and relations of Hawkins and Kandel's account. The ontologies of the two theories are about the same things—the real-world systems in their intended empirical applications overlap—although they describe these things at different theoretical levels. What we have in the reduction of Rescorla and Wagner's theory to Hawkins and Kandel's theory is a smooth intertheoretic reduction with heterogeneous ORLs: a reduction that vindicates the ontology of the reduced theory by virtue of structuring its amorphous, functionally specified base elements into their underlying component parts and the dynamics of these lower-level kinds.[8]

Given that the reduced theory in this case meets the standard mark of the cognitive, have I now established the second plank of my agenda? Perhaps this conclusion would be too quick. Someone might counter my argument by pointing out that Hawkins and Kandel's choice of an anatomical and physiological model, the sea slug, is significant. To conclude that I have refuted the "put up or shut up" challenge by the reduction just discussed, don't I also have to show that it is reasonable to suppose that sea slugs have representations, and more important, that sea-slug representations are relevantly similar to the representations that most of cognitive psychology purports to be about, namely, those of humans and other higher organisms? Put tersely, this worry is that all I have shown is that sea-slug cognition reduces to neurobiology. But that doesn't meet the "put up or shut up" challenge for the creatures that cognitive psychology typically purports to be about.

Thus framed, this is an insensitive criticism. Without question, cognition in humans and higher organisms has some special properties not shared by sea slugs: considerably richer content, special combinatorial capacities, productivity, systematicity, consciousness, and special access. However, this counter first ignores the fact that the sea slug is a neuro-biological *model* on Hawkins and Kandel's account.[9] This is important for several reasons. Hawkins and Kandel use sea-slug anatomy and physiology to investigate the fundamental intracellular processes, the "letters" of the cell-biological "alphabet," because sea-slug anatomies and physiologies are so much simpler and easier to explore. Notice also that the use of these processes in theoretical explanations of higher-order features of associative learning occur only with anatomical and physio-logical assumptions known to hold in higher nervous systems.

There is a deeper point as well. Since the mechanisms serving as "letters" of the neurophysiological "alphabet" out of which Hawkins and Kandel build explanations of higher-order cognitive processes are *internal to individual neurons*, an argument for their applicability to types of learning unique to organisms higher than sea slugs can appeal to evolutionary considerations. Hawkins and Kandel offer exactly this appeal:

We propose that higher forms of learning may utilize the mechanisms of lower forms of learning as a general rule; and second, we speculate that this may occur because higher forms of learning *have evolved* from lower forms of learning.... Thus, whereas individual neurons may possess only a few fundamental types of plasticity that are utilized in all forms of learning, combining the neurons in large numbers with specific synaptic connections (as occurs, e.g., *in mammalian cortex*) may produce the much more subtle and varied processes required for more advanced types of learning. (1984b, 391)

Notice that this appeal is directly in keeping with new-wave reductionism. Hawkins and Kandel propose that the fundamental forms of intracellular neural plasticity, in various sequences and combinations permitted by increasingly complex nervous systems, underlie all higher forms of learning. This applies even to types of learning *specific* to higher organisms, since their nervous *systems* implement complex *sequences and combinations* of these forms of intracellular plasticity beyond simpler systems' capabilities. This is a reduction of the function-to-structure-plus-dynamics variety (chapter 4, section 5). Higher-level theories postulating functional kinds lacking internal structure (from the higher-level perspective) reduce in a domain-relative (and if need be, token-token) fashion to theories explaining the underlying structure of lower-level kinds and their theoretically important dynamic interactions. As far as the evolution of cognition goes, this story makes perfect sense. Evolution typically builds complexity onto what is already present in existing organisms to produce novel structures and functions. It rarely starts from scratch.

The applicability of these evolutionary considerations is one key advantage behind seeking what I'll call "combinatorial" ("neurophysiological alphabet") reductions of cognitive psychological theories to neuroscientific counterparts. If we can uncover the fundamental forms of intracellular plasticity and processes in simpler creatures and then show how combinations and sequences of these forms permitted by increasingly complex nervous systems explain psychological data, we will generate neurophysiological explanations that cohere with evolutionary considerations. We will thus have not only neuroscientific reductions of cognitive theories but also biologically acceptable accounts of how these cognitive processes came to exist.

I can say more about the worry of mere sea-slug cognition. This worry also ignores how important the higher-order features of associative learning are for the unique capacities of human and higher-mammalian cognition. We often think of associative learning as a low-level psychological phenomenon (after all, sea slugs can do it!). But one must bear in mind, from the perspective of modern cognitive accounts like Rescorla and Wagner's, the task performed by the mechanisms of higher-order associative learning. These mechanisms are involved in the *detection of correlations* between past, present, and future events. This latter task is a necessary component of a further task of crucial cognitive significance, one that we humans have a special capacity for: the ability to track *causal relationships*. Dickenson explicitly notes this connection between lower and higher forms of learning. Remarking on the extent to which experimental variations of the blocking theme led to developments of the modern account of associative learning, which might suggest that the latter are "of little general import or relevance," he insists, "It should be remembered, however, that failures of learning, such as are seen in the blocking experiment, underlie the important capacity of animals, and probably ourselves, to detect the overall correlation between events. It is this ability which lies at the heart of the problem of tracking causal relationships" (1980, 142–143).

Notice that we can also iterate the combinatorial reduction strategy. The simplest forms of cellular plasticity, completely explainable in neurophysiological terms internal to neurons, produce, in various sequences and combinations, higher-order associative phenomena (like blocking). We might similarly explain more complex cognitive phenomena (like the ability to track causal relations) with sequences and combinations of higher-order associative phenomena (where we can fully characterize the anatomical and physiological components of these sequences and combinations in purely neurophysiological terms). The result is similarly reductive. There exist a few fundamental forms of cellular plasticity, each fully explained at the cell-physiological level but implemented in novel sequences and combinations by increasingly complex nervous systems to produce the rich variety of learning found throughout the class of cognizers. This includes forms only implementable in the complexity afforded by the human brain. Insisting that reduction can't reach cognitive theories applicable only to humans and other higher mammals requires pointing out the limits of this "interactive combinatorial" form of reduction. Any such limits seem far from obvious.

Finally, this "only sea-slug cognition" charge ignores more recent discoveries about other fundamental forms of intracellular plasticity that we can add to our neurophysiological alphabet. Over the past decade much intracellular research has focused on events known to occur in neural structures specific to higher organisms (cortex, cerebellum, hippocampus) and important for the unique cognitive capacities of higher organisms (learning, memory). The most well studied of these processes is *long-term potentiation* (LTP), a process that strengthens synaptic connections. Several features of LTP make it an excellent cellular substrate for memory. LTP is *selective*: it occurs only in synapses undergoing high-frequency bursting activity, leaving less active neighboring synapses unchanged. Its *time course* is appropriate: synaptic changes wrought by LTP can last for weeks, while these changes result in less than a second and stabilize in seconds to minutes. It is *associative*: LTP induction requires near-simultaneous activation of some minimal number of contacts on a cell, which requires activity in several input axons. Finally, two pharmacologically very different drugs that block LTP induction also induce a selective impairment of certain forms of memory.[10]

Recent work on the intracellular and biochemical mechanisms inducing LTP reveals the importance of a set of voltage-dependent postsynaptic receptors, the N-methyl-D-aspartate (NMDA) receptors. Quantitative studies using a fixed number of electrical bursts to hippocampal cells in vitro reveal that the optimal interburst interval (the time between the deliverance of electric bursts) for producing LTP is 200 msecs. This number is intriguing because it corresponds to the period of the theta rhythm, an EEG pattern prominent in the hippocampus of mammals engaged in exploration. This discovery grounds the "theta pattern" account of LTP induction (Lynch et al. 1988, 186–189). A burst of presynaptic activity "primes" the postsynaptic neurons, producing a suppression of normally occurring inhibitory postsynaptic potentials (IPSPs) that truncate subsequent excitatory postsynaptic potentials (EPSPs). This prolongs the EPSPs evoked in the postsynaptic cell by the theta bursting pattern 200 msecs. later, which produces enhanced spatial and temporal summation and ultimately enhanced depolarization of the postsynaptic cell. This enhanced depolarization in turn releases (postsynaptic) NMDA receptors on the active contact sites from voltage-dependent magnesium blockage. These open receptor sites allow an influx of calcium into the postsynaptic cell. The calcium triggers biochemical reactions that result in structural changes in the dendritic spines or new synapse formation. These changes increase the future likelihood that presynaptic activity will induce postsynaptic cell firing, and ultimately (in combination with LTP induction at many other sites) behavioral change.

Using this "neurophysiological letter" while mimicking the anatomical connectivity of the mammalian telencephalon yields impressive results. Gary Lynch and his colleagues (Lynch et al. 1988; Granger et al. 1989) demonstrate this point using artificial neural networks. Their networks' architecture mimics the anatomy of the rat olfactory bulb and layers I and II of piriform (olfactory) and entorhinal cortex, and it employs a learning algorithm for readjusting connection strengths derived from the theta-pattern account of LTP induction. Training proceeds by presenting a network with a series of simulated training "odors," 19- to 20-element vectors with each element representing the strength of a chemical component of the simulated odor. Because connection strengths are initially identical, the network first produces an informationally void response to each simulated odor that is a "signature" firing pattern of cells in simulated cortex. But owing to connection-strength changes produced by the "winner-take-all" learning algorithm mimicking NMDA-receptor-induced LTP, which incrementally strengthens highly activated connection sites (within known biological limits), training produces informationally rich activation patterns upon subsequent presentations of both training and novel inputs. The same cells of simulated cortex fire—the same "firing signature" occurs—to inputs grouped within the same category.[11]

Grouping sensory representations into meaningful categories is an important cognitive task. If an organism treats every distinct input as novel, then information will be lost because distinct inputs are often just novel presentations of a familiar object or state of affairs. If it groups every novel input into an already existing category, then it will not devise new categorical groupings when appropriate (and so will be unable to *learn*). It will probably also be unable to draw behaviorally important distinctions between individual representations grouped within the same category. Somehow cognizers must find a middle ground, and Lynch and Granger's networks do so merely by simulating LTP within realistic cortical anatomies. Early experiments also showed that their networks can alter existing categories discovered during initial training after later encountering new training inputs. With each new set of training inputs, the network discovered the optimal partitioning of all cues. "Optimality" was measured information-theoretically, and calculated via a standard "beam search" technique (Fisher 1987). The networks arrived at optimal partitions in linear computational time. This contrasts with the factorial time required by the computerized beam search, since it needs to repeat the entire computational process with the addition of each new training cue (Lynch et al., 1988, 212).

Lynch and Granger's networks also display "hierarchical recognition memory," the capacity to represent items in memory at multiple levels. "First sniff" responses to initial inputs at the onset of the simulated theta rhythm group inputs into broad categories. The same cells of simulated layer II piriform cortex fire to several distinct input patterns. Responses to later presentations during the simulated theta rhythm serve to individuate the inputs that first sniffs group together. By the third sniff in the theta sequence, the network represents each input initially grouped together on the first sniff by a different cell-firing signature (Granger et al. 1989). As Lynch and his colleagues point out, this suggests a form of higher memory well studied by cognitive psychologists. We can recognize a given object as a vehicle, an automobile, or a Mustang. Such a higher cognitive capacity emerges in Lynch and Granger's networks as the direct outcome of the simulated cellular processes involved in the induction of LTP implemented in anatomically realistic neural architectures.

Lynch and his colleagues' own account of their project suggests that the "combinatorial" ("neurobiological alphabet") model of reduction is at work. They write,

Our strategy does not take as its starting point a set of prespecified functional operations (e.g., perception of angles, detection of moving objects, or recognition of degraded cues) and then seek to explain how a network (cortical or otherwise) might solve these operations. Rather, we are attempting to identify and characterize the physiological and behavioral properties of learning and memory that emerge when detailed neurobiological features are incorporated into circuities containing salient anatomical characteristics found in specific areas. (Lynch and Granger 1989, 205)

That they derive the features incorporated into their models directly from processes and events that occur in mammalian (including primate) brains, especially in areas involving higher cognition, and that the resulting models display activity uniquely suggesting higher cognition show that the reductive approach defended in this chapter has already moved far beyond sea-slug cognition.

Notice also that and Lynch and his colleagues put the combinatorial-reduction strategy to work within a more bottom-up research methodology than did Hawkins and Kandel. Unlike Hawkins and Kandel, they are not trying simply to implement a higher-level, psychological theory in a set of neural mechanisms. Rather, they are simply starting with the lower-level intracellular mechanisms and seeing what happens with increased network and connectionistic complexity. This is an important methodological difference because the success of any neurobiological account constructed simply to mimic or "mechanize" a particular higher-level theory will be only as good as the higher-level theory employed. I've already mentioned, for example, that a number of competing theories built on problematic experimental results challenge Rescorla and Wagner's theory. If psychologists ultimately reject Rescorla and Wagner's theory, then Hawkins and Kandel's theory in the form presented above goes down with it. Working with a more bottom-up research methodology raises the probability that the combinatorial reductions achieved will be less smooth, since one isn't explicitly trying to mimic explanatory resources at a lower level of theorizing. But the biological nature of real cognizers might force this result upon us. Even the best psychological theories might only approximate the real neural dynamics driving behavior (see the discussion of revisionary reductions in the next chapter).

It is important to be clear about why I introduce Lynch and Granger's work in this section.[12] The issue in question is the potential explanatory power of a combinatorial reductive approach (involving a neurophysiological alphabet) toward cognitive psychological theories. How far into the realm of cognitive psychology can we reasonably expect this reductive approach to go? That is, how much cognitive phenomena can we reasonably hope to explain by postulating a few cellular processes that modify synapses and then embedding these basic processes in nervous systems of sufficient connective complexity to be capable of implementing those processes in a variety of sequences and combinations? So long as we stick with the presynaptic processes of Hawkins and Kandel, our "neurophysiological letters" might be sufficiently limited to take us not much beyond the cognitive aspects of associative learning. But results like those of Lynch and Granger, based on postsynaptic cellular processes known to occur and be important for learning and memory in mammals, extend the potential reach of a combinatorial (neurophysiological alphabet) approach to reduction. Given the explanatory accomplishments of theories based on these postsynaptic processes, we add a potentially vast dimension to the prospects for combinatorial reduction of cognitive phenomena when we add these additional cellular processes to our neurophysiological "letters." Remember, the context here is the "only sea-slug cognition" challenge to combinatorial reduction. Enriching our repertoire of cellular building blocks, especially with ones known to exist and be cognitively important in mammals and primates, greatly enriches the potential of combinatorial reductions to explain cognitive phenomena by embedding these basic processes in increasingly complex sequences and combinations afforded by bigger and more connectively complex nervous systems. This is my reason for introducing Lynch and Granger's work at this time.

I thus take it that the second plank of my agenda is established. Some currently accepted psychological theories, including ones that employ cognitivist resources suggestive of uniquely higher organisms, have reduced (in a domain-relativized fashion) to purely neurophysiological theories. Furthermore, combinatorial reduction offers a promising strategy for generating additional reductions, employed either in the more top-down fashion of Hawkins and Kandel or the more bottom-up fashion of Lynch and Granger. I have met the first "put up or shut up" challenge to new-wave reductionism, and the pursuit of combinatorial reductions is a promising strategy for finding additional future reductions. It remains an open question how much more of cognitive psychology might reduce to neuroscience. But some already has, as a matter of accomplished scientific fact. The new-wave reductionist predicts that all of psychology will ultimately reduce. At this point, we cannot assess the correctness of this claim beyond examining cases of reductions already in place, ones looming on the horizon, and the general promise of strategies like combinatorial reduction. But notice that we can now locate questions concerning the scope of psychoneural reductionism exactly where they belong: out of the realm of philosophical armchair speculation and directly in the area of further empirical developments in the brain and behavioral sciences. If new-wave reductionism only accomplishes this much, that is intellectual progress (even if it winds up losing its bet on comprehensive reducibility of psychology to neuroscience). But we can't stop yet. There is a second part to the "put up or shut up" challenge that seeks to drive a wedge between the foundations and applications of the new-wave account of intertheoretic reduction.

3   Is the Foundational Model of Theories and Theory Reductions Applicable to the Cognitive and Brain Sciences?

The worry here is that the foundations of new-wave reductionism are too far removed from the structure and dynamics of actual theories in the cognitive and brain sciences to be of much relevance. We have seen that theories in physics can be fruitfully reconstructed in terms of the formal accounts of theories and reduction sketched in chapter 3. But what reason do we have for thinking that the same holds for theories in the cognitive and brain sciences? One need not even argue for a qualitative difference between theories in physics and theories in cognitive psychology and neurobiology to worry whether the application of a philosophy of science appropriate for the former is appropriate for the latter. At the very least, we need to see what cognitive-and-brain-science theories and their interrelations look like through the lens of our foundational philosophy of science.

To show this, I'll borrow from structuralist-inspired accounts I offered in Bickle 1993a. However, since the context has changed, the analysis must change as well. In that article I was concerned with the relationship between folk psychology and connectionist cognitive science. Here I am concerned with theories from intentional-psychology and theories from computational neuroscience. This will require a somewhat different, more detailed, structuralist-inspired analysis. I'll present accounts of cognitive representation and computation from a schematic intentional-psychological theory and from a schematic neuroscientific theory that focuses on synaptic modifiability. What follows is a recipe for formulating reductive pairs from these two disciplines in the account of theory structure outlined in chapter 3. Where possible, I will illustrate the schematic account with details from the reductive cases presented in the earlier sections of this chapter.

I begin with a schematic theory of intentional-psychology. Here I have in mind the sorts of theories most naturally interpreted as employing a "language of thought" (Fodor 1975). A psychological state is a relation between a subject and a propositionally structured mental representation. A psychological process is a transformation from one state to some other that respects the logical relations obtaining between the propositionally structured contents. The minimal conditions on the account of mental representation in such theories are the following:

• The contents of mental representations have propositional structure (and are usually taken to have a combinatorial syntax and semantics).
• Distinct types of mental representations (e.g., beliefs, desires) can involve the same propositional content.
• Mental representations are causally efficacious, giving rise to actions and/or other mental representations.
• These causal relations are isomorphic to various logical relations (equivalence, entailment, consistency, relevance [?]) holding between the propositional contents of the action commands and/or other mental representations (with different propositional contents).

How can we capture these conditions in the structuralist-inspired account of theory structure providing the foundation for a new-wave reduction?

Here I axiomatize, set-theoretically, intentional psychology's account of mental representation and computation. On intended empirical applications, the singleton member of S is the subject, $MR_1 \ldots MR_n$ are sets of different types of mental representations (e.g., beliefs, desires, etc.), *Act* is a set of action commands (to the subject's motor systems), *Prop* is a set of propositions, *Cont* is the content-assigning function for a subject's mental representations and action commands, and *Cause* is the causation relation holding from a subject's mental representations to other mental representations (with different contents) and/or to action commands. The set-theoretic axiomatization is then the following:

x is a potential model of intentional psychology ($x \in M_p(\text{IP})$) iff

(1) $x = \langle S, MR_1, MR_2, \ldots, MR_n, Act, Prop, Cont, Cause \rangle$,

(2) S is a singleton set,[13]

(3)   for all i ($1 \le i \le n$), MR_i is a finite, possibly empty set, but for some i, MR_i is nonempty,

(4)   *Act* is a finite, possibly empty set,

(5)   *Cont*: $S \times MR_1 \cup \cdots \cup S \times MR_n \cup S \times Act \rightarrow Prop$,

(6)   *Cause*: $\mathscr{P}(S \times MR_1 \cup \cdots \cup S \times MR_n) \rightarrow$
$\mathscr{P}(S \times MR_1 \cup \cdots \cup S_n \cup S \times Act)$.

(In English, (5) says that *Cont* is a function from the union of the Cartesian products of *S* and the *MRs* and of *S* and *Act* into *Prop*, an auxiliary base set of propositions, and (6) says that *Cause* is a function from the power set of the Cartesian products of *S* and the *MRs* into the power set of the union of the Cartesian products of *S* and the *MRs* and *S* and *Act*.)

  S, the *MRs*, and *Act* are the empirical base sets of potential models of intentional psychology (**IP**), *Prop* is an auxiliary base set, and *Cont* and *Cause* are the fundamental theoretical relations typified over the base sets. Actual models *M*(**IP**) in addition require *Cause* to mimic or reflect various logical relations in accordance with some appropriate propositional logic L(*Cause*). The details of L(*Cause*) will, of course, depend upon the particular **IP** theory at issue. Schematically, however, it will have the following structure:

(7)   For all $m_1, \ldots, m_n \in MR_1 \cup \cdots \cup MR_n$, $a \in MR_1 \cup \cdots \cup$
$MR_n \cup Act$, $s \in S$, if $Cause(\langle s, m_1 \rangle, \ldots, \langle s, m_n \rangle) = \langle s, a \rangle$, then
$Cont\langle s, m_1 \rangle$ & $\cdots$ & $Cont\langle s, m_n \rangle$ stands in relation L to $Cont\langle s, a \rangle$.

Here $m_1, \ldots, m_n$ are token mental representations, *a* is a token action command or other mental representation, *s* is the subject, and *L* is some logical relation sanctioned by the propositional logic appropriate for the particular application in question.[14] (In English, (7) says that if a subject's having a set of mental representations causes him or her to have some action command or other mental representation, then the conjunction of the contents of the former stands in the appropriate logical relation to the content of the latter.)

  To illustrate this schematic axiomatization, consider how it applies to Rescorla and Wagner's account of blocking. A pretrained rat has already acquired the expectation that a shock will occur when the light flashes. This is $Cont\langle s, m_1 \rangle$, where $m_1 \in s$'s MR^e ("e" for expectations). Hence when the combined CSs start during the second phase of blocking, the pretrained rat acquires the belief that the light flashed. This is $Cont\langle s, m_2 \rangle$, where $m_2 \in s$'s MR^b ("b" for beliefs). Conjoined, these cause the further expectation that the shock will occur. $Cont\langle s, m_1 \rangle$ conjoined with $Cont\langle s, m_2 \rangle$ stand in L (derivation, in this case) to $Cont\langle s, a \rangle$. In keeping with the special law of Rescorla and Wagner's model that learning (i.e., developing a new expectation) does not occur unless previous expectations are violated, a pretrained animal develops no new expectation during phase-two training. In this application, the special learning law has the following form:

(8) $Cause(\langle s, m_1^e \rangle, \ldots, \langle s, m_n^e \rangle, \langle s, m_1^b \rangle, \ldots, \langle s, m_m^b \rangle) = \langle s, m_{n+1}^e \rangle$ when and only when $Cont\langle s, m_1^e \rangle$ & $\cdots$ & $Cont\langle s, m_n^e \rangle$ & $Cont\langle s, m_1^b \rangle$ & $\cdots$ & $Cont\langle s, m_m^b \rangle$ stand in L to $Cont\langle s, m_{n+1}^e \rangle$ and there is some $\langle s, m_i^e \rangle$ $(1 \leq i \leq n)$ such that $\neg\, Cont\langle s, m_i^e \rangle$

(In English, a subject's expectations and beliefs cause a further expectation when and only when the contents of those expectations and beliefs stand in L to the further expectation and the content of at least one of the initial expectations is false ["violated"].) Assuming a standing expectation of no shock in a novel environment, a naive animal that undergoes no phase-one training will have an expectation violated by the shock following the compound CS and so will develop new expectations of the shock to both components of the compound CS during phase-two training.

On to a structuralist rendering of neurobiological theories of Hawkins and Kandel's sort. The fundamental features are these:

• A set of neurons
• For each neuron, a state of activation and an output function
• A pattern of connectivity among the neurons
• An intraneuron activation rule for combining the inputs to a neuron with its current activation state to produce a new activation state
• Various intraneuronal processes for adjusting the synaptic strengths between a neuron and others receiving its output as part of their input

Representations are usually characterized in one of two ways: as patterns of activation values (values of nonnegative real numbers representing the firing rates of some or all of the neurons in the network), or as patterns of synaptic weight values that regulate activation values in all but the input neurons of the network (see again the quote from Hawkins and Kandel 1984a on p. 179 above).[15]

Here I give a structuralist-inspired schematic representation of a neurobiological theory of this sort. First let me define my notation. In empirical applications, N is a network (hence the well-ordering condition) of neurons (n). *Act* is a set of action commands (to the motor system). T is a set of time instances (t). AV is the activation-value relation, taking neurons at times into positive real values. O is the neurons' output at times, determined by some mathematical function A on each neuron's activation value. I is input at times coming into any neurons from outside the network (e.g., from the sensory periphery). CW is the connection-weight relation at times, with the restriction that no unit is actively connected to itself. *Cause* is the causation relation from the activation values of a subset of neurons (seemingly without exception a proper subset, the output neurons) onto action commands. The schematic representation of the neurobiological theory is then the following:

x is a potential model of a computational neuroscientific theory (**CNT**) iff

(1) $x = \langle N, Act, T, \Re, AV, O, I, CW, Cause \rangle$,

(2) N is a finite, nonempty, nonsingleton, well-ordered set,

(3)   *Act* is a finite, possibly empty set,

(4) T is a finite, nonempty, nonsingleton, well-ordered set,

(5) $AV : N \times T \to \Re^+$,

(6) $O : N \times T \to \Re$, and for all $n \in N, t \in T, O(n,t) = A(AV(n,t))$,

(7) $I : N \times T \to \Re$,

(8) $CW : N \times N \times T \to \Re$, and for all $n \in N, t \in T, CW(n,n,t) = 0$,

(9)   *Cause* $: AV^* \to Act$, where $AV^* \subseteq AV$ (seemingly without exception, $AV^* \subset AV$).

Actual models of **CNT** must also meet the following condition on AV:

(10)   For all $n_1, n_2 \in N, AV(n_1, t) =$
$F(CW(n_2, n_1) \cdot O(n_2) \times I(n_1) \times AV(n_1, t - 1))$.

(In English, (10) states that the activation value of each neuron at some time is the result of some arithmetical function F on connection weights multiplied by the output of all neurons actively connected with the one in question, inputs to the neuron from outside the network [if any], and the neuron's activation value at the time instant just before.) To adequately capture activation values in real nervous systems, F typically must be a differentiable, quasi-linear function.

In addition to (10), the actual models of any application of **CNT** must meet a change condition on either O or CW. The particular condition will differ, depending on the **CNT** at issue, since different accounts will employ different intracellular processes as their basic neurophysiological letters.(Recall the discussion from the previous section about the explanatory potential of adding an additional postsynaptic modification process to the exclusively presynaptic processes of Hawkins and Kandel's model.) Still, we can provide the basic form of the weight-change law and examine a specific application of it in Hawkins and Kandel's theory. The basic idea is that weight change over time is a function of the inputs to the system:

(11)   If R obtains between $I(N)$ at t & $I(N)$ at $t-1$ & $\cdots$ & $I(N)$ at $t-n$, then $CW(N)$ at t times $O(N)$ at t differs by D from $CW(N)$ at $t-n$ times $O(N)$ at $t-n$.

Here R is the relation between inputs to the network over time necessary to produce learning (synaptic-weight change), and $I(N)$ at t, $CW(N)$ at t, and $O(N)$ at t are the set of all $I(n)$, $CW(n,n')$, and $O(n)$ at t. (In English, (11) says that if the right relation obtains between inputs to the network over time, then the connection weights times outputs of the presynaptic units differ by quantity D from those products at an earlier time.) On Hawkins and Kandel's theory, for example, continued presentation of a stimulus produces habituation, a reduction in the output of the sensory neurons to the same stimulus. Hence

(12)   If $I(N)$ at $t = I(N)$ at $t-1 = \cdots = I(N)$ at $t-n$, then $O(N)$ at t differs from $O(N)$ at $t-n$ in that for some $n \in N$, $O(n,t) < O(n,t-n)$.

(In English, if identical inputs to the network obtain over time, then the outputs of some units will be less at a later time in comparison with the earlier time.) Neurobiologically, the output is less in the output neurons because less transmitter is released by their presynaptic counterparts. Other types of synaptic processes, like the LTP processes discussed by Lynch and Granger, produce changes to the actual connection weights CW over time. These will require a different application of (11). Similar applications of (11) hold for the other two intracellular processes that make up the neurophysiological letters of Hawkins Kandel's model. Sensitization produces a general increase in O from a particular pattern of inputs, while classical conditioning produces subnetwork, selective increases in O.

We then establish the reduction of an intentional-psychological theory to its computational neuroscientific counterpart by showing that the conditions on ρ can be met (chapter 3, secs. 2 and 4). The application of those conditions to the illustrated case is straightforward. The onto-logical-reduction-link (ORL) condition is interesting. The empirical base set S (the subject set) of **IP** will be linked to the entire set N (the set of network neurons) in ρ-related potential models of **CNT**, since these are the respective seats of cognitive activities in the related models. Set inclusion will not obtain here: $S \not\subseteq N$. So this ORL is heterogeneous. The sets MR_i will be linked to either AV (typically some proper subset of AV) or to CW in the ρ-related potential models of **CNT**, depending on which of these elements the theory builds its account of cognitive representation upon. Either way, set inclusion will not obtain here, since the MRs are sets of unstructured elements, while both AV and CW are sets of ordered pairs. This ORL is also heterogeneous, and we here have a case of elements "structured through reduction" (chapter 3, sec. 5). Finally, the set Act in ρ-related potential models of **IP** and **CNT** will be linked by a homogeneous ORL. The behavioral consequences explained by the two theories remain the same. In the next chapter I'll explore the ontological consequences of these results.

With this result, both versions of the "put up or shut up" challenge are met. There are instances of the reduction of genuinely cognitive intentional-psychological theories to neuroscientific counterparts. There is real promise that the combinatorial-reduction strategy employed in these cases will carry actual psychoneural reductions further. And there is no uncrossable gap between actual theories in the cognitive and brain sciences and the foundational philosophy of science underwriting new-wave reductionism. But we can't stop here. In the final chapter we plunge back into that old philosophical quagmire, the mind-body problem, reformulated in the fashion of intertheoretic reduction (IR) (chapter 2, secs. 3 and 4).

6

Revisionary Physicalism

The intertheoretic-reduction (IR) reformulation of the mind-body problem asserts that ontological conclusions are secondary to and dependent on the nature of the IR relation obtaining (or failing to obtain) between folk psychology and some developed scientific successor. We saw the case for why folk psychology, our commonsense conception of the mental, is the appropriate theory to be reduced. All of the traditional solutions to this problem—dualisms, identity theory, functionalisms, eliminativism— emerge as predictions about the relation that will or won't obtain. Failure to reduce warrants our asserting the ontological autonomy and independence of the kinds referred to by folk psychology, and hence dualism. Smooth reduction warrants claims of cross-theoretic property identities, and hence either functionalism or a theory of mind-brain identity, depending on which science provides the smooth successor. Bumpy reduction warrants eliminativism. These conclusions rest on the relations between scientific theories generally, as illustrated by the top and bottom arrows of figure 2.1. (All of these claims were developed and defended in chapter 2.)

We've also seen both the foundations and some applications of new-wave reductionism. Now it is time to see what our empirical examples of psychoneural reduction suggest as the prediction of where (if anywhere) the reduction of folk psychology to neuroscience will fall on the new-wave intertheoretic spectrum and what the ontological consequences will be. Not only will this account round out and complete my discussion of new-wave reduction, it will also enable me to clarify the ontological status of intentional properties, as these are characterized by folk psychology.[1]

One caveat before I begin. I'm going to be exploring folk psychology in the light of computational neuroscientific theories that focus on synaptic modeling and modifiability. This is not the only up-and-running approach in theoretical neuroscience. It is the one with which I am most familiar. It is also one that is quite popular nowadays. *But readers should not take my exclusive focus on this approach to mean that I am letting it stand for all of neuroscience.* What I am doing here is seeing what status folk-psychological kinds have through the lens of one current approach to neuroscientific theorizing. For all I know, their status might be quite different if one adopts a different neuroscientific approach as the potential reducer. I welcome others to carry out such a task.²

1   The Core Properties of Propositional Attitudes

Before we can seriously assess the fate of folk psychology, we must decide on the central features of propositional attitudes, its key explanatory resource. It requires stipulation to state the properties that a vindicating scientific successor must by and large preserve. Fortunately, there is general agreement in the literature about folk psychology.³

The sentential account of content

The central debate between realists and eliminativists about the propositional attitudes is over the structure of mental content, over whether a "sentential" account of content will provide the best account of cognitive representation and computation.⁴ Borrowing from Patricia Churchland, I will call a psychological theory "sentential" if it conforms to the following two conditions:

• The representational content of a cognitive state is identified by (as) a sentence or proposition.
• The transformations from one state to another (the cognitive processes) are characterized by a logic (either deductive or inductive) specifying appropriate relations between the sentences or propositions identifying the contents of the states.⁵

Interestingly, many realists who defend the scientific viability of folk psychology agree on these central properties of its fundamental explanatory resource. Recent remarks by Jerry Fodor illustrate this:

I will view a psychology as being commonsensical about the attitudes—in fact, as endorsing them—just in case it postulates states (entities, events, whatever) satisfying the following conditions:

(i) They are semantically evaluable.

(ii) They have causal powers.

(iii) The implicit generalizations of commonsense belief/desire psychology are largely true of them.

In effect, I'm assuming that (i)–(iii) are the essential properties of the attitudes. (1987, 10)

Fodor's constraints on a vindicating successor for folk psychology closely resemble Churchland's. While Fodor does not explicitly mention sentential contents, sentences and their constituents are the paradigmatic "semantically evaluable" entities. And the logiclike interactions of sentential contents determine the causal powers of the attitudes. Hence for Fodor and Churchland, prime movers on either side of the realist-eliminativist divide, vindication of folk psychology's propositional attitudes amounts to the same thing: the scientific viability of the sentential account of content and computation.

Folk psychology is deeply committed to a sentential account of content and computation. Its central explanatory posits are, after all, *propositional* attitudes. This warrants the primacy of this feature in the realist-eliminativist debate. Yet I want to emphasize two additional core properties of folk psychology's propositional attitudes. The status of these other features will be critical for distinguishing eliminativism from a related ontology, *revisionary* physicalism.

The functional profiles of cognitive states
As we've already seen, folk psychology consists of generalizations that systematically relate propositional attitudes to sensory inputs, other propositional attitudes, and behavioral outputs. My seeing a bottle of beer in the refrigerator produces in me the belief that there is a bottle of beer in the fridge. This belief, coupled with my desire to drink a beer, produces my intention to remove the beer. This intention produces behavior that removes the beer. By characterizing the relevant cognitive states in this fashion, folk psychology attributes to each such state a causal role in an abstract, systematically interconnected network according to the states that cause its occurrence and the states it further causes.

Folk psychology attributes an *abstract functional profile* to each state, connecting each to other states and ultimately to sensation and behavior. The functional profile of a state is the set of causal paths running through it.

By virtue of its sentential account of content and computation, folk psychology also *explains* why each state has its particular functional profile. This has to do with the logical relations obtaining between the contents of the states. Yet it is crucial to keep the abstract functional profile that folk psychology attributes to each state separate from folk psychology's explanation of why each state has the profile it has. It is possible that folk psychology attributes the correct functional profile to many cognitive states, that it gets correct the abstract causal structure of the cognitive network mediating sensation and behavior, but gets wrong the explanation of this feature (in terms of the logiclike relations between the sentential contents of the states).

A functionalist ontology of mind takes the functional profile of a cognitive state as *the* essential property of the state, as *the* mark of what it is to be a cognitive state of that type. The functional (causal) profile of the state exhausts what it is to be, e.g., the belief that there is a bottle of beer in the fridge. Any state in a suitably endowed information-processing network realizing this abstract functional profile is a belief that there is a bottle of beer in the fridge, whatever the physical stuff realizing the network. However, that a core feature of folk psychology's propositional attitudes is their functional profiles does not imply that folk psychology is committed to a functionalist ontology of mind. Nor does it imply that, from the IR-reformulation perspective, only a cognitive/computational scientific psychology could vindicate its ontology. The functional profile that folk psychology attributes to a cognitive state is *just one* of its central properties. It is also a property that could be vindicated even by a science that restricted its domain to a particular type of physical system, if the abstract causal network that the system's states figured in mostly matched that attributed by folk psychology.

Intentionality

By characterizing cognitive states as propositional attitudes, folk psychology attributes a specific directedness to each state, to the object or affair the state is of or about. This is apparent in states closely connected to sensory or behavioral peripheries. For example, the state folk psychology characterizes as my belief that this computer before me is on is about this computer and the state of its being on. Similarly with the state characterized as my intention that I get a cup of coffee. That state has a specific sort of aboutness. It is directed to events resulting in my getting a cup of coffee.

Besides specifying the object or state of affairs that a particular cognitive state is of or about, folk psychology also provides an explanation of a state's intentionality. Since cognitive states are *propositional* attitudes, the resources of linguistic analysis can pick out the object of the state. One can use theories of reference, denotation, description, and predication, applied to the propositional content of the state. My belief that Salzburg is a beautiful city is about Salzburg (and not about Boston, or Suzy, or this desktop) because of the referential properties of the name "Salzburg" that occurs in its content. As with functional profile, however, it is important to keep separate the attribution of intentionality to cognitive states (what the state is of or about) from the explanation of this property that folk psychology provides. Folk psychology might be mostly correct concerning what particular cognitive states are of or about, while wrong in its explanation of their aboutness in terms of the referential features of their sentential contents.

2 Revisionary Physicalism

Our question now is whether and to what extent these core properties of propositional attitudes are present in the explanatory posits of one promising theoretical approach in neuroscience. We saw in chapter 5, section 2, that one promising strategy in computational neuroscience focuses on the changes wrought by experience on synaptic events in real brains. Experience, encoded by firing rates in input neurons, affects the amount of neurotransmitter released by presynaptic neurons and/or the receptive properties of postsynaptic neurons. This changes the firing rates in postsynaptic neurons and ultimately changes behavior. We even saw in Hawkins and Kandel's and Lynch's work how a few simple mechanisms of synaptic modifiability, embedded in increasing complex neural circuitry that enables novel sequences and combinations of these intra-cellular processes to occur in parallel, can produce behavior that at the psychological level of explanation requires the resources of cognition (representations and computations over their content). This strategy is becoming a cornerstone of contemporary cognitive neurobiology. What implications does it carry concerning the ontological status of folk psychology's propositional attitudes?

I contend that developments like this support a *revisionary physicalism* about our commonsense conception of the mental. As we've seen, the theory of intertheoretic reduction underwriting new-wave reductionism and its IR reformulation of the mind-body problem recognizes a spectrum of possible outcomes. These range from perfectly smooth reductions out to extremely bumpy ones (figure 2.1, top arrow, and chapter 3, sec. 6). Lying between these two extremes is a continuum, with cases in between. In these intermediate cases, the ontological consequences entailed by the reduction resemble those associated with the endpoint more closely approximated: there are some cross-theoretic identifications, some straightout eliminations, and some *conceptual changes or revisions* to the posits of the reduced theory T_R, depending on where and to what extent T_R stands corrected (i.e., the sizes of the blurs required to meet the conditions on the reduction relation ρ).

One well-studied reduction that occupies an intermediate position between the extremes of retention and replacement is that of the simple thermodynamics of gases to the kinetic theory (chapter 2, section 3; chapter 3, section 5). This case illustrates three conditions separating revisionary from retentive and replacement reductions. My statement of each condition is followed by a brief commentary.

1. *Explanations generated by T_R approximate the actual events causing the observable phenomena.* In the reduction of simple thermodynamics of gases to kinetic theory, this approximation is due to the fact that the reduction obtaining is a limit reduction, where the limits at which cross-theoretic identities are exact never actually obtain (these limits involve, e.g., an infinite number of molecules, a volume indefinitely large compared to the average distance between molecular collisions). Any cross-theoretic "identities" thus hold only under an open class of boundary conditions satisfying extensive and empirically unrealizable constraints.

2. *Key explanatory concepts of* T_R *fragment into several distinct concepts of* T_B, *and often each of the latter appropriate candidates for cross-theoretic "identification" lie at appropriate limits or within particular domains of application of* T_B. Clifford Hooker (1981, 48) cites (macroscopic) entropy as an example in the reduction of simple thermodynamics of gases to kinetic theory. It fragments via the reduction into Boltzmann entropy and the fine- and coarse-grained Gibbs entropies.

3. *Revisionary cases of reduction display mutual evolutionary feedback between* T_R *and* T_B, *where developments within each theory serve to mutually constrain and promote fruitful development within the other, but especially within* T_R. The long quote from Hooker at the end of section 4 of chapter 4 points out that problems confronting classical thermodynamics spurred initial development and application of statistical mechanics. At the same time, the injection of statistical-mechanical results back into equilibrium thermodynamics in turn yielded corrections that enabled it to overcome some previous explanatory limits.

These three conditions serve as marks of a revisionary intertheoretic reduction, in contrast to a straightforward retentive or replacement reduction. The resulting intertheoretic relation is (new-wave) reduction (not mere historical theory succession), but a "significantly corrective" one, in the sense developed in chapter 3, sections 5 and 6.

The semiformal details of a "significantly corrective" (although nonetheless genuine) reduction relation ρ motivates each of these marks. Approximation obtains because although the ORLs (partly) comprising ρ are heterogeneous for at least some empirical base sets of T_R, the size of the blurs required to meet the conditions on ρ are not huge (in comparision with bumpier replacement reductions). This is what "intertheoretic approximation" amounts to, in the terminology of chapter 3. Fragmentation is suggested by the heterogeneous nature of the ORLs for some empirical base sets of T_R and by how concepts of the reduced theory become "structured" through reduction (chapter 3, section 6). It often turns out that a reduction associates an unstructured, "functional" concept of the reduced theory with theoretically related yet distinct processes, sequences, and complex entities of the reducing theory (combinations of empirical base sets, auxiliary base sets, and theoretical functions of T_B). Finally, the relatively close approximation between reduced and reducing theory, in terms of the size of the blurs required, makes possible fruitful mutual coevolutionary feedback. Because the approximation is relatively close, this facilitates initial fruitful development of the reducing theory. If meeting the conditions on ρ ultimately requires big blurs, the reduced theory won't have provided a very fruitful guide for initial development of the reducing theory. Close approximation (in new-wave sense) also makes both feasible and fruitful injection of some structure that the reducing theory uncovers back into the reduced theory.

What are the ontological consequences of revisionary reductions? Hooker's own statement about the thermodynamics case is a clear statement of a revisionary ontological outcome: "In a fairly strong sense thermodynamics is simply conceptually and empirically wrong and must be replaced.... On the other hand, the situation is evidently not one of radical replacement, as say in the case of phlogiston-to-oxidation reduction, in which only the neutrally described observations are retained" (1981, 49). The outcome is *conceptual change*, not straightforward retention nor outright elimination of the posits and kinds of the reduced theory. The revisionary physicalist predicts a similar fate for the propositional attitudes of folk psychology. Some of their central properties will not find close analogs in the key posits of its neuroscientific successor, so in this "fairly strong" sense, folk psychology is "conceptually and empirically wrong and must be replaced." In the terminology of chapter 3, the ORLs (partly) composing the reduction relation ρ are heterogeneous. At least some empirical base sets of reduced T_R do not include elements of the potential models of reducing T_B, although ORLs link the ontologies of the two theories (as shown by overlap in their intended empirical applications). This is the eliminativist strand in revisionary physicalism. The properties corresponding to those sets are abandoned as lacking actual extension. However, the revisionist also predicts that other central properties of folk psychology's propositional attitudes will be preserved via homogeneous ORLs. (Hence in the terminology of chapter 3, section 4, the ORLs partly composing ρ are "mixed.") The revisionist also foresees the need for only moderately big blurs to meet the conditions on ρ. Hence he denies that this will be a case of "radical replacement" (either bumpy reduction or mere historical succession of theories). The case thus will not be comparable in the size of the requisite blurs and the nature of the ORLs to caloric-fluid heat theory and phlogiston chemistry to their successors. While there won't be straightforward property identity between reduced and reducing kinds, primarily since the reduced, functionally specified kinds become structured through the reduction, nevertheless the replacing kinds will resemble (approximate) the replaced kinds in significant fashion.

My contention is that recent work on the biology of synaptic modifiability and the resulting accounts of higher cognitive behavior makes a strong empirical case for the revisionist's prediction. To defend it, I reconsider the status of the three central properties of folk psychology's propositional attitudes in light of the scientific developments described in chapter 5, section 2. Bear in mind the three marks of revisionary reductions: approximation, fragmentation, and mutual coevolutionary feedback. Since Hawkins and Kandel's neurophysiological-alphabet account of higher-order associative learning was presented in the most detail, I'll focus explicitly on it. The arguments generalize in obvious fashion to other scientific developments employing mechanisms of synaptic modifiability and the strategy of combinatorial reduction.

The sentential account of content

Here the implication is straightforward. In its *theoretical explanations*, the computational-neurobiological strategy of synaptic modifiability and combinatorial reduction wholly eschews both the sentential account of content and the logiclike account of cognitive processing (computation). As the long quote from Hawkins and Kandel (chapter 5, section 2) shows, the approach does posit representational states. But it identifies the contents and causal powers of these states in terms of synaptic strengths, connectivity in the neural network, and resulting firing patterns, not by way of sentences. The processes operating over these representations are intracellular neurophysiological processes that modify synaptic strengths and connections and ultimately result in changed patterns of cellular activity, which in turn change behavioral responses. In the terminology of chapter 3, ORLs link the base set of propositional attitudes in potential models of folk psychology to these features of the potential models of cognitive neuroscience, since the intended empirical applications of the two theories overlap. However, these ORLs are heterogeneous. Neither set inclusion nor (set) identity obtains for this empirical base set of folk psychology.

Given the centrality of sentential content in folk psychology, any eschewal of it will have significant negative consequences for the ontological status of folk psychology's propositional attitudes. To the extent that this theoretical approach in the neurosciences proves fruitful, it follows that there is no need to posit *propositional* attitudes to do any causal work in generating cognition and behavior. Hence explanatory generalizations adverting to propositional attitudes are, strictly speaking, false. Such generalizations fail to correctly describe the actual cognitive dynamics of the real-world cognitive systems under investigation. Those systems operate on an entirely different basis. In Hawkins and Kandel's account of blocking, for example, there are no propositional attitudes—e.g., surprise that the shock occurred, expectation that a shock is coming—doing any causal work. Instead, there are a few basic intracellular neurophysiological mechanisms producing changes in the strengths of certain synapses, which leads to increases or decreases in neurotransmitter-release rates. In combinations allowed by complex neural circuitries, these events ultimately cause the behavioral changes that are the higher-order features of associative learning. These processes operate over states representing knowledge of the training environment, encoded in the changing synaptic strengths. These specific events, each fully describable at the cell-biological level, are doing all the causal work. This approach to neuroscientific theorizing, as a fundamental working hypothesis, completely ignores the sentential account of content (though, to reiterate, it need not eschew propositional attitudes in its methodology during the construction of an explanation appealing to synaptic modifiability).

Eschewing the sentential account of content is consistent with a strong brand of caloric-fluid/phlogiston-type eliminativism. How, then, do these scientific developments support revisionism? Clearly, folk psychology does not recognize enough propositional attitudes to pair an attitude with each neurophysiological state that figures in a neurobiological-alphabet type explanation of some cognitive event. We might "identify" the synaptic strengths in the sensory and facilitator interneurons produced by early occurrences of a novel US with the folk-psychological propositional attitude "is surprised that the shock occurred." I here use "identify" in a loose sense, and I justify this use by the fact that these folk-psychological states closely approximate the explanatory function of the correlated neurophysiological states. We might comfortably "identify" the relevant synaptic strengths following training upon presentation of the CS with the folk attitude "expects that the shock is about to occur." Shortly we'll even see reasons for why we can rest comfortably with these loose identities. But that about exhausts the extent to which we will find cross-theoretic identities tenable. From the perspective of folk psychology, when exactly does the surprise state give way to expectation during training? What attitudes occur between the initial states and the later trained states? The only ones that come to mind are essentially vague characterizations like "is somewhat surprised that the shock just occurred" or "now to some extent expects that a shock is coming." These folk-psychological "attitudes" are not candidates for even loose identity with the continuous range of cell-biological states (changing states of synaptic strengths, in terms of neurotransmitter-release rates) as training proceeds. We can precisely characterize the latter in terms of synaptic strengths (neurotransmitter-release rates, changing probabilities and rates of postsynaptic responses). This feature yields precise predictions about subsequent behavioral effects (exactly how much these changes will affect baseline behavior). The folk-psychological characterizations ("is somewhat surprised that" and "to some extent expects that") do neither.

This is not to say, however, that neurobiological resources can't be injected back into folk psychology, with fruitful consequences. Quite the contrary. We should expect folk psychology to spawn more precise, *although revised*, explanatory posits because of these neurobiological developments. There is no barrier to mutual evolutionary feedback here. That initial and final states approximate their neurophysiological cou terparts provides the toehold for such enrichment. The fruitfulness of such feedback, recall, is one mark of a revisionary reduction.

The functional profiles of cognitive states

While folk psychology appears to have gotten wrong the actual structure of cognitive content, it appears to have gotten right the basic functional profile it assigns to many states. Recall from above that folk psychology assigns states a place in an abstract, systematically connected network running from sensory to behavior peripheries, in terms of the states or events that cause their occurrence and the subsequent states or events they cause. What folk psychology appears to have gotten right is the *gross abstract structure of this network*, the coarse-grained web of relations obtaining between (some) cognitive states.

This point requires some spelling out. Consider first an analogy with my familiar example of a revisionary reduction. The simple thermodynamics of gases recognizes the mathematical relationship obtaining between pressure p, volume V, and temperature T of a gas: $pV = nrT$, where n is the number of moles and r is the gas constant (chapter 2, section 2). The kinetic theory preserves *in a coarse-grained fashion* this mathematical relationship among the appropriate analogs of p, T, and the ideal gas: respectively, mean rate of momentum per unit area, mean molecular kinetic energy, and a collection of molecules having 0 distant-dependent intermolecular forces. This is because the analog of the classical gas law is derivable in the thermodynamic limit (equation 1 of chapter 2, section 2). In actual, nonlimit situations, however, the classical gas law only *approximates* kinetic-theory explanations. It fails to capture the kinetic theory's more *fine-grained* analysis and explanation of the actual events and processes, in terms of statistical properties of the myriad molecular collisions. For most practical purposes, of course, the approximation is sufficient.

A similar relation holds between the functional-level story provided by folk psychology and the more fine-grained account emerging from neurobiological theories like Hawkins and Kandel's. According to folk psychology, perception of the occurrence of a shock causes the cognitive state identified as surprise that the shock occurred. This state of surprise in turn causes shock- and surprise-associated behavior, including suppression of activity. Repeated presentations of the shock in the same setting and in temporal sequence with some conditioned stimulus causes the state of surprise finally to give way to a state of expectation when the conditioned stimulus occurs. As noted above, folk psychology has no real story to tell about the attitudes lying between the initial surprise and the final expectation. That's what makes its specification only coarse-grained, as compared with the causal story a cognitive-neuroscientific account provides. Finally, when the subject is in a state of expectation, his behavior changes in response to the conditioned stimulus to include a suppression of activity before the shock.

Much the same *coarse-grained* network of causal relations between sensory inputs, representational states, and behavioral outputs obtains on Hawkins and Kandel's explanations, despite the differences in their characterization of the states' contents. Initial presentations of a bio-logically noxious stimulus coupled appropriately with a neutral stimulus produces a series of intracellular events that strengthen certain synapses, in terms of increased rates of neurotransmitter release. Ultimately, this culminates in a defensive behavioral response. Repeated presentations of the noxious stimulus paired with the conditioned stimulus result in long-term changes to synaptic strength between appropriate neurons. These produce changes in motor output and ultimately behavioral changes to particular sensory inputs.

The abstract processing structure of the two networks is very similar, at least at a coarse-grained level of analysis. The gross causal flow, from sensations through representational states to behavior, is mostly the same. Imagine the two accounts diagramed as nets of nodes, with each node representing a representational state occurring in the explanation, connected by arrows representing causal effects. If we overlay the nets, landmark nodes and arrows of the two would largely lie one on top of the other. In the terminology of chapter 3, the lawlike axioms in the set-theoretic definitions of models of folk psychology and cognitive neuroscience describe a similar causal flow from input through related representations ultimately to behavior. Of course, the functional profiles assigned to cognitive states on Hawkins and Kandel's neurobiological account are much more fine-grained and detailed, for that account rec-ognizes distinctions and connections that folk psychology either lumps together or leaves extremely vague. (For instance, many states brought on by early occurrences of the shock during training get lumped together under the state of "surprise that the shock occurred," whereas Hawkins and Kandel's account distinguishes these states. In the area of vagueness, e.g., "is still somewhat surprised that the shock occurred" is about the best folk psychology can do during training, whereas Hawkins and Kandel's account assigns precise content to these states in terms of syn-aptic strengths and resulting firing rates.) Here again, however, we can expect that injection of some neurobiological details back into folk psychology would fruitfully enrich the latter, and thus allow development of a more fine-grained folk-psychological account that better matches the detailed functional profiles that neurobiology assigns to its representational states. There is no principled reason against such enrichment.

Functionality also displays the second mark of a revisionary reduction: the fragmentation of key reduced kinds into a variety of related but distinct reducing kinds. For example, states that folk psychology lumps together as "is surprised that *p*" fragment into several distinct neurobiological states in terms of changing synaptic strengths and connections. Each of the latter shares a similar functional profile at a coarse-grained, approximative level of analysis but exhibits important functional differences at the more fine-grained level of changing synaptic strengths (changing neurotransmitter-release rates). Similarly for the rest of the representational states recognized by a folk-psychological explanation of the data.

Recall, however, the possibility noted above that folk psychology could get right the basic functional profile of some cognitive states but get wrong the explanation of this feature in terms of the logical relations obtaining between the sentential contents of the states. On Hawkins and Kandel's account, this possibility obtains. It is changing synaptic strengths and connectivity of the neural network that explains why each state has the functional profile it has, not its sentential content.

Intentionality

Along with getting the coarse-grained functional profiles of some cognitive states largely correct, folk psychology also appears to have correctly characterized the intentionality of many cognitive states: their directedness toward specific objects or states of affairs external to them, what the states are of or about. For example, following initial presentations of a shock, folk psychology adverts to the "surprise that the shock occurred." So identified, this cognitive state is of or about the shock, but is not of or about other features of the environment.

The same directedness gets attributed to the counterpart neurobiological state. The changing strengths of particular synapses encode information *about the shock*. The representational state characterized neurobiologically is directed toward that same external event. Because we replace the sentential account of content with a neurophysiological one, we can no longer explain the intentionality of these states in terms of reference, denotation, or other linguistic/semantic properties of their contents. Folk psychology got the *explanation* of the intentionality or "aboutness" of cognitive states wrong. What makes these states directed toward, of, or about specific objects and states of affairs is not what folk psychology implies. Instead, we account for the directedness of a state by the effects of sensory inputs on changing synaptic strengths and changing behavior keyed to specific features of the environment. The mathematical theory of information might provide the key resource. What folk psychology did get right, however, is the external object or state of affairs that many cognitive states are of or about.

It is surely this sense of intentionality that Patricia Churchland refers to when she writes, in response to John Bishop, "Finally, Bishop is concerned about whether representational states characterized within cognitive neuroscience would be intentional states. My answer is *no*, in the narrow sense of intentionality that is precisely tied to the linguistic model (i.e., nontruth-functionality, failure of existential generalization, and failure of substitutivity). But my answer is yes, in the very loose sense that neurobiological representations are *about* things. And it is this loose sense which I see yielding to a richer explanatory theory as cognitive neuroscience evolves" (1988, 401). Intentionality in this loose sense—a core property of cognitive states characterized as propositional attitudes —appears headed for clear preservation in the explanatory posits of developing neuroscience. This holds even if the explanation of this aboutness or specific directedness in terms of the resources of linguistic analysis goes the way of sentential contents.

I can now cobble together the vision of revisionary physicalism. First, the preserved central features of folk psychology's propositional attitudes within a powerful developing neuroscience (a given state's coarse-grained functional profile and its intentionality in the loose sense) support the claim that folk psychology *approximates* the actual cognitive dynamics (with "approximation" characterized in terms of the "intertheoretic approximation" of chapter 3, sections 5 and 6). These two preserved features even show *when* folk psychology's approximation will be methodologically useful. Cognitive scientists are still trying to piece together a coarse-grained account of information processing in the mind-brain. In such investigations, the propositional attitudes can provide useful simplifications for initial theory construction because of the features of cognition that folk psychology appears to have gotten right. Second, we should expect that theoretical developments in the neurosciences will produce *fragmentation* of the propositional attitudes into families of more fine-grained neurobiological successors. Members of these families will share similar coarse-grained functional profiles, while more fine-grained analyses at the neuroscientific level will reveal important differences in their actual causal powers. Third, we can expect the fruitful *mutual coevolutionary feedback* between folk psychology and its neurobiological successors that is typical of revisionary reductions. The coarse-grained functional profiles and the intentionality that folk psychology attributes to cognitive states can help constrain and focus initial neurobiological theorizing. Hawkins and Kandel (1984a, 1984b) themselves used folksy explanatory intuitions about the higher-order features of associative learning to get their cell-biological-alphabet explanations off the ground. Finally, injection of some details of cognition revealed at the neurobiological level back into the propositional attitudes will plausibly yield fruitful enrichment of folk psychology. All three marks of a revisionary reduction obtain in this projected case.

Ontologically speaking, revisionary physicalism predicts enough conceptual change to rule out cross-theoretic identities between propositional attitudes and neurophysiological posits and their theoretically relevant properties. (Recall Hooker's remarks about the ontology of the simple thermodynamics of gases at the beginning of this section.) Revisionary physicalism thus differs from standard realism about the attitudes. This is its eliminativist strand. However, it also rejects the radical eliminativism encapsulated in appeals to the ontological fate of, e.g., caloric fluid and phlogiston. And it rejects this by appeal to the broadly empirical grounds over which contemporary eliminativists (e.g., the Churchlands) wage the debate. Revisionary physicalism appeals directly to influential theorizing in recent neurobiology, armed with a rigorous, grounded account of intertheoretic reduction. Perhaps the clearest way to state the revisionist's position is this. One kind of representation concept (one kind of belief concept, one kind of desire concept), the folk psychological one, is being replaced by another kind of representation concept, the cognitive-neurobiological one. This is exactly the ontological outcome in historical revisionary reductions. Special relativity theory still employs a mass concept, a length concept, a velocity concept, only not the specific *classical* mass, length, and velocity concepts. Significant conceptual change, yes. Strict cross-theoretic entity and property identities, no. Total elimination of the caloric-fluid/phlogiston variety, again no.

Notes

Chapter One

1. This book is concerned exclusively with *psychoneural* reduction: reduction of mind to brain mechanism and/or of psychology to neuroscience. Philosophers often understand the term "reductionism" more broadly, to encompass a view of all ontology (including, e.g., the status of numbers, propositions, etc.). I admonish the reader to understand "reduction" and all of its cognates as they occur here in the narrower sense. A similar restriction of scope holds for "physicalism."

2. For those who think that this restriction too narrowly limits the scope of this book, take heed of a quotation from Jerry Fodor. Speaking on behalf of his earlier functionalism, Fodor writes, "It seems to me, for what it's worth, that functionalism does not provide an adequate account of qualitative content; that, in fact, we have no adequate materialist account of qualitative content. Since I have nothing at all to add to this discussion.... I shall simply assume that the functionalist program applies at most to the analysis of propositional attitudes" (1981, 17). Fodor is rarely accused of being overly narrow in scope!

3. Chapters 7 and 9 of Patricia Churchland's *Neurophilosophy* (1986) are closest to a comprehensive account. Yet she neglects some important features of a general theory of intertheoretic reduction necessary to ground the account adequately and gives up on providing a formal model of the relation. And with the rising popularity of nonreductive physicalism over the past few years, her defense is now a bit dated.

4. Thanks to the manuscript reviewers, Ronald Endicott in particular, for helping me clarify this initial statement of the differences between classical and new-wave reductionism. However, as we will see in the next section, there is a firm limit to the conciliatory attitude of new-wave reductionism toward antireductionist tenets.

5. Citing Moore in this context goes back to Davidson (1973). Davidson is universally acknowledged as having introduced supervenience into the philosophy of mind. See Heil 1992, chapter 3, for an excellent overview of the use of supervenience in philosophy of mind.

6. John Searle (1992, chapter 5) is sensitive to it, and Searle does deny being something he labels a "reductionist." Numerous commentators have labeled Searle a property dualist. But once I articulate new-wave reductionism, Searle's "biological naturalism" will turn out closely related to it. So Searle is not the sort of antireductionist I am targeting here. In fact, I see no reason why Searle would challenge new-wave reductionism as an acceptable relation between psychological and neurobiological theories, especially given his distinction between two senses of "causally relevant emergent properties" in chapter 5 of his *Rediscovery of the Mind* (1992). For more on Searle and new-wave reductionism, see the discussion at the beginning of the next section.

7. Horgan's supervenience thesis (S) reads, "There do not exist any two P-worlds which are exactly alike microphysically but which differ in some other respect" (1984, 20). P-worlds are physically accessible possible worlds. They share the same microphysical laws as our world, and their natural kinds "either are, or are fully decomposable into, entities whose most specific natural kinds are actual-world natural kinds" (1984, 19). (S) is in keeping with what philosophers now call "global" supervenience. See, e.g., Heil 1992, chapter 3.

8. The passage from Fodor is this: "Some monetary exchanges involve strings of wampum. Some involve dollar bills. And some involve signing one's name to a check. What are the chances that a disjunction of physical predicates which covers all these events ... expresses a physical kind?" (1974, 134).

9. Kim himself saw this problem many years ago. See section 2 of his "On the Psycho-physical Identity Theory" (1966). I thank Ronald Endicott for pointing this out to me.

10. Lombard 1986, especially chapter 3, provides a good introduction to various theories of events.

11. This is part of Kim's argument for the "instability" of nonreductive physicalism. I myself don't think that nonreductive physicalism is "unstable," except in its label. Most of it is clearly committed to a property- (or event-) dualistic ontology of mind.

12. This is a good time to note explicitly a presupposition that I will not defend in this book. I presuppose a minimal scientific-realist interpretation of scientific theories. Theories purport to represent the structure of unobservable reality as well as observable reality. I'm confident that I can presuppose this on the part of most readers, at least "for argument's sake."

13. Oppenheim and Putnam's account of microreduction obtains between *branches* of science, not theories. But branch reduction is itself built upon Kemeny and Oppenheim's (1956) general account of theory reduction, so I will speak of microreduction as an inter*theoretic* relation.

14. Going this route raises another worry, however. One must then hold that psychological phenomena are "wholes" composed of cell-network "parts." I myself find this claim puzzling. It seems to me that the "parts" of an intentional mental state are its mode of presentation and its propositional content. But this is a big issue, and I won't pursue it here.

Chapter Two

1. This discussion of true and false theories takes place against a backdrop, already mentioned, of at least a minimal scientific realism.

2. To keep my notational conventions consistent with Hooker's, I employ his symbol T_R^* to denote the analog structure specified within and derived from reducing theory T_B. However, the reader must not confuse Hooker's T_R^* with Schaffner's! They differ on the very point at issue, namely, the theory from whose vocabulary and resources they are constructed. For Hooker, T_R^* is constructed out of the resources and vocabulary of the *reducing* theory T_B. For Schaffner, it is constructed out of the *reduced* theory T_R. I emphasize the importance of this difference in the discussion that follows.

3. In his reviewer remarks, Ronald Endicott suggested that I am slighting Schaffner (1967) in attributing this insight to Hooker. Although historical precedent is secondary to the conceptual point, still I do strive to keep the former straight. It seems to me that Schaffner's insistence and conditions on the reduction functions—the conditions being so similar to those on the connecting principles of the received view—belie Endicott's suggestion. If T_R^* is already specified in the vocabulary and conceptual resources of T_B, there is no need for these reduction functions as part of the reduction proper.

4. I borrow figure 2.1 from Bickle 1996.

5. This is not, however, the only result of the reduction of classical equilibrium thermodynamics in its entirety to microphysics via statistical mechanics. See, e.g., Nagel 1961, 359–360.

6. Here I follow standard scientific notational convention using the subscript 1 to denote the initial state and the subscript 2 to denote the final state.

7. Bear in mind, again, that the relation between the combined ideal gas law and features of the kinetic theory and statistical mechanics is but a part of the full intertheoretic reduction.

This is a good point to mention (and then postpone discussion of) Lawrence Sklar's careful work on the reduction of thermodynamics to the kinetic theory and classical mechanics. One might think that my demonstration and claims based on the argument above conflict with some of Sklar's conclusions. I do not think that they do. But I wish to postpone discussion until the next chapter, after I have embedded Hooker's insights in a broader approach to the structure of scientific theories and intertheoretic relations. I can then more fruitfully investigate comparisons between my account and Sklar's.

8. Some material in the next two sections draws heavily on Bickle 1989 and 1991.

9. I coined this term in Bickle (1989).

10. As we shall see later in this section, this choice does not beg the question against dualism or functionalism.

11. Paul Churchland offers a list of folk-psychological generalizations, including ones relating mental states to perceptions of the external environment, to other mental states, and to behaviors. See Churchland 1979, 92–93, and 1987, 58–59.

12. For the simulation versus the theory theory debate, a good place to start is Gordon 1986 and Goldman 1989. Stich and Nichols 1992 contains a good overview of more recent work on this issue, including empirical studies.

13. To my knowledge, Paul Chruchland first explicitly noted how each traditional solution emerges as a prediction about the reductive fate of folk psychology when the mind-body problem is reformulated as an issue in intertheoretic reduction. (See Churchland 1979, chapter 4, section 15.) My arguments in the rest of this section owe much to Churchland's account, yet I do carry the details of the discussion beyond where Churchland leaves off.

14. The terms "a priori functionalism" and "psychofunctionalism" (introduced below) are borrowed from Block 1978.

15. I won't discuss explicitly the IR reformulation of philosophical behaviorism. (There aren't too many left on the current landscape.) Put briefly, it amounts to the claim that folk psychology ultimately will intertheoretically reduce to some behavioristic psychology.

16. Although in chapter 10 of his 1983 work Stick offers some arguments against protoversions of the IR reformulation as they occur in the writings of the Churchlands up to that time. These criticisms miss the mark against a careful statement of the Churchlands' early version of the IR reformulation. See Bickle 1989, chapter 3.

17. Twin Earth thought experiments originate in Putnam 1975. Their proliferation in philosophy of mind stems from Burge 1979. Woofield 1982 is a good early collection of their application to philosophy of mind. The literature since then is voluminous. Baker 1987 is a useful landmark. Interestingly, Putnam (1988) has recently stressed that the Twin Earth argument is applicable to a critique of functionalism, an ontology of mind he was so instrumental in developing.

Chapter Three

1. In these postmodern times, this name is unfortunate. The "structuralists" I refer to are formalistic philosophers of science located primarily in Germany and eastern Europe. Please do not confuse them with, e.g., the French structuralists.

2. The next six paragraphs draw heavily on Bickle 1993a, 361–365.

3. This is a simplified version of the presentation in Balzer, Moulines, and Sneed (1987, 96–99). I present the same account for illustrative purposes in Bickle (1993a, 362).

4. I supply the figures in this chapter to help those who are a bit rusty on their set theory. For the same reason, I'll also provide English translations of the more

complicated set-theoretic conditions. Thanks to Morton Winston and Valerie Hardcastle for recommending these aids.

5. This stronger reading is important, though, if one is attempting to capture some points urged by "radical" critics of logical empiricism within the structuralist formalism.

6. To keep the record straight with the structuralist literature, what I've provided is a simplified account of their notion of *theory element*, the "smallest set-theoretic entities that may have empirical claims associated with them" and out of which "more complex, non-elementary, 'molecular' empirical theories are built" (Balzer, Moulines, and Sneed 1987, 36). Structuralists further distinguish theory elements into *cores*, their purely formal components (models and potential models, in my simplification), and the partly informal, ultimately only pragmatically specifiable set of intended empirical applications. I've ignored three other components of theory cores: The partial potential models $M_{pp}(T)$, the global constraint $GC(T)$, and the global link $GL(T)$ belonging to $M_p(T)$. The *partial potential models* $M_{pp}(T)$ is a set consisting of the potential models stripped of their "T-theoretic functions." The *global constraint* $GC(T)$ is the intersection of all admissible combinations of potential models. (For example, in the **CCM** case, a given particle p might be an element of different sets $P_1, P_2, \ldots, P_n$ of different potential models. We must then require that the mass function m assigns the same value to p in all admissible cases. Only those potential models that make this assignment count as admissible in the empirical applications and claims of **CCM**. This is an example of a constraint $C(T)$. The global constraint $GC(T)$ is the intersection of all the constraints, i.e., the set of all sets of potential models of T satisfying all of T's constraints taken together.) The *global link* $GL(T)$ belonging to $M_p(T)$ is a set of intertheoretic links between T and surrounding theories that both determine T's nontheoretical structure and narrow the choice of admissible theoretical functions of T by tying them to the theoretical functions of other theories with which T functions to generate predictions and explanations. The second and third components of the full structuralist account of theory core affect the exact structuralist definition of a theory's theoretical content $Cn_{th}(T)$, the subset of potential models that are actual models and accord with the global constraint and the global link of T—in other words, those potential models meeting all of T's empirical laws (expressed by the axioms distinguishing the models from the potential models), "higher order" laws (expressed by the global constraint), and "linking" laws (linking T with other theories related to T in explanations, expressed by the global link). All three of these additional components are crucial for the structuralist solution to the problem of theoreticity, but with one exception they are irrelevant to concerns about intertheoretic reduction. The exception is that on Balzer, Moulines, and Sneed's (1987) full account of theory structure, $I(T)$ is actually a subset of the theory's partial potential models $M_{pp}(T)$. So their global-reduction relation ρ is a mapping from the partial potential models of the reducing theory $M_{pp}(T_B)$ into the partial potential models of the reduced theory $M_{pp}(T_R)$. I will instead specify the reduction relation ρ as a mapping from the potential models of the

reducing theory $M_p(T_B)$ into the potential models of the reduced theory $M_p(T_R)$. Nothing of philosophical interest hangs on my simplification. Its only purpose is to avoid some complexities in specifying the reduction relation that could distract from my particular concerns. These simplifications on theory structure are common in the structuralist literature on reduction. For example, C. U. Moulines (1984, 53) makes exactly these simplifying assumptions when presenting his notion of an ontological reductive link, a notion that will be very important in section 4 below.

7. See Rott 1987 and Mormann 1988 for good overviews, comparisons, and contrasts between the various accounts.

8. Once again, these are adaptations of Balzer, Moulines, and Sneed's (1987) conditions. Balzer, Moulines, and Sneed do not develop the notion of an analog structure T_R^*. For this reason, I will refer to these conditions as BMS-*inspired*.

9. For the full structuralist account of theory elements, including the theory's global constraint and global link (see again note 6 of this chapter), conditions similar in import to condition (1) must be introduced for both additional components, so that the "higher order" and "linking" laws of reduced and reducing theory stand in the same relation to one another as do the "empirical" laws related by condition (1).

10. Their reconstructions of these reductions do not make use of my construal of Hooker's analog structure T_R^* but can be easily modified to include it.

11. This is not Mayr's definition. His definition (1976, 291–292) is a relation on partial potential models, which I have left out of my simplification of structuralist theory elements. Mayr also defines an anomaly for a theory in terms of an empty intersection between the theoretical expansions of an intended empirical application of T (where the T-theoretical functions have been added onto the partial potential models contained in $I(T)$ and $M(T)$). His and my definitions are set-theoretically equivalent.

12. "Mayr-*inspired*" because Mayr does not develop the notion of an analog structure T_R^*.

13. If one seeks to capture more precisely Kuhn's or Lakatos's notion of anomaly in structuralist terms, one will probably wish to place some restriction on $I(T)$ in the definition, separating the *paradigmatic* intended empirical applications from the more peripheral ones. Genuine anomalies could then be restricted to elements of this special subclass of paradigmatic intended empirical applications that have not or cannot be shown to be models of T_R For an early structuralist attempt to explicate the paradigmatic applications of a theory, see Stegmüller 1976, chap. 15.

14. This is Suppes's definition 2 (1956, 262). Hence it is puzzling that Schaffner (1967, 141) felt compelled to cite Church's general definition of an isomorphism (which is nothing more than a generalization of Suppes's definition 2) in order to "give some sense of exactness" to Suppes's use of the term. Church's formulation does, however, make more elegant Schaffner's proof of a theorem

relating Suppes's reduction paradigm to that of Nagel, Woodger, and Quine (discussed in the text that follows).

15. It isn't obvious, though, that the conditions on p are *logically* stronger than those on isomorphism. See Day 1985, 169–171, for an interesting discussion relating Suppes's account to E. W. Adams's (1955, 1959) account (whose account is very similar to that of Balzer, Moulines, and Sneed [1987], from which my conditions (1) and (2) on p are inspired). Day concludes that "neither analysis entails the other." But there are actual historical cases that are not genuine reductions but that meet Suppes's condition while failing to meet Adams's. Hence Adams's analysis is "more adequate." Day's argument also sheds interesting negative light on whether Schaffner (1967) is correct to count Adams's theory as part of Suppes's reduction paradigm.

16. In private correspondence, Moulines informs me that Schaffner's essay was "not before his conscious mind" when he wrote the essay from which the quote to follow is drawn.

17. Moulines is not the only structuralist to notice that the too-weak-to-be-adequate worry (though not under that name) arises for many of these accounts (though Schaffner never gets mentioned in the structuralist literature). Balzer, Moulines, and Sneed note, "Mere formal comparison cannot determine any kind of reduction," because if such requirements were sufficient, "then many theories would reduce to other theories in quite unexpected ways" (1987, 264). One example they explicitly cite is exchange economics reducing to thermodynamics, "an obviously unintended result." Their response is to explicate the notion of successful applications of a theory and then add onto the conditions on p the additional condition that the reducing theory "should be able to deal successfully with all successful applications" of the reduced. They dub this condition an important additional "pragmatic" requirement. Its semiformal explication requires one of the additional components of a theory element, the partial potential models, that I have left out of my simplified presentation. (This is because, as I already stated, in Balzer, Moulines, and Sneed's full account of theory structure the set of intended empirical applications is a subset of the partial potential models, not the potential models as I am treating them.) For the details of this alternative structuralist attempt to address what amounts to Schaffner's challenge, see Balzer, Moulines, and Sneed 1987, 264–267.

18. My discussion in the next few paragraphs draws upon, and expands, the presentation of ORLs in Bickle 1993a.

19. A typification is a construction procedure for building an *echelon set* by applications (possibly iterated) of power-set and Cartesian-product operations on the base sets.

20. See Kamlah 1984 for a structuralist reconstruction of the relation between phlogiston chemistry and oxygen chemistry. Kamlah's reconstruction does not include T_R^* or ORLs.

21. For the arguments in the rest of this section, the reader must bear in mind that potential models of a theory, including intended empirical applications, are

the things depicted by the theory: the things represented, not the representations of the things. The arguments that follow only make sense when this point is borne clearly in mind.

22. See Balzer, Moulines, and Sneed 1987, chapter 3, for detailed structuralist reconstructions of **SETH** and **PEE**.

23. Because P_x depends on density and on the number of molecules striking the wall per unit time (with the latter also depending on density), $P_x = aD^2$, where a is the proportionality constant and D is the density of the gas (see chapter 2, section 2). For a given quantity of gas, density is inversely proportional to volume (the denser the gas, the less volume taken up by a given quantity of it). So we can write the above equation as $P_x = a/V^2$. Thus $P_i = P + a/V^2$. The second expression of the equation (a/V^2) is one key part of the *van der Waal's equation* for real gases, which changes the ideal gas law so as to take account of the weak attractive forces (called *van der Waal's forces*) present in real gases. Values for a are quite small and differ from gas to gas, since different types of gas molecules exert forces of different characteristic sizes among themselves.

24. This value for V_i is the second important component in van der Waal's equation (see footnote 23 above). The full equation, with these values substituted for P_i and V_i in the ideal gas law, is thus $(P + a/V^2)(V - b) = nRT$, where, as with a, the value of b is very small and differs from gas to gas, as different gases have different characteristic molecular volumes.

25. So in a full structuralist reconstruction of thermodynamics, its empirical base sets must include states indexed to various types of gases.

Chapter Four

1. Some of the arguments in this section draw heavily on Bickle 1992a.

2. Brian McLaughlin (1985, secs. 2 and 9) also suggests that Davidson has Nagel's account of intertheoretic reduction in mind when he makes his anti-reductionist claims. McLaughlin writes, "Davidson concludes from the fact that the conditions for the application of psychological concepts cannot be stated in a purely physical vocabulary that: 'There is no important sense in which psychology can be reduced to the physical sciences.' ... *The important sense of reduction is reduction via bridge laws*" (1985, 356; my emphasis).

3. Unfortunately, Horgan and Woodward don't see that Churchland (1981) had already moved away from the orthodox logical-empiricist model of intertheoretic reduction. They speak of folk psychology probably not enjoying a "smooth *term-by-term* absorption" into some future physical science (1985, 202; my emphasis). Churchland assumes no such account of reduction. I overlook this slip, however, since I can easily reconstruct Horgan and Woodward's point using the account of "smooth intertheoretic reduction" that Churchland hints at in his 1981 essay, which new-wave reductionism has further developed.

4. To keep the record straight, Horgan and Woodward's argument against Churchland's eliminativism also fails, for the same reason. Davidson's anomalous monism does not count as a nonreductive, noneliminative physicalism, even on Churchland's earlier and less sophisticated account of intertheoretic reduction. See Bickle 1993b, sec. 1.

5. "Conceptual" and "empirical/methodological" are used here to mark out segments of a spectrum. Conceptual arguments make less of an appeal to results from, or consequences for, the empirical cognitive and brain sciences, empirical/methodological arguments make more direct appeals to these.

6. Paul and Patricia Churchland make the same point using this case. See P. M. Churchland 1987, 41, and P. S. Churchland 1986, 356.

7. Kim defends an even stronger thesis in sec. 3 of his 1989b essay. He argues that nonreductive physicalists who talk of "physical realizations" of mental properties *commit* to the existence of species-specific bridge laws, and hence to the species-specific strong connectivity of psychology to neuroscience. (This is one reason why he titles his essay "The *Myth* of Nonreductive Physicalism.") However, he points out that he needs only the weaker claim about the consistency of species-specific strong connectivity with multiple realizability to block any antireduction conclusion.

8. The antireductionist might in turn deny that reduction obtains in the textbook case. But this move is inconsistent with the philosophy of science adopted by new-wave reductionism (see again the discussion in the first paragraph of chapter 2).

9. Thanks to Ronald Endicott for this way of phrasing the worry.

10. Terry Horgan (private correspondence) first suggested this way of framing the worry. An anonymous referee for the MIT Press also put it this way, albeit in condensed form.

11. I make a similar point about multiple realizability in PDP systems, albeit toward a slightly different end, in Bickle 1995a. Some of the discussion that follows draws on that essay, although new material is added here.

12. My discussion of this simple connectionist net abstracts from an example of Paul Churchland's (1987, 157–162; 1989, 164–169). *A* and *B* are variables for classifiable features, not names for letters of the alphabet. In Churchland's example (which he draws from Rosenberg and Sejnowski 1987), the network is taught to distinguish sonar echoes of underwater rocks (*A*) and sonar echoes of submerged explosive mines (*B*) lying on the bottom of an enemy harbor. Although Churchland appeals to PDP resources to illustrate and defend a variety of ambitious philosophical and scientific claims (see especially the essays in 1989, part 2), he never mentions their application to multiple-realizability arguments against psychoneural reduction, as I expound in 1995a and am about to expand here.

13. This is all standard connectionist fare. There are by now numerous clear, nontechnical introductions to connectionism besides the presentations of Church-

land already cited. John Tienson (1988) emphasizes several important philosophical issues, and Bechtel and Abrahamsen (1991) provide extended treatment. For a more technical introduction, Rumelhart et al. 1986, especially chapters 1–4 and 8, remains difficult to beat.

14. This apparent difference in turn constitutes the connection between connectionism and eliminative materialism. See, e.g., Ramsey et al. 1990; P. S. Churchland 1986, chap. 7, sec. 5; and Bickle 1993a.

15. However, Shavlik et al. (1991) also found that ID3, a symbolic algorithm, performed comparably, while requiring only a single pass through the training data. (NETtalk was allowed 100 passes.)

16. At numerous places Churchland has tried to put this increase in quantitative terms (see, e.g., 1989, 190, and 1995, 4–7). The numbers are eye-opening.

17. Recall from the previous section that the most determinate specification of a gas is at the "microcanonical" level, which individually fixes the location and momentum of each molecule. Analogously, a "microcanonical neurobiological" level of description will individually specify the firing rate and frequency of each neuron comprising the layer in question.

18. The arguments in this section draw heavily on Bickle 1996.

19. It is worth pointing out that any reductionist willing to formulate the thesis as a broadly based empirical prediction about the relationship to expect between developed special and basic scientific theories can adopt my responses to the methodological criticisms. Nothing in the arguments in this section hinges on the specific nature of the new-wave intertheoretic-reduction relation. The influence that these methodological criticisms have enjoyed, however, shows that classical reductionism didn't stress this formulation of the thesis strongly enough.

20. For the record, the quotes from Fodor are these. First, "The reason it is unlikely that every kind corresponds to a physical kind is just that (a) interesting generalizations (e.g., counterfactual supporting generalizations) can often be made about events whose physical descriptions have nothing in common; (b) it is often the case that *whether* the physical descriptions of the events have anything in common is, in an obvious sense, entirely irrelevant to the truth of the generalizations, or to their interestingness, or to their degree of confirmation, or indeed, to any of their epistemologically important properties; and (c) the special sciences are very much in the business of formulating generalizations of this kind" (1974, 133; quoted by Horgan 1993b, 306). Second, "Suppose, for example, that Gresham's 'law' really is true. (If one doesn't like Gresham's law, then any true and counterfactual supporting generalization in any conceivable future economics will probably do as well.) Gresham's law says something about what will happen in monetary exchanges under certain conditions.... Banal considerations suggest that a physical description which covers all such events must be wildly disjunctive. Some monetary exchanges involve strings of wampum. Some involve dollar bills. And some involve signing one's name to a check.... What is interesting about monetary exchanges is surely not their commonalities under *physical*

description" (1974, 113–114; quoted by Horgan 1993b, 306). Here we see a glimpse, mentioned at the end of chapter 3, of why philosophers often conflate this methodological criticism with arguments from multiple realizability. Fodor himself is not always clear about what sort of argument he is offering. See especially the discussion in the remainder of the paragraph in the text.

21. The same anonymous referee for Bickle 1996 who suggested this worry also suggested a second way in which new wave reductionism might reasonably constrain methodology in special sciences like psychology. Reductionism *as a general program in science* might become so well-supported empirically that specific reductionist theories should be sought in all special sciences. I defer discussion of this possibility until after I have offered a methodological approach connected with new-wave reductionism.

22. In certain restricted experimental situations, it is even expedient to calculate heat transfers using fluid-mechanical equations, though the reduction of caloric fluid to thermodynamics falls well out toward the bumpy endpoint of the intertheoretic-reduction spectrum (top arrow of figure 2.1).

23. These questions and objections are entirely without force against new-wave reductionism. For the rather obvious arguments for this claim, see Bickle 1991.

24. In chapter 6, I will introduce mutual coevolutionary feedback as one condition on a "revisionary" intertheoretic reduction and show how it obtains in the relation between propositional-attitude cognitive psychology and one recent influential approach toward theorizing in cognitive neuroscience.

25. Fodor states the same point in his typically pithy fashion: "Physics develops the taxonomy of its subject matter which best suits its purposes.... But this is not the only taxonomy which may be required *if the purposes of science in general are to be served*—e.g., if we are to state such true, counterfactual supporting generalizations as there are to state. So there are special sciences, with their specialized taxonomies, in the business of stating some of these generalizations" (1974, 145; my emphasis).

26. Fodor draws the same conclusion from the same point. The quotation in note 25 concludes, "If science is to be unified, then all such taxonomies *must apply to the same things*. If physics is to be the basic science, then each of these things had better be a physical thing. But it is not further required that the taxonomies which the special sciences employ *must themselves reduce* to the taxonomy of physics. It is not required, and it is probably not true" (1974, 145; my emphases).

27. The account of token-token reduction about to be presented draws on Bickle 1992b, sec. 5.

28. Hooker's full account of cross-categorical reduction is broader than what I present and develop here. In addition to token-token reduction, he also develops a special theory of "cross-categorical coevolution" to handle cases involving reduced theories postulating "whole system" properties from the perspective of the reducing theory.

Chapter Five

1. Material in the first two sections of this chapter draws heavily on Bickle 1995b.

2. Some philosophers have begun to notice the importance of recent work on associative learning for broader issues in the philosophy of science, as well as for more specialized issues in the philosophy of biology, psychology, and cognitive science. These include Kenneth Schaffner (1992), George Graham (1991), and J. Christopher Maloney (1991).

3. John Anderson gets mentioned in the text, but only in a brief discussion of the distinction between "procedural" and "declarative" memory. Jerry Fodor gets mentioned, but only in a brief discussion of the language-of-thought hypothesis (and here Dickenson insists, "What is clear ... is that the study of animal cognition and learning may well illuminate the nature of a general, internal 'language of thought'" [1980, 12]).

4. My choice is motivated by the fact that a discussion of this result occurs in virtually every learning-theory text and the fact that it receives explicit discussion in many important subsequent papers. Lessons similar to those in the text follow from several other results from the study of higher-order features of associative learning.

5. To my knowledge, no one has made an explicit attempt to account for any of Rescorla and Wagner's competitors neurobiologically, in the fashion discussed in the next section. For good overviews of the two initial alternatives (by Macintosh and by Pearce and Hall), see the final two sections of chapter 4 in Dickenson 1980. For more recent competitors, see Klein and Mowrer (1989), especially the chapters by Durlach, Miller, and Matzel and by Wagner and Brandon.

6. Hawkins and Kandel use the term "cell-biological" where I have and will continue to use "neurophysiological." The latter has more currency in the recent literature.

7. In addition to simple reflexive conditioning, the "letters" of Hawkins and Kandel's neurophysiological learning "alphabet" contain processes underlying habituation (in which an organism dampens response to a recurring harmless stimulus) and sensitization (in which an organism strengthens all of its defensive responses in response to a particular noxious stimulus). The intracellular mechanisms for reflexive conditioning is an elaboration of the mechanism for sensitization.

8. The reduction is smooth because Hawkins and Kandel's theory doesn't correct Rescorla and Wagner's at any point. The former simply takes the latter's mathematical account as correct for the data in question and seeks to show how sequences and combinations of known cellular processes embedded in real anatomies could produce the behavioral dynamics predicted by the latter. This

is a problem for a neurophysiological theory if the behavioral/cognitive theory turns out to be faulty—a real possibility in the case at hand, since a number of competitors to Rescorla and Wagner's theory have arisen over the past two decades. For this reason, perhaps an even more bottom-up research methodology, e.g., that of Lynch and his colleagues described below, will provide a more promising application of the "neurophysiological alphabet" approach to cognitive neuroscience.

9. I here use "model" in the scientific sense, rather than the logical/mathematical sense, as meaning an experimentally manipulable structure (real or imagined) deemed relevantly similar to the phenomena being studied.

10. See Landfield and Deadwyler 1988 for an important collection of review articles on LTP. My discussion to follow draws heavily on Lynch et al. 1988, Lynch and Granger 1989, and Granger et al. 1989.

11. For an especially impressive display of this capacity in one of their earlier networks, see Lynch et al. 1988, 211–217.

12. In her capacity as manuscript referee, Valerie Hardcastle emphasized the worry I am about to express. Thanks to her for doing so. Her attitude did contrast with that of a reviewer for Bickle 1995b, where I first addressed the "put up or shut up" challenge. That reviewer explicitly recommended Lynch and Granger's work to buttress my response to this challenge of only sea-slug cognition.

3. C. U. Moulines (private correspondence) informs me that within model-theoretic reconstructions, the fact that a base set is a singleton usually indicates that it can be dispensed with. While this raises interesting ontological questions for the case at hand, I retain this set in my axiomatization, since intentional psychology is committed to the idea that mental representations and actions are always some cognizer's.

14. To account for "term attitudes" (e.g., "desires a cold beer"), one can add a second auxiliary base set (a set of terms) to the potential models of **IP**, enrich the *Cont* relation appropriately, and make the underlying logic determining the actual models of **IP** a term logic.

15. See also Paul Churchland 1989, chapters 9 and 11, for a good discussion of the relative merits of adopting either of these accounts.

Chapter Six

1. This chapter draws heavily on Bickle 1992c.

2. Thanks to Valerie Hardcastle for raising the worry that prompts this caveat.

3. There are some important dissenters, e.g., Terry Horgan and George Graham's (1991) "austere" conception of folk psychology, and Frank Jackson and Richard Pettit's (1990) account.

4. The debate is not, and never has been, over the existence of representations, as some critics of, e.g., the Churchlands, have insisted. For clear textual evidence that the Churchlands' search has always been for alternative accounts of the structure of cognitive representations, see Patricia Churchland 1988.

5. I distill these conditions from Patricia Churchland 1980 and 1986, chapter 9. She also specifies a sententialist account of cognitive virtue (rationality), but these two conditions are paramount for the realist-eliminativist controversy.

References

Adams, E. 1955. *Axiomatic Foundations of Rigid Body Mechanics*. Unpublished doctoral dissertation, Stanford University.

Adams, E. W. 1959. "The Foundations of Rigid Body Mechanics and the Derivation of Its Laws from Those of Particle Mechanics." In L. Henkin, P. Suppes, and A. Tarski (eds.), *The Axiomatic Method*, 250–265. Amsterdam: North-Holland.

Baker, L. R. 1987. *Saving Belief*. Princeton: Princeton University Press.

Balzer, W., Moulines, C. U., and Sneed, J. 1987. *An Architectonic for Science*. Dordrecht: Reidel.

Balzer, W., Pearce, D. A., and Schmidt, H. J., eds. 1984. *Reduction in Science*. Dordrecht: Reidel.

Bechtel, W., and Abrahamsen, A. 1991. *Connectionism and the Mind*. New York: Basil Blackwell.

Bickle, J. 1989. "Toward a Contemporary Reformulation of the Mind-Body Problem." Doctoral dissertation, University of California, Irvine.

Bickle, J. 1991. "Contemporary Reflections on the Mind-Body Problem." In L. Pojman, ed., *Introduction to Philosophy: Classical and Contemporary Readings*, 333–342. Belmont, Calif.: Wadsworth.

Bickle, J. 1992a. "Mental Anomaly and the New Mind-Brain Reductionism." *Philosophy of Science* 59, no. 2: 217–230.

Bickle, J. 1992b. "Multiple Realizability and Psychophysical Reduction." *Behavior and Philosophy* 20, no. 1: 47–58.

Bickle, J. 1992c. "Revisionary Physicalism." *Biology and Philosophy* 7, no. 4: 411–430.

Bickle, J. 1993a. "Connectionism, Eliminativism, and the Semantic View of Theories." *Erkenntnis* 39, no. 5: 359–382.

Bickle, J. 1993b. "Philosophy Neuralized: A Critical Notice of P. M. Churchland's *Neurocomputational Perspective*." *Behavior and Philosophy* 20, no. 2; 21, no. 1 (double issue): 75–88.

Bickle, J. 1995a. "Connectionism, Reduction, and Multiple Realizability." *Behavior and Philosophy* 23, no. 2: 29–39.

Bickle, J. 1995b. "Psychoneural Reduction of the Genuinely Cognitive: Some Accomplished Facts." *Philosophical Psychology* 8, no. 3: 265–285.

Bickle, J. 1996. "New Wave Psychophysical Reduction and the Methodological Caveats." *Philosophy and Phenomenological Research* 56, no. 1: 57–78.

Bishop, J. 1988. "Is a Unified Science of the Mind-Brain Possible?" *Biology and Philosophy* 3: 375–391.

Block, N. 1978. "Troubles with Functionalism." In C. W. Savage, ed., *Perception and Cognition: Issues in the Foundations of Psychology*, Minnesota Studies in the Philosophy of Science, no. 9. Minneapolis: University of Minnesota Press.

Burge, T. 1979. "Individualism and the Mental." In P. A. French, T. E. Uehling, and H. K. Wettstein, eds., *Studies in Metaphysics*, Midwest Studies in Philosophy, no. 4. Minneapolis: University of Minnesota Press.

Burge, T. 1982. "Other Bodies." In Woodfield 1982, 97–120.

Burge, T. 1986. "Individualism and Psychology." *Philosophical Review* 45: 3–45.

Churchland, P. M. 1979. *Scientific Realism and the Plasticity of Mind*. Cambridge: Cambridge University Press.

Churchland, P. M. 1981. "Eliminative Materialism and the Propositional Attitudes." *Journal of Philosophy* 78, no. 2: 67–90. Reprinted as chapter 1 in P. M. Churchland 1989.

Churchland, P. M. 1982. "Is 'Thinker' a Natural Kind?" *Dialogue* 21, no. 2: 223–238.

Churchland, P. M. 1985. "Reduction, Qualia, and the Direct Introspection of Brain States." *Journal of Philosophy* 82, no. 1: 1–22. Reprinted as chapter 3 in P. M. Churchland 1989.

Churchland, P. M. 1987. *Matter and Consciousness*. Revised edition. Cambridge: MIT Press.

Churchland, P. M. 1989. *A Neurocomputational Perspective*. Cambridge: MIT Press.

Churchland, P. S. 1980. "Language, Thought, and Information Processing." *Noûs* 14: 147–170.

Churchland, P. S. 1986. *Neurophilosophy: Toward a Unified Science of the Mind-Brain*. Cambridge: MIT Press.

Churchland, P. S. 1988. "Replies to Corballis and Bishop." *Biology and Philosophy* 3, no. 4: 393–402.

Churchland, P. S., and Sejnowski, T. J. 1991. *The Computational Brain*. Cambridge: MIT Press.

Davidson, D. 1970. "Mental Events." In L. Foster and J. W. Swanson, eds., *Experience and Theory*. Amherst: University of Massachusetts Press. Reprinted as chapter 11 in Davidson 1980.

Davidson, D. 1972. "Psychology as Philosophy." In S. C. Brown, ed., *Philosophy of Psychology*. New York: Macmillan. Reprinted as chapter 12 in Davidson 1980.

Davidson, D. 1973. "The Material Mind." In P. Suppes, L. Henkin, G. C. Moisil, and A. Joja, eds., *Proceedings of the Fourth International Congress for Logic, Methodology, and Philosophy of Science*. Amsterdam: North-Holland. Reprinted as chapter 13 in Davidson 1980.

Davidson, D. 1980. *Essays on Actions and Events*. Oxford: Oxford University Press.

Day, M. 1985. "Adams on Theoretical Reduction." *Erkenntnis* 23: 161–184.

Dickenson, A. 1980. *Contemporary Animal Learning Theory*. Cambridge: Cambridge University Press.

Dretske, F. 1983. *Knowledge and the Flow of Information*. Cambridge: MIT Press.

Enç, B. 1983. "In Defense of the Identity Theory." *Journal of Philosophy* 80: 279–298.

Feigl, H. 1967. *The "Mental" and the "Physical": The Essay and a Postscript*. Minneapolis: University of Minnesota Press.

Feyerabend, P. K. 1962. "Explanation, Reduction, and Empiricism." In H. Feigl and G. Maxwell, eds., *Scientific Explanation, Space, and Time*, Minnesota Studies in the Philosophy of Science, no. 3, 28–97. Reprinted as chapter 4 in Feyerabend 1981.

Feyerabend, P. K. 1977. "Changing Patterns of Reconstruction." *British Journal for the Philosophy of Science* 28: 351–382.

Feyerabend, P. K. 1981. *Philosophical Papers*. Vols. 1 and 2. Cambridge: Cambridge University Press.

Fisher, D. 1987. "Knowledge Acquisition via Incremental Conceptual Clustering." *Machine Learning* 2: 139–172.

Fodor, J. A. 1974. "Special Sciences." *Synthese* 28: 77–115. Reprinted as chapter 5 in Fodor 1981.

Fodor, J. A. 1975. *The Language of Thought*. New York: Thomas Crowell.

Fodor, J. A. 1981. *Representations*. Cambridge: MIT Press.

Fodor, J. A. 1985. "Fodor's Guide to Mental Representation." *Mind* 96. Reprinted as chapter 1 in Fodor 1991.

Fodor, J. A. 1987. *Psychosemantics*. Cambridge: MIT Press.

Fodor, J. A. 1991. *"A Theory of Content" and Other Essays*. Cambridge: MIT Press.

Garfield, J. L., ed. 1990. *Foundations of Cognitive Science: The Essential Readings*. New York: Paragon House.

Giere, R. 1988. *Explaining Science*. Chicago: University of Chicago Press.

Goldman, A. 1989. "Interpretation Psychologized." *Mind and Language* 4.

Gordon, R. 1986. "Folk Psychology as Simulation." *Mind and Language* 1, no. 2: 158–171.

Gorman, R. P., and Sejnowski, T. J. 1988. "Analysis of Hidden Units in a Layered Network Trained to Classify Sonar Targets." *Neural Networks* 1: 75–89.

Graham, G. 1991. "Connectionism in Pavlovian Harness." In Horgan and Tienson 1991, 143–166.

Granger, R., Ambros-Ingerson, J., and Lynch, G. 1989. "Derivation of Encoding Characteristics of Layer II Cerebral Cortex." *Journal of Cognitive Neuroscience* 1: 61–87.

Hawkins, R. D. 1989. "A Simple Circuit Model for Higher-Order Features of Classical Conditioning." In J. H. Byrne and W. O. Berry, eds., *Neural Models of Plasticity: Experimental and Theoretical Approaches*, 74–93. San Diego: Academic Press.

Hawkins, R. D., and Kandel, E. R. 1984a. "Is There a Cell-Biological Alphabet for Simple Forms of Learning?" *Psychological Review* 91: 375–391.

Hawkins, R. D., and Kandel, E. R. 1984b. "Steps Toward a Cell-Biological Alphabet for Elementary Forms of Learning." In G. Lynch, J. L. McGaugh, and N. M. Weinberger, eds., *Neurobiology of Learning and Memory*, 385–404. New York: Guilford Press.

Hebb, D. O. 1949. *The Organization of Behavior*. New York: Wiley.

Heil, J. 1992. *The Nature of True Minds*. Cambridge: Cambridge University Press.

Hooker, C. A. 1979. "Critical Notice: R. M. Yoshida's *Reduction in the Physical Sciences*." *Dialogue* 18: 81–99.

Hooker, C. A. 1981. "Towards a General Theory of Reduction. Part I: Historical and Scientific Setting. Part II: Identity in Reduction. Part III: Cross-Categorial Reduction." *Dialogue* 20: 38–59, 201–236, 496–529.

Horgan, T. 1984. "Supervenience and Cosmic Hermeneutics." *Southern Journal of Philosophy* 22, suppl.: 19–38.

Horgan, T. 1993a. "From Supervenience to Superdupervenience: Meeting the Demands of a Material World." *Mind* 102: 555–586.

Horgan, T. 1993b. "Nonreductive Materialism and the Explanatory Autonomy of Psychology." In S. Wagner and R. Warner, eds., *Naturalism: A Critical Appraisal*. Notre Dame, Ind.: University of Notre Dame Press.

Horgan, T. 1994. "Physicalism (1)." In S. Guttenplan, ed., *A Companion to Philosophy of Mind*, 471–479. New York: Basil Blackwell.

Horgan, T., and Graham, G. 1991. "In Defense of Southern Fundamentalism." *Philosophical Studies* 62: 107–134.

Horgan, T., and Tienson, J., eds. 1991. *Connectionism and the Philosophy of Mind*. Dordrecht: Kluwer.

Horgan, T., and Tienson, J. 1992. "Cognitive Systems as Dynamical Systems." *Topoi* 11, no. 1: 27–44.

Horgan, T., and Woodward, J. 1985. "Folk Psychology Is Here to Stay." *Philosophical Review* 94, no. 2: 197–226.

Jackson, F. 1982. "Epiphenomenal Qualia." *Philosophical Quarterly* 32: 127–136.

Jackson, F., and Pettit, R. 1990. "In Defense of Folk Psychology." *Philosophical Studies* 59: 31–54.

Kamin, L. 1968. "Predictability, Surprise, Attention, and Conditioning." In B. A. Campbell and R. N. Church, eds., *Punishment and Aversive Behavior*, 279–296. New York: Appleton-Century-Crofts.

Kamlah, A. 1984. "A Logical Investigation of the Phlogiston Case." In Balzer, Pearce, and Schmidt 1984, 217–238.

Kemeny, J. G. and Oppenheim, P. 1956. "On Reduction." *Philosophical Studies* 7: 6–19.

Kim, J. 1966. "On the Psycho-physical Identity Theory." *American Philosophical Quarterly* 3: 227–235.

Kim, J. 1969. "Events and Their Descriptions: Some Considerations." In N. Rescher et al., eds., *Essays in Honor of Carl G. Hempel.* Dordrecht: Reidel, 198–215.

Kim, J. 1976. "Events as Property Exemplifications." In M. Brand and K. Walton, eds., *Action Theory.* Dordrecht: Reidel, 159–177.

Kim, J. 1985. "Psychophysical Laws." In E. LePore and B. McLaughlin, eds., *Actions and Events: Perspectives on the Philosophy of Donald Davidson.* New York: Basil Blackwell.

Kim, J. 1989a. "Mechanism, Purpose, and Explanatory Exclusion." In J. Tomberlin, ed., *Philosophy of Mind and Action Theory*, Philosophical Perspectives, no. 3, 77–108. Atascadero, Calif.: Ridgeview. Reprinted as chapter 13 in Kim 1993.

Kim, J. 1989b. "The Myth of Nonreductive Materialism." *Proceedings and Addresses of the American Philosophical Association* 63, no. 3: 31–47. Reprinted as chapter 14 in Kim 1993.

Kim, J. 1992. " 'Downward Causation' in Emergentism and Nonreductive Physicalism." In A. Beckermann, H. Flohr, and J. Kim, eds., *Emergence or Reduction? Essays on the Prospects of Nonreductive Physicalism*, 99–138. New York: Walter de Gruyter.

Kim, J. 1993. *Supervenience and Mind.* Cambridge: Cambridge University Press.

Klein, S. B., and Mowrer, R. R., eds. 1989. *Contemporary Learning Theories: Pavlovian Conditioning and the Status of Traditional Learning Theory.* Hillsdale, N.J.: Lawrence Erlbaum.

Kremer, E. F. 1978. "The Rescorla-Wagner Model: Losses in Associative Strength in Compound Conditional Stimuli." *Journal of Experimental Psychology: Animal Behavior Processes* 4: 22–36.

Kuhn, T. 1976. "Theory-Change as Structure-Change: Comments on the Sneed Formalism." *Erkenntnis* 10: 179–199.

Kuhn, T. 1977. *The Essential Tension: Selected Studies in Scientific Tradition and Change.* Chicago: University of Chicago Press.

Lakatos, I. 1970. "Falsification and the Methodology of Scientific Research Programs." In I. Lakatos and A. Musgrave, eds., *Criticism and the Growth of Knowledge.* Cambridge: Cambridge University Press.

Landfield, P. W., and Deadwyler, S. A., eds. 1988. *Long Term Potentiation: From Biophysics to Behavior.* New York: Alan R. Liss.

Lehky, S. R., and Sejnowski, T. J. 1988. "Network Models of Shape from Shading: Neural Function Arises from Both Receptive and Projective Fields." *Nature* 33: 452–454.

LePore, E., and Loewer, B. 1989. "More on Making Mind Matter." *Philosophical Topics* 17: 175–191.

Lewis, D. 1969. "Review of *Art, Mind, and Religion.*" *Journal of Philosophy* 66: 23–35.

Lombard, L. 1986. *Events.* London: Routlege and Kegan Paul.

Lynch, G., and Granger, R. 1989. "Simulation and Analysis of a Simple Cortical Network." *Psychology of Learning and Motivation* 23: 204–241.

Lynch, G., Granger, R., Larson, J., and Baudry, M. 1988. "Cortical Encoding of Memory: Hypotheses Derived from Analysis and Simulation of Physiological Learning Rules in Anatomical Structures." In L. Nadel, L. Cooper, P. Culicover, and R. N. Harnish, eds., *Neural Connections, Mental Computations*, 180–224. Cambridge: MIT Press.

Maloney, J. C. 1991. "Connectionism and Conditioning." In Horgan and Tienson 1991, 167–197.

Margolis, J. 1979. *Persons and Minds.* Dordrecht: Reidel.

Mayr, D. 1976. "Investigations of the Concept of Reduction, I." *Erkenntnis* 10: 275–294.

McClamrock, R. 1992. "Irreducibility and Subjectivity." *Philosophical Studies* 67: 177–192.

McLaughlin, B. 1985. "Anomalous Monism and the Irreducibility of the Mental." In E. LePore and B. McLaughlin, eds., *Actions and Events: Perspectives on the Philosophy of Donald Davidson.* New York: Basil Blackwell.

Mormann, T. 1988. "Structuralist Reduction Concepts as Structure-Preserving Maps." *Synthese* 77: 215–250.

Mormann, T. 1991. "Husserl's Philosophy of Science and the Semantic Approach." *Philosophy of Science* 58, no. 1: 61–83.

Moulines, C. U. 1984. "Ontological Reduction in the Natural Sciences." In W. Balzer, D. A. Pearce, and H. J. Schmidt 1984, 51–70.

Nagel, E. 1961. *The Structure of Science*. New York: Harcourt, Brace, and World.

Nagel, T. 1989. *The View from Nowhere*. Oxford: Oxford University Press.

Oppenheim, P., and Putnam, H. 1958. "Unity of Science as a Working Hypothesis." In H. Feigl, M. Scriven, and G. Maxwell, eds., *Concepts, Theories, and the Mind-Body Problem*, Minnesota Studies in the Philosophy of Science, no. 2, 3–36. Minneapolis: University of Minnesota Press.

Post, J. F. 1987. *The Faces of Existence: An Essay in Nonreductive Metaphysics*. Ithaca, N.Y.: Cornell University Press.

Putnam, H. 1960. "Minds and Machines." In S. Hook, ed., *Dimensions of Mind*. New York: NYU Press.

Putnam, H. 1964. "Robots: Machines or Artificially Created Life?" *Journal of Philosophy* 61, no. 2: 668–691.

Putnam, H. 1967. "Psychological Predicates." In W. H. Capitan and D. D. Merrill, eds., *Art, Mind, and Religion*. Pittsburgh: University of Pittsburgh Press. Reprinted in Putnam 1975.

Putnam, H. 1975. *Mind, Language, and Reality*. Vol. 2 of *Philosophical Papers*. Cambridge: Cambridge University Press.

Putnam, H. 1988. *Representation and Reality*. Cambridge: MIT Press.

Pylyshyn, Z. W. 1984. *Computation and Cognition*. Cambridge: MIT Press.

Ramsey, W., Stich, S., and Garon, J. 1990. "Connectionism, Eliminativism, and the Fate of Folk Psychology." In J. Tomberlin, ed., *Action Theory and Philosophy of Mind*, Philosophical Perspectives, no. 4, 499–533. Atascadero, Calif.: Ridgeview Press.

Rescorla, R. A. 1988. "Pavlovian Conditioning: It's Not What You Think It Is." *American Psychologist* 43: 151–160.

Rescorla, R. A., and Wagner, A. R. 1972. "A Theory of Pavlovian Conditioning: Variations in the Effectiveness of Reinforcement and Nonreinforcement." In A. H. Black and W. F. Prokasy, eds., *Classical Conditioning. II: Current Research and Theory*, 64–99. New York: Appleton-Century-Crofts.

Richardson, R. 1979. "Functionalism and Reductionism." *Philosophy of Science* 46: 533–558.

Rorty, R. 1965. "Mind-Brain Identity Theory, Privacy, and Categories." *Review of Metaphysics* 19: 24–54.

Rosenberg, C. R., and Sejnowski, T. J. 1987. "Parallel Networks That Learn to Pronounce English Text." *Complex Systems* 1: 145–168.

Rott, H. 1987. "Reduction: Some Criteria and Criticisms of the Structuralist Concept." *Erkenntnis* 27: 231–256.

Rumelhart, D. E., McClelland, J. L., and the PDP Research Group, eds. 1986. *Parallel Distributed Processing.* Vols. 1 and 2. Cambridge: MIT Press.

Schaffner, K. 1967. "Approaches to Reduction." *Philosophy of Science* 34: 137–147.

Schaffner, K. 1992. "Philosophy of Medicine." In M. H. Salmon, J. Earman, C. Glymour, J. G. Lennox, P. Machamer, J. E. McGuire, J. D. Norton, W. C. Salmon, and K. Schaffner, eds., *Introduction to the Philosophy of Science.* Englewood Cliffs, N.J.: Prentice-Hall.

Searle, J. 1984. *Minds, Brains, and Science.* Cambridge: Harvard University Press.

Searle, J. 1992. *The Rediscovery of the Mind.* Cambridge: MIT Press.

Sellars, W. 1962. "Philosophy and the Scientific Image of Man." In R. Colodny, ed., *Frontiers of Science and Philosophy,* 35–78. Pittsburgh: University of Pittsburgh Press.

Shaffer, J. 1968. *Philosophy of Mind.* Englewood Cliffs, N.J.: Prentice-Hall.

Shavlik, J. W., Mooney, R. J., and Towell, G. G. 1991. "Symbolic and Neural Algorithms: An Experimental Comparison." *Machine Learning* 6, no. 1: 111–143.

Sklar, L. 1993. *Physics and Chance.* Cambridge: Cambridge University Press.

Smart, J. J. C. 1963. "Materialism." *Journal of Philosophy* 60: 651–662.

Smart, J. J. C. 1967. "Comments on the Papers." In C. Presley, ed., *The Identity Theory of Mind.* St. Lucia, Brisbane: University of Queensland Press.

Smolensky, P. 1988. "On the Proper Treatment of Connectionism." *Behavioral and Brain Sciences* 11: 1–74.

Sneed, J. 1971. *The Logical Structure of Mathematical Physics.* Dordrecht: Reidel.

Stegmüller, W. 1976. *The Structure and Dynamics of Theories.* Berlin: Springer-Verlag.

Stich, S. 1983. *From Folk Psychology to Cognitive Science.* Cambridge: MIT Press.

Stich, S., and Nichols, S. 1992. "Folk Psychology: Simulation vs. Tacit Theory." *Mind and Language* 7, nos. 1 and 2: 29–65.

Suppe, F. 1974. *The Structure of Scientific Theories.* Urbana: University of Illinois Press.

Suppes, P. 1956. *Introduction to Logic.* Princeton: van Nostrand.

Suppes, P. 1967. "What Is a Scientific Theory?" In S. Morgenbesser, ed., *Philosophy of Science Today.* New York: Basic Books.

Tienson, J. 1988. "An Introduction to Connectionism." *Southern Journal of Philosophy* 26, suppl.: 57–84.

Trout, J. D. 1991. "Reductionism and the Unity of Science." In R. Boyd, P. Casper, and J. D. Trout, eds., *Philosophy of Science*. Cambridge: MIT Press.

Van Fraassen, B. 1970. "On the Extension of Beth's Semantics of Physical Theories." *Philosophy of Science* 37, no. 3: 325–339.

Van Fraassen, B. 1972. "A Formal Approach to the Philosophy of Science." In R. Colodny, ed., *Paradigms and Paradoxes*. Pittsburgh: University of Pittsburgh Press.

Van Fraassen, B. 1980. *The Scientific Image*. Oxford: Clarendon Press.

Van Fraassen, B. 1987. "The Semantic Appropach to Scientific Theories." In N. Nersessian, ed., *The Process of Science*. Dordrecht: Martinus Nijhoff.

Wilson, M. 1985. "What Is This Thing Called 'Pain'—The Philosophy of Science Behind the Contemporary Debate." *Pacific Philosophical Quarterly* 66: 227–267.

Woodfield, A., ed. 1982. *Thought and Object*. Oxford: Clarendon Press.

Index